# The Wianno Senior Story

*A Century on Nantucket Sound*

# The Wianno Senior Story

*A Century on Nantucket Sound*

Stan Grayson

Foreword by Llewellyn Howland III

The Wianno Senior Class Association

Tilbury House, Publishers, Gardiner, Maine

Published by
The Wianno Senior Class Association
PO Box 1242
South Yarmouth, MA  02664
www.wiannosenior.org

ISBN 978-0-88448-365-6

Book design and production by Jon Albertson, www.albertson-design.com

Distribution by Tilbury House, Publishers
103 Brunswick Ave.
Gardiner, Maine  04345
800-582-1899, www.tilburyhouse.com

Printing and binding by Versa Press, E. Peoria, Illinois, USA

*Frontispiece: Action at
Edgartown, July, 2006.*

# Contents

# Foreword

*Llewellyn Howland III*

In the great yacht race that is life, not all one-design sailboat classes are born equal. The work of even the best designers and builders often falls short. Even the most dedicated owners, skippers, and class sponsors sometime lack the resources to inspire a thriving fleet of one-designs — or, just as important, the fortitude to lead a class through the storms of wind, war, fire, fad, and fashion that inevitably test the works of humankind. This is why the effective life span of most one-design classes may be measured in years, not decades. This is why fewer than a dozen American one-design classes still active today can claim to have been in existence for a century or more and to compete under their original rig. Of these, the Wianno Senior Class is surely the largest and most famous.

Stan Grayson's superb history of the Wianno Seniors thus begins with a miracle. For, truly, it *is* a miracle that Wianno Seniors are still being raced and sailed in such large numbers so many years after the first boats in the class made their first appearance in the summer of 1914.

And from the miracle come the all-important questions: who, what, why, when, and where? These are the questions that any historian worthy of the name must ask. Labor-intensive though it is, however, finding the answers is the easy part. Making an entertaining, coherent, convincing, and responsible narrative from the answers is where the hard work and art begin.

Credit for the conception of the Wianno Senior belongs to two men: Osterville boatbuilder H. Manley Crosby and Boston financier and Wianno developer and summer resident Henry Brown Day. It was Day who recognized that the Wianno summer community would likely support a class of 25′, one-design knockabouts — and he asked Crosby to design and build boats for such a class at an affordable price. It was Crosby who had the local knowledge and the intuitive understanding and technical skill to produce a boat that would be fast, able, safe, and competitive for skippers and crews of even limited sailing experience and judgment.

But if Manley Crosby (and others in that webfooted boatbuilding family) deserve credit for

*The beauty of a Wianno Senior race: this image is from the July, 2012, Scudder Cup event at Osterville and shows #174* Sea Lyon, *#190* Golden Summer, *and #162* Odin.

creating and maintaining early boats in the Wianno Senior fleet, and H. B. Day and other early Wianno Senior owners deserve credit for their sponsorship of the class, it is, as Stan Grayson makes clear, the scores, hundreds, and by now thousands of subsequent owners, skippers, and crew members who have given the story of the class its real meaning and its power. In the end, it is the boats themselves in this most fortunate class that command our greatest admiration and affection.

What were the origins of this gaff-rigged, one-design, knockabout sloop? How does the Wianno Senior as a type fit into the larger history of one-design racing in America? Fixed as the Wianno Senior may be in hull design, why does it continue to carry an antiquated gaff rig ninety years after the marconi rig came into general use on American racing sailboats? How is it possible for an aging Wianno Senior built the traditional way of wood to compete on a fair and equal basis with a newer Wianno Senior built of fiberglass? And if class rules allow a Wianno Senior to be built of fiberglass, how come her spars still have to be made of wood, instead of lighter, stronger, maintenance-free aluminum, carbon fiber, or the like?

How, in sum, has the class maintained its identity and character through one hundred years of relentless social, political, economic, and technological change? What does its survival say about the intrinsic merits of the boats? Just as important, what does it say about the values and aspirations of the owners themselves?

For the scientifically minded, sailboats are all about hydrodynamics and aerodynamics, skin friction and metacentrics, righting arms and prismatic coefficients. For yacht-racing fanatics, they are simply machines for winning, waterborne chess pieces, wind-powered tactical weapons. For those who enjoy unpressured daysailing and cruising, they are family jalopies, companions in pleasure, transports of delight.

For the past century, the Wianno Senior has somehow, and miraculously, managed to be all these things and more. It has done so not through a process of constant change and reinvention but by remaining pretty much the same boat that it always was. It has done so despite the frequent, mostly well-meaning, and almost always misguided efforts of those owners who thought they knew better.

Even as he weaves an astonishing quantity of names, dates, race results, and class particulars and statistics into the fabric of his narrative, Stan Grayson never loses sight of the larger patterns, the deeper meanings of the story he tells. He renders the land and sea marks of upper Cape Cod as they were in 1914 — and are today. He traces the evolution of the extended Wianno Senior family from its infancy to the present. He shows how local, national, and international events — including, lest we forget, the assassination of a U.S. president and a U.S. attorney general — have affected the class. He gives class leaders their due. Also-rans may be surprised to find that they, too, rate a mention and a kind word or two in this comprehensive and very generous history.

Through it all, the Wianno Senior holds to its course, providing daunting starts and dramatic finishes, good sport upwind and downwind, a snug cabin for sudden squalls and weekend cruising, plenty of brightwork to sand and varnish, and memories to cherish for a lifetime. I suspect that this book may help ensure the survival of the Wianno Senior Class for at least another century, and I am betting that Wianno Seniors will still be gaff-rigged in 2114.

# Introduction

"It's no fish ye're buying," wrote the great Scottish novelist Sir Walter Scott, "it's men's lives." So it is with boats. The story of the Wianno Senior is the story of the lives of those who conceived and built her and of the generations of families for whom the boat became an integral part of life. This story had its beginnings over one hundred years ago now, and a final chapter does not appear to be anywhere on the horizon.

The decision by the Wianno Senior Class to sponsor this centennial commemoration of its cherished boat must be recognized for what it is — a once-in-a-lifetime opportunity. The decision came none too soon. Much of this story has long since passed into history. Boats are gone. People have passed on. Often enough, details of their lives have faded from the memory of even their most devoted progeny. The written record, never voluminous to start with, has become elusive, incomplete and, at times, inconsistent. Even the landmarks and landscapes known to the first generation of Wianno Senior owners have undergone profound change or disappeared.

Serious works about the history of American yachting are regrettably rare. At their best, such books offer fascinating insights into American culture, society, and technology. The story of the Wianno Senior is about much more than a highly skilled group of one-design sailors. It's about those who started the class and those who followed. It's about the development of small-boat racing as we know it today, the boat's many-faceted designer/builder, the vessel itself, and the development of Cape Cod.

*The Wianno Senior Story* may be seen as a kind of mirror in which all who have ever owned or sailed aboard a Wianno Senior will see reflected an important part of their lives. But it's my hope that readers, Wianno Senior sailors or not, Cape Codders or not, will find in these pages a truthful book, one that offers insights into the way things were and how they evolved to become what they are today.

Stan Grayson
Marblehead, Massachusetts
August 2013

*In July, 2013, on the eve of the 100th anniversary of the Wianno Senior Class, #222 Beltane won the class's premier award, the Frederic F. Scudder Memorial Trophy. From the bow: Paul Revere, Stew Roach at hatch, Karl Anderson, and skipper Jim Cunningham at the tiller.*

# Prologue
# Carolyn's Window

Memories, for most, fade. But not always, not for everyone. Ninety-five years after she was born, Carolyn Rowland's recall, once prompted, could open a window onto a bygone world that once existed in a magical little corner of Cape Cod. It was a vibrant place of people and boats and summer days that came, for children and adults alike, with the promise of new adventures. It was the world she had known as a girl, when she was what the local newspaper once called a "young lady of Wianno."

In those days she was Carolyn Crossett, and well-born. Her father Edward could afford what he wanted and could live where he chose. Shortly before America entered the Great War, Edward Crossett began bringing his family to Cape Cod for the summer. By the year of Carolyn's birth in 1916, development had begun on the Cape, but it was still a world apart, a place of sand roads and ponds, forests and wind-ruffled green marsh, all made more wonderful by glistening bays and the restless waters of Nantucket Sound. Carolyn's memories of those days were of all the people and boats that she knew.

"Mr. Paine used the bulkhead next to Mr. Day's for his boat, and I put my motorboat there, too," she remembered. "It was a real community." When Carolyn was six years old in 1922, her father bought a 25' sailboat designed eight years earlier but just newly referred to as a Wianno Senior. Her father saw that she began learning the ropes under the watchful eye of the family's skipper. It was the beginning of an association with the boat and those who sailed it that would last all her long life.

Many of those who most influenced Carolyn belonged to the Wianno Yacht Club, as did her father. "The Wianno Yacht Club and then the Wianno Club were remarkable for their longevity," Carolyn said. "They were remarkable for the importance they represented in the lives of those like my father, Mr. Day, and Mr. Hornor. They all gave of themselves freely to run the club and make it what it was." The manners she learned from that generation persisted. It took some time before she might drop the formal "Mr." and, bit by bit, communicate on a first-name basis.

Looking back on the years between then and World War II, Carolyn never lost her appreciation for the gift she'd been given. "Life," she said, "was different before the war. Life was smaller. The world was smaller. I'm so glad I experienced that time and glad I knew all the people in Osterville and still do. They were friends. And then there was Uncle Manley, of course. He used to sit in his old shed on a rocking chair and watch the goings-on in the harbor." Uncle Manley was Horace Manley Crosby, the man behind the boat.

Carolyn was a small woman. It was hard to picture her at the tiller for several hours in a big breeze of wind, battling weather helm on a long, wet slog to the Vineyard. But it became less hard when one recognized her determination. In fact, she could seem fierce, even intimidating. But beneath that lay an independence and a sensitivity born of a lifetime's learning and an interest in art and photography instilled by her father. As a young woman, she studied with great men, Alfred Stieglitz and Ansel Adams. Memories of the two, like memories of old Osterville, were very much alive in her home, where some of Adams's prints hung.

Even after she stopped sailing, Carolyn kept up with developments in the Wianno Senior fleet. She was in attendance, of course, for the fiftieth anniversary of the year Manley Crosby had launched the first boats. She was there, too, for the seventy-fifth anniversary, a gathering that, like so much else in her life, she never forgot. On the big day, like an answer to an unspoken prayer, the wind went north, perfect for the much-anticipated parade of yachts. It was a Saturday and the skippers of all the boats milling around West Bay were doing their best to get organized. The northerly breeze helped, providing an easy broad reach as they fell into a long line arranged according to sail number.

"I stood on the dock at the Wianno Yacht Club and the only sound was the *ssssssh* of the boats through the water," Carolyn said. "The wind was a God-given gift, and I knew that as I watched the boats using it to parade out through the cut. Well, I started thinking of all the boats I had known and all the people I had known who had sailed Wianno Seniors. I cried."

It was an emotion that anyone who's been part of the one-hundred-year-old Wianno Senior family, whether skipper, spouse, crew, child, or descendant, would understand.

*Carolyn Crossett Rowland, 1916–2012*

*Heavy going aboard #142* Eight Ball *at the 1996 Edgartown regatta: (l–r) Ian McNiece, Karl Anderson, Rick Bishop, Henry Dane. "It was blowing 25 plus," Karl remembered. "We led the race at the weather mark. Unfortunately, the leeward mark floated onto the beach and the race was canceled. Still, it was a great day of sailing!"*

# CHAPTER ONE

# The Village and the Club

*"Not the least of the attractions of the Cape are the excellent facilities for yachting. Regattas are sailed each season at various points around the shore...."*

— *Simeon L. Deyo, ed.* History of Barnstable County, Massachusetts, *1890*

*Sailing and bathing were principal attractions that drew summer people to Osterville starting in the late nineteenth century. From the pier at the Wianno Club, one can see the bathing pavilion at "Wianno Beach." This rare image is believed to have been made in 1916. The photographer was Louis Maynard Huntress (1873–1962) whose Cape Cod scenes were popular as postcards.*

"Pioneers" is what they came to be called, the families who began purchasing property for summer residences in Osterville in the early 1880s and, with increasing frequency, the 1890s. There was a lot to like about the village, still known to some of the old, resident families as Oysterville. Of all the villages on Cape Cod, this one enjoyed a uniquely beautiful location, bounded on one side by East Bay and on the other by West Bay, which offered access to the shallow waters of Nantucket Sound. A train ride from Boston to the station at West Barnstable followed by an hour-long stagecoach journey over sandy roads brought one to the village, where visitors could relax and enjoy the salt air, go bathing, fishing, or sailing with a local skipper.

The *Barnstable Patriot* reported on most aspects of village life, the comings and goings of family and friends, the arrivals of vacationers at rented cottages or hotels like the Cotocheset House (a regular advertiser starting in the 1880s), civic gatherings, accidents and illnesses, births and deaths. The paper also reported on the village baseball teams — Osterville and Wianno each fielded its own team — and other sporting events. On July 19, 1881, the *Patriot* noted the victory of local boatbuilder Wilton Crosby, then twenty-five years old, in a sailboat race. In an era when betting on such events was routine — wealthy yachtsmen in Newport, Boston, and New York might wager hundreds or even thousands of dollars — Crosby pocketed $12, a good take worth just over $280 in today's money.

In 1885 the Wianno Yacht Club was organized and a number of the pioneers became members. The clubhouse was located at the corner of Sea View Avenue and Wianno Avenue. Although none of the club's nineteenth-century records have surfaced, its general focus was in keeping with the trend to smaller boats rather than big yachts initiated in 1872 with the founding of the Beverly Yacht Club. The impetus for Beverly was the refusal of Marblehead's Eastern Yacht Club to accept boats less than 30' on the waterline, a bylaw that existed at the New York Yacht Club as well.

THE WIANNO YACHT CLUB was formally chartered by the state of Massachusetts in 1901. That May, WYC member William Bradford Homer Dowse joined the chairman of the Barnstable Board of Selectmen, the local state representative, and others in petitioning for permission to dredge a 3'-deep cut into East Bay. The cut was seen as necessary to both improve access to Nantucket Sound and boost the local economy by making Osterville even more attractive as a yachting venue. Since Dowse owned the land through which the cut would be dredged, he stressed to the Committee on Harbors and Public Lands that there "would be no expense in consequence of land damages." The petition was eventually approved and the cut completed in December, 1905.

As at Beverly, a variety of racing classes had by now emerged at the WYC for catboats and jib-and-mainsail yachts — the term then used instead of "sloop" to distinguish such craft from cat-rigged types. The boats were grouped according to size, but all of them were well under 30' on the waterline. By 1902, the club's roster included three jib-and-mainsail classes. These included Class A, ranging from around 23' length-of-waterline (LWL) to 35' overall; Class B, ranging from 18' LWL to about 21' overall; and Class D, ranging from 17' LWL to about 26' overall. Class C — catboats — also raced, with waterlines of from about 20' to 22'8".

The WYC class designations were fluid. The club's Class C catboats had, by 1904, become jib-and-mainsail boats while Class E was for catboats. By 1908, O. D. Lovell's 19'6" LWL catboat *Ibis* was competing in Class D. Dr. Walter Woodman's 23'1" LWL *Sheila*, Class A in 1902, was Class B in 1908. The accompanying table shows the WYC classes as of 1904.

The Class D yachts of 1904 appear to have been the first one-design class at the WYC, and they

*The Wianno Yacht Club's home was known locally as the "Red Onion" thanks to its red-painted shingles. The building was located at the corner of Wianno Avenue and Seaview Avenue. The club had its own pier similar to the one at the Cotocheset House (later the Wianno Club) located not far away down Seaview Avenue.*

were built starting that winter by Daniel Crosby who received an order for five or more of the boats. Such a class was affordable by local sailors, and one boat was owned by Nelson Bearse, the son of a successful Centerville contractor. In *Stranger*, Nelson became a strong competitor, and by 1913 he had amassed a collection of nine trophies.

The class evolutions continued. What had been Class D in 1904 was Class G by 1908. By 1913, Class C, limited to a maximum LWL of 18' in 1904, was permitting larger boats. We know the details of one such WYC Class C boat because it had been designed and built in 1911 by America's greatest yacht designer, Nathanael Herreshoff. Captain Nat, as he

| A Snapshot in Time: WYC Classes in 1904 | |
|---|---|
| Class | Boat Type |
| A | Jib-and-mainsail: 21' to 25' LWL |
| B | Jib-and-mainsail: 18' to 21' LWL |
| C | Jib-and-mainsail: 15' to 18' LWL |
| D | One design: 15' knockabouts |
| E | Catboats |

was known to many, had built *Oleander* for his own use during winter visits to Bermuda where oleander is a common, flowering shrub. Herreshoff later sold the boat to WYC member Philip Sawyer and, in the summer of 1913, Herreshoff visited the club and sailed the three-year-old boat in that Saturday's Class C race. Herreshoff won in an impressive fashion. *Oleander* was an open boat that measured 23'7" LOA × 20' LWL × 6'10" beam × 1'9" draft (board up).

AMONG THOSE who became active in the WYC, and among the earliest pioneers to build in the southeast section of Osterville known as Wianno, was George N. Talbot. A Brookline entrepreneur who owned a Fall River dry goods store and was later involved in founding the Talbot chain of clothiers, Talbot was in his mid-thirties when he built his house on Wianno Avenue. He soon joined the WYC. By 1902, Talbot owned a 26'5"-long Class D knockabout named *Dotty*, and as of 1905 he was on the regatta committee.

While some who followed bought property elsewhere in Osterville, as development hastened in the early 1900s, many newcomers purchased in Wianno. That they did so was due to the impetus of Boston financier and local property investor Henry Brown Day, who had recognized the area's very special location. Day himself had a fine home there overlooking Nantucket Sound and, as of 1902, owned what was then labeled a Class B knockabout (20'7" LWL × 27'8" LOA) named *Dolly*.

"Mr. Day was sort of the leader around here," remembered Carolyn Crossett Rowland, "and he persuaded his friends to build." One of those friends was Carolyn's father Edward Crossett. Crossett had made a substantial fortune in the lumber business in Arkansas where a town in the southeast part of the state was named in his family's honor.

The development activity initiated by the enthusiastic Henry Day was welcomed in the village as it created jobs for tradesmen of all specialties. The *Barnstable Patriot* on January 28, 1901, noted that "Those who are not skilled in the trades find employment in clearing a large tract of land for Day at Wianno…. Altogether Osterville is a busy place this winter, and everyone ought to be thankful."

The family whose project generated this particular thankfulness was that of William P. Halliday. The son of a highly successful Cairo, Illinois, businessman — the senior Halliday had been a steamboat captain before concluding a contract with his friend Ulysses S. Grant involving river trade during the Civil War — Halliday was first brought to Osterville during summers by his parents in the 1880s.

As the friends of Henry Day settled in, it didn't take long for some to join the Wianno Yacht Club. By 1912, the club was becoming a comparatively robust organization requiring a more sophisticated level of planning, promotion, and management. In 1914, the first recorded commodore was elected. William Bradford Homer Dowse had been born in Sherborn in 1852 and, after graduating from Harvard, he became a very successful patent attorney. Later, he left his practice to become a major force in a variety of manufacturing companies.

Civic-minded, Dowse used his wealth to build a war memorial in his hometown of Sherborn, and

in 1914 he gave the town a library. By then, Dowse was dividing his time between his West Newton home opposite the BraeBurn Country Club and the big house he'd built overlooking the water at the end of East Bay Road, not far from Henry Day. In 1902, the WYC's biggest boats were three Class A knockabouts — 35' overall and with 803 square feet of sail area — and Dowse owned one of these. He also became involved in the affairs of the club. In 1908, he presented a bronze and silver trophy as the prize for a race from the yacht club to the Succonesset lightship and back.

Directly abutting Dowse's property was that of Andrew Adie, a Brookline textile manufacturer. Adie owned several boats — among them a Class C — and joined the WYC while also devoting meaningful energy on the Cape to the Barnstable Agricultural Society. In 1910, Adie made improvements to his Wianno home that included an addition with a large kitchen, new servants' quarters, and new windows.

If Talbot, Day, Dowse, and Adie were Bostonians and thus reasonably close to their summer

*It is early summer 1905 and catboats cluster around the pier at the Wianno Yacht Club in this L. M. Huntress photo. The club had seventy-four members at this time.*

places, others had a significant journey to make. The Hallidays came to the village and the Wianno Yacht Club from Memphis. Frank Hagerman was a nationally prominent attorney—he'd been admitted to the Iowa bar at age nineteen—from Kansas City, Missouri. Franklin Robinson came up to the village from New York City where he worked as a composer, lecturer, and writer about music. Percy Melville came from Chicago where his family was involved in steel manufacturing.

Charles M. and Mary Gaff Hinkle moved to the village from Cincinnati in the 1880s, eventually building a big house they named Green Bays overlooking the Bumps River in an area of the village known as the Bluffs. "They didn't think they were wealthy enough to make a ripple in Newport," Charles's grandson Jim Hinkle, Jr. recalled in 2011, "but this wasn't an issue in Osterville." In 1894, the Hinkles' daughter Jean was born in Boston and, four years later their son James Gaff Hinkle was born at Green Bays. James was crewing aboard his uncle's 28-footer in Padanaram in 1906 when he got his first taste of winning a sailboat race. The *Barracouta* took home 1st prize, Class B. "My dad was a natural sailor," said Jim Hinkle, Jr., who still has the cup.

Whatever the success of the WYC's racing events, the alphabet soup nature of the classes would not have provided the level playing field of the sort offered by one-design boats, which began appearing with some frequency at the start of the twentieth

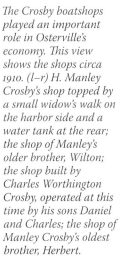

*The Crosby boatshops played an important role in Osterville's economy. This view shows the shops circa 1910. (l–r) H. Manley Crosby's shop topped by a small widow's walk on the harbor side and a water tank at the rear; the shop of Manley's older brother, Wilton; the shop built by Charles Worthington Crosby, operated at this time by his sons Daniel and Charles; the shop of Manley Crosby's oldest brother, Herbert.*

century. The New York Yacht Club introduced its immediately popular New York 30 (30' LWL, 43'6" LOA) in 1905. Nat Herreshoff designed that boat, as he did the little "12½", initially created for the Beverly Yacht Club and launched in 1914. Both these early one-design classes are still active.

By the 1913 sailing season, it is possible that the matter of running races for a variety of classes, most with non-identical boats that required handicapping — the 1902 roster lists time allowances per mile and per 8 miles — had become an issue at the WYC. It is entirely possible, too, that Henry Day, with the support of Commodore Dowse, envisioned a new one-design class to finally replace the club's various knockabouts and catboats. Such a new yacht could be created exclusively for the WYC and the local waters. If a one-design, the new boat would eliminate handicapping and emphasize sailing skill rather than a design advantage, benefits likely to attract support from a wider base of potential club applicants.

Day and Dowse didn't have to look far to find a builder. Many of the towns and villages that dotted coastal Massachusetts then had a resident boatbuilder or two. Osterville had the Crosbys, whose several boatshops on West Bay represented perhaps the most dynamic business enterprise in the village. The Crosbys were renowned as builders of the Cape Cod catboat and other yachts, due in part to the popularity of *The Rudder* magazine, whose pioneering reporting spread the word.

The only surviving direct quote about the reason why a new boat was wanted at the WYC came from the boat's designer, Wilton Crosby's younger

The Wianno Yacht Club yearbook of 1905.

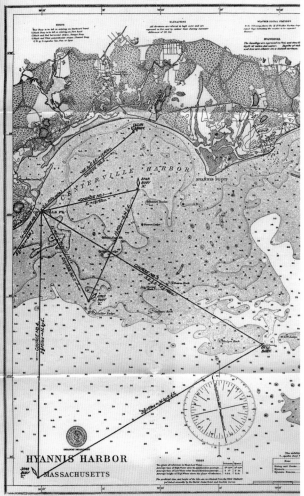

These are the Wianno Yacht Club's race courses as laid out in Centerville Harbor in 1905.

brother Manley. Looking back on the event during an interview with the *New Bedford Standard Times* in the 1930s, Horace Manley Crosby stated: "In the old days, the Wianno Club had a fleet of racing boats built so light they wouldn't stand up. Fritz B. Day, who was interested in these racers, came to me

one day and asked me to design a boat which would stand the gaff and not pound the sea."

For Manley Crosby, the timing of the WYC's commission couldn't have been much better as demand for catboats had slackened off considerably by about 1910 and then dwindled further. "When my uncles were young," Wilton "Bill" Crosby said in a September 2001 interview, "they would tow a string of catboats down to customers in Long Island Sound. When World War I came, that was the end."

As 1913 faded and the short winter days of 1914 commenced, Manley Crosby began organizing to build the WYC's new boats, which would be designated by the WYC as Class P. Although Class P (the P Class at the WYC had no relation to the big Class P yachts built to the Universal Rule) may have been the boat's official name, it would be referred to variously in the press as the Class P One-Design Knockabout, the Wianno Yacht Club One Design, the Wianno 18-foot Class, the Crosby Seventeen, and the Wianno One Design. Finally, when the club introduced a smaller one-design class in 1922 as a new training boat for kids, the Class P yacht was relabeled the Wianno Senior and the smaller boat — also designed by Manley Crosby — the Wianno Junior.

When the idea for the new boat was first presented to WYC members, they responded in a lukewarm manner, and Day, Dowse, and perhaps one other were the only ones voicing support. However, it is likely that during the summer of 1913, Henry Day turned his promotional gifts from real estate to drumming up interest in the new club boat. The one-design aspect with its implicit suggestion of a level playing field apparently played an important role. At any rate, three more members who owned an existing yacht got on board with the project: William Halliday, Andrew Adie, and Franklin Robinson. The group soon expanded with the support of Talbot, Hagerman, Melville, the Hinkles, and several others including a couple of local men. All agreed to purchase a boat sight unseen.

*Commodore Dowse's home circa 1920s. Destroyed in the 1944 hurricane, the house overlooked Phinney Bay with East Bay on the opposite side. A boardwalk connected it to the original Wianno Yacht Club and continued down to the Wianno Club.*

The first Wianno Seniors cost about $600 each, roughly equivalent to $15,000 in today's money. The $600 price was an amount roughly equal to about a half-year's wages for a well-paid working man and more than a year's income for many others. That said, the Senior was a lot of boat for the money. A Herreshoff 12½ was comparatively more expensive for its size, typical of the Manufacturing Company's boats, costing $420. The Senior's price was a sum that with two or three possible exceptions, the buyers could well afford. Most had been born to well-off families and went on to attain good educations and then developed their own successful careers in the professions or in business.

Years after the fact, Manley admitted that he expected interest in the boats to last about a decade. But the owners proved him mistaken and became a steady clientele on which, it turned out, the Crosbys would rely for many years. The men, the founding fathers who made it all happen, had unknowingly begun a sailboat class that would still flourish a century later.

# Chapter Two

# The Builder, the Boat, and the Bet That Never Was

*"...prospective owners called for approximately the following modest requirements: a fast, able, good-looking, unsinkable, seaworthy, light-draught knockabout, to have cruising room for two, of stout material and good workmanship...."*

— The Rudder, *April 1915*

C. Worthington Crosby (1823–1898) stands in the doorway of his shop on West Bay circa 1880. New shingles indicate how the shop's roofline had been modified to create more room inside.

Twenty-six years after its founding, the Beverly Yacht Club's roster of less-than-30'-waterline yachts had grown from perhaps a dozen in 1872 to 132 boats; of that total, the club's 1898 roster listed 70 catboats. By the mid-'90s, catboat racing had entered a kind of golden age, and each season saw the launching of new designs for owners from Massachusetts to New York and New Jersey. To cite but one example, in 1895 the Pavonia (Bayonne) Yacht Club's annual regatta had *six* classes of catboats divided according to length overall and whether or not the boat had a cabin. All this activity kept a number of specialist builders, including the Crosbys, quite busy.

The man who won the 1895 Pavonia Yacht Club regatta event for Class 5 Cabin Catboats (under 23' long) was named Frank M. Randall. A wealthy businessman and real estate developer, Randall was a staunch advocate of the Crosbys. He'd won his class at the 1893 PYC regatta in a Crosby catboat named *Hit or Miss*, bought a new 24-footer — *Win or Lose* — from Herbert Crosby for the '94 season, and purchased *Ethel* for '95. In the spring of 1894, while sailing *Win or Lose* from Osterville to New York, Randall found himself weathered-in at a New London dock. Weary of cruising his new catboats home, and seeing the enthusiasm for catboat racing in New York and New Jersey, Frank Randall conceived the idea of starting a company to build fast catboats right in the heart of his local market. What's more, he convinced Horace Manley Crosby that he was the perfect man for the job.

Manley Crosby was twenty-four years old and already a skilled designer and builder when he left Cape Cod for the Bay Ridge section of Brooklyn in October 1895, having previously shipped his household goods to New York in the schooner *Luella*, owned by his friend Captain C. Nickerson. When Manley and his wife Velina set up housekeeping in Bay Ridge, they did so aboard a decommissioned steamboat. Accompanying the Crosbys were Manley's thirty-five-year-old brother Joseph and two Osterville boatwrights, Oliver Coffin and Frank Williams. Capitalized at $10,000 — at least $270,000 in today's money — The Crosby Catboat and Yacht Building Company had four directors. They included the two Crosby brothers together with Frank M. Randall and Frank Williams of South Brooklyn.

Long accustomed to a busy but quiet life in Osterville, the Crosbys now found themselves in a different world entirely. The boatyard was established initially at the 55th Street premises leased from well-known yacht builder John Mumm and in close proximity to the beautiful, shingled headquarters of the very active Atlantic Yacht Club. Thrust into this hotbed of activity, Manley Crosby became witness to the latest trends in yachting. Orders began flowing in immediately, and by May 1896 the *Brooklyn Eagle* reported that "The Crosby Catboat and Yacht Building Company [now at 56th St.] is building a bicycle boat… an auxiliary knockabout…several catboats." Among the latter was the 34' × 25' × 12' × 2'6" *Step Lively*, built for Randall himself, a boat that immediately became so successful that she may have stifled the very interest Randall hoped to promote.

Manley Crosby's design and building commissions during the period 1896–99 included a variety of yachts. His work ranged from catboats as large as 33 feet to the increasingly popular knockabout sloops of various sizes, and a 75' cruiser for the Globe Engine Company of Philadelphia, one of the great pioneers of gasoline marine engines. All this activity does not suggest whether the Crosby Catboat and Yacht

Building Company was financially successful or whether the move to Bay Ridge and association with Randall were happy events. In all likelihood, the answer to these matters was "no." For one thing, Joseph immediately became homesick and quickly returned to Osterville, bought a shallow-draft schooner, and successfully established himself in the oyster business. Everyone else was homesick, too. The *Barnstable Patriot* reported the regular visits to Osterville of the Crosbys and of boatbuilders Williams and Coffin. Velina's mother regularly visited Brooklyn.

In 1898, Velina gave birth to her third son, Wilton, aboard the steamboat in Bay Ridge. By then, Frank Randall's notion that building racing catboats would result in a viable business had already been proved overly optimistic, for the Crosby Catboat and Yacht Building Company had ceased to exist. Now Manley was doing business under his own name. He had also changed his address, setting up shop in a new location at the foot of 43rd Street, a move that may have been prompted by John Mumm's sale of his boatyard.

By January 1899, Manley Crosby had concluded that building boats profitably in Brooklyn was unlikely. He purchased a retired 250' Hudson River steamboat named the *Walter Brett* and proceeded to start a massive remodeling project. The plan was to moor the "house boat" in Gravesend Bay, a popular yachting venue, as a floating resort with a dance floor and café. The *Brooklyn Eagle* reported on this ambitious project in May 1899, and on its outcome in June 1900. At that time, the paper listed Horace Manley Crosby among several men who had been discharged

from bankruptcy. By then, Manley had returned to Osterville with his family and reopened his boatshop, which had been leased since late 1898 to a Barnstable acquaintance, land surveyor and small-boat designer Vaughan D. Bacon. That October, the *Barnstable Patriot* reported that "Messrs. Wilton and H. Manley Crosby have enlarged their boat shops…. They have added electric lights to the shop also. These are the first to appear in this part of the country." In fact, the Crosby installation of electricity predated by more than a decade its more widespread introduction at Hyannis and elsewhere. Now, Manley quickly settled in. He was once again building catboats and other vessels, teaching village kids to build model yachts

*The Crosby who left Osterville: This portrait of Horace Manley Crosby was made in Brooklyn during the period 1896–99 when the boatbuilder was in his twenties.*

and full-size skiffs, organizing a village orchestra, and generally establishing himself as one of Osterville's best-liked and most successful figures.

SEEMINGLY AS FAST as catboat racing declined during the late 1890s, interest in new knockabout designs grew, and Manley Crosby was well aware of the type's popularity. By 1898, knockabouts accounted for two-thirds of the regattas around New York, and the Atlantic Yacht Club was a leading proponent. Although pervasive and doubtless understood by sailors in the period before and after the turn of the twentieth century, the original meaning of the term "knockabout" can now be rather perplexing, as it was applied variously to sloops and to schooners. Knockabout schooners dispensed with the "widow-maker," as bowsprits had come to be known. Many knockabout sloops did too, but not all of them. Some carried short sprits to permit a larger jib and to ease anchor handling.

The original meaning of the term "knockabout" becomes easier to understand when considered in the context of the Eastern or New York Yacht Club's bylaws regarding members' boats. The NYYC's rule was that boats were to be a minimum "thirty feet load waterline length, if single-masted, and she is a full-decked vessel, reasonable cockpit excepted; and, further by her design and construction she is well suited to accompany the Squadron on a cruise." Viewed in that light, the knockabouts can be seen for what they were: smaller, less-expensive boats intended primarily for day racing with very minimal or no accommodations. They were boats intended for "knocking about."

The original Knockabout Class was developed in the Eastern Yacht Club's hometown of Marblehead in 1892. The boats were 25'6" long with a 21' waterline, a 7'8" beam, and a full keel that resulted in a 4'2" draft. As the original Knockabout Class's popularity grew, it was found necessary to impose certain design restrictions to keep the boats from becoming as extreme, or more extreme, than catboats like *Step Lively*. (*Step Lively*'s overall length was 34'9" but her waterline length was just 25', and her main sail area totaled 1,050 square feet.) These restrictions involved sail area and waterline length. How extreme could such a boat become? In March 1916, "one of the famous 18-foot Knockabout Class boats" was offered for sale in *The Rudder*. This yacht had been built by Charles C. Hanley, among the leading designers and builders of his day. The boat was 30' long on a waterline of only 18'2".

In general, however, the various knockabout classes that quickly developed tended to be less dramatic. "They are free from freakiness," wrote sailor/

The 34' racing catboat
Step Lively *was among
Manley Crosby's most
triumphant designs
built in Brooklyn.* Step
Lively *(1896) and
similar boats would
gradually be replaced
by more moderate
one-design knockabouts,
among them Manley's
own Wianno Senior.*

194

author A. J. Kenealy in his popular book *Boat Sailing*, first published in 1895. The emerging one-design knockabouts were generally moderate yet sporty boats. B. B. Crowninshield's Manchester 17 (better known as the Dark Harbor 17) introduced in 1906 was a good example. Its dimensions were 17½' (LWL) × 25'10" (LOA) × 6'3" (beam) × 4'3" (draft).

The fact that most knockabouts had waterlines that ranged from around 16' to 22' should not suggest that the boats lacked design sophistication, for these were racing "machines" that reflected the best thinking of their day. From roughly 1894 until 1930, knockabouts of various classes were designed by Nat Herreshoff, Bowdoin B. Crowninshield, W. B. Stearns, Fred Lawley, the John Alden office, Charles D. Mower, and other capable men.

A one-design knockabout made eminent sense to many yacht clubs for obvious reasons. Other than ensuring that such boats were identical, a club measurer had little else to concern him, and the need for calculating racing length or time allowances was gone. The one-design aspect meant, in theory, that sailing skill would be the determining factor on race day. The boats were generally affordable, and could be skippered by the owner and crewed by his or her friends. At the Wianno Yacht Club, the decision to establish a new one-design class would prove to be the single greatest key in sparking renewed interest in racing among members.

By the time he was approached by Henry Day about a new boat for the WYC, Horace Manley Crosby had, thanks to his sojourn in New York, already built a number of knockabouts, and had seen many more including those built by his cousin Daniel Crosby. However, the boat Manley envisioned differed in one crucial aspect from the knockabouts designed by the big-name naval architects. Those boats generally had artfully shaped fin keels. Manley's boat instead possessed a keel/centerboard, a stroke of genius born of the builder's innate understanding of his local waters. Among other considerations, the entrances to East Bay and West Bay then had a controlling depth of less than 3' and Nantucket and Vineyard Sounds were, of course, as *The Rudder* reported, "everywhere astonishingly shallow."

Manley Crosby may well have started carving the half-model for his new design in the spring or summer of 1913. Certainly, he had largely finalized the boat's half-model by September, for that is when the *Barnstable Patriot* published the very first mention of the boat. "A large class of one-design Knockabouts is to be built this winter from designs of H. Manley Crosby, 17'6" × 25' × 8' × 2'6", with cabin and water-tight cockpit and centerboard in keel, which is to have an iron bulb for ballast of boat." The term "bulb" was incorrect, at least according to today's understanding of the term. The "keel" was a wooden structure housing a ballast shoe. The ballast shoe was an iron casting with a slot for the centerboard. Shallow though it was, the keel (and deadwood) was sized and shaped to permit the boat to make some windward progress in shallow water without lowering the board.

In April 1915, *The Rudder* published an article entitled "The Wianno Y.C. One-Design," a piece that remains the single most important period source

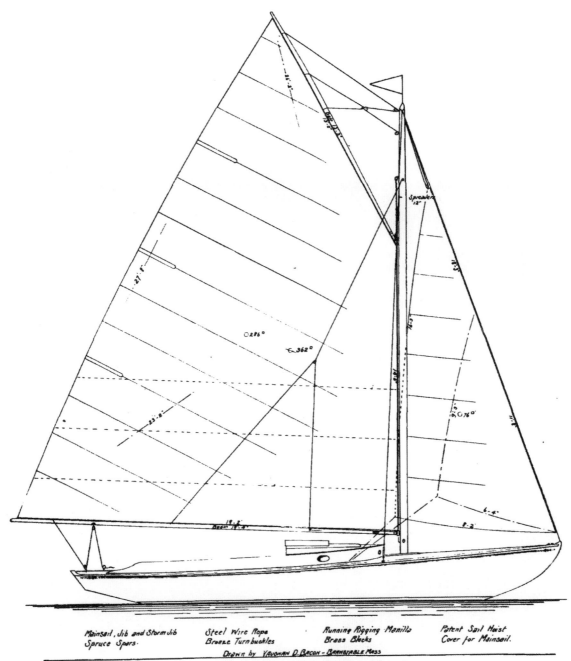

*This profile and sail plan for the Wianno Yacht Club's new one-design was drawn by Barnstable draftsman and small-boat designer Vaughan D. Bacon. It appeared in* The Rudder's *April 1915 issue.*

Mainsail, Jib and Storm Jib Spruce Spars.

Steel Wire Rope Bronze Turnbuckles

Running Rigging Manilla Brass Blocks

Patent Sail Hoist Cover for Mainsail.

Drawn by VAUGHAN D. BACON · BARNSTABLE MASS

**Sail Plan of Wianno Y. C.'s One-Design Class Boats**

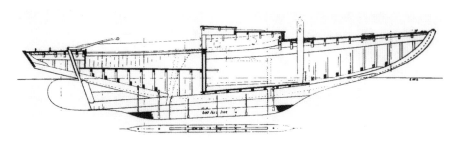

*This drawing, published in* The Rudder *in April 1915, shows the Crosby knockabout's keel and rudder in their original configuration. They would later be revised.*

regarding the boat's design and construction. It is unfortunate that the article carried no byline but it was clearly written by someone with reporting skills who understood what questions to ask. The only name associated with the piece is that of Vaughan D. Bacon, who had been one of the magazine's early contributors and who, of course, knew Manley and the other Crosbys. It is possible but speculative that Bacon wrote the article, but there is no question about who made the article's profile drawing and sail plan — "Drawn by Vaughan D. Bacon — Barnstable, Mass."

"The Wianno Y.C. One-Design" makes fascinating reading today because, among other things, it so clearly portrays how the boat was viewed in the context of its design era and what that generation of small-boat sailors expected. In a time when extreme overhangs and enormous rigs had doubtless contributed to the decline of interest in racing catboats, rules limiting overhangs and sail area in previously unrestricted knockabout classes had to be adopted. The WYC's new boat was intended as a one-design from the outset, explicitly limiting such challenges, and the author of *The Rudder*'s commentary, probably echoing Manley Crosby, noted the design as having "easy, but not extreme overhangs in order to take

the short but sometimes rather choppy seas that are prevalent in Wianno waters."

By today's standards the boat would be considered as having modest freeboard, but that was not the sense in 1915. "The freeboard is higher than the average, which is another aid toward making them good sea-boats, and which also makes possible the cabin with two fair-sized transoms [berths] and a moderate amount of headroom for boats of such a size."

The new knockabout was built with materials long familiar to the Crosbys and shared basic construction techniques with their catboats. Some eighty-five years after the first boats were launched, restorer Chris Mattoon of Berkshire Wooden Boat remarked on the keel structure. "She is built on a heavy timber keel, with a horn timber aft to the transom. To machine the keel, a straight 12" tall by 6" wide by 20' long white oak timber that is relatively free from any defects is required."

In the Crosbys' day, such timber could be procured locally on Osterville Grand Island or, later, from a sawmill in Branford, Connecticut. By the latter years of the twentieth century, however, oak stock of this size and quality had become rare and sought by others than boatbuilders, increasing costs and further challenging availability. The yacht's 1½"-square frames were steamed white oak bent over the mold using metal compression straps to help make the curves on all frames from the transom to those just forward of the centerboard trunk.

The trunk itself was a formidable structure attached to the keel with a tongue-and-groove joint and 6" iron drifts. The wood used for construction evolved over time. Initially, the boats were built of pine planking over oak frames from trees harvested on Grand Island. Later, planking was cypress that was ordered, according to Ted Crosby, from "down South." Although at least one boat had mahogany planking, mahogany became standard in the early 1930s. Cockpit and cabin coamings were oak. Like most Crosby products, the boat was iron-fastened until about the same time as mahogany planks became standard. Then bronze was used. As was typical, the decks were canvas covered. Surprising, however, was *The Rudder* article's note that the self-bailing cockpit and cockpit seats were also canvas-covered. Sails were built by the highly regarded Ratsey & Lapthorn of City Island, New York, and this firm continued to supply replacement sails for many years, sometimes ordered through Crosby's and, on occasion, from orders received directly from the owner.

The design brief for an unsinkable boat was addressed by making the cabin essentially watertight. *The Rudder* reported that "The cabin, by the way, is arranged to shut up completely, thus forming an air bulkhead."

Manley Crosby apparently was not overly concerned that the boat would either capsize or sink. Among the apocryphal legends that grew up around the new knockabout is that Manley offered owners a bet suggesting he'd pay $1,000 to anybody who managed to capsize the boat. Although Manley's son Malcolm "Max" Crosby was definitive that his father had never made such a wager, the challenge on occasion proved irresistible to some.

"Bruce and David Steere would get their crew together and try and capsize their boat to see if they could win the $1,000 bet," remembered Mark Robinson, who crewed regularly for the competitive and successful Lew Gunn. "But they said they felt the spar would break before a Wianno Senior ever tipped over." Others agree. "In my view," said boat designer and longtime Senior owner John Kiley III, "the Senior is nearly impossible to capsize because of the combination of its ballast and the gaff-rigged mainsail. When the boat heels over in a big blow, all the pressure spills out of the mainsail once the boat reaches 70 to 80 degrees. At that point, there is no more pressure on the boat and, the hull design and distribution of its ballast keeps it from going over."

The fact remains that despite decades of hard racing — sometimes in winds of 40-plus knots with unreefed mainsails and some very impressive cruising — no Wianno Senior has ever capsized, and nobody ever attempted to claim the mythical $1,000.

*A new backbone for an old Wianno Senior. Built in 1924, #60 passed through the hands of eight owners before Chris Mattoon of Berkshire Wooden Boat acquired the boat in 2004. A total restoration including the stem, keel, and horn timber was completed in 2008.*

# CHAPTER THREE

# A Family Affair

*"Many young ladies of Wianno handle the boats sailing now and will have one of the new boats."*

— Barnstable Patriot, *September 15, 1913*

In August 1898, while Manley Crosby was in the midst of his Brooklyn sojourn, his cousin Daniel presented a 16½' catboat named *Waltz* to daughter Myrtle. Then Myrtle began receiving sailing lessons from her father in West Bay so that, soon enough, she could skipper the boat herself. By the 1890s, if not before, it was generally accepted that small-boat sailing was a healthful, instructive sport for both sexes. What's more, parents — including the pioneers at Wianno and those who followed — recognized that the skills involved in learning to handle a sailboat could provide their children with important life lessons about responsibility, politeness, fair play, and respect for others, knowledge that would serve them throughout their lives.

*Wianno Senior #4 A.P.H. was a gift from Memphis businessman and Osterville summer resident William Halliday to his daughter, Anne Pillow Halliday. Anne sailed the boat for the next thirteen years and maintained a lifelong connection to the class.*

"WELL," CAROLYN ROWLAND remembered, "the adults then were generous with the children in terms of instructing. They always made us feel welcome and treated us with respect, and we learned to do the same. Then there were Manley Crosby and 'Uncle Bill' [Manley's older brother Wilton B.]. Being around them taught us a lot of things." One of the things Manley taught Carolyn was how to troubleshoot the engine in the 16' motorboat he'd built for the family. "My father didn't want me out in that boat unless I knew something about how it worked. He made sure I knew how to tear that motor down," she said.

When his father Charles died in 1913 at age fifty-three, James Gaff Hinkle was fifteen years old and his sister Jean was nineteen. Seven years earlier, Charles had bought his children a knockabout from Daniel Crosby. Now, in the wake of Charles's passing, his widow Mary added her name to the list of buyers for the WYC's new knockabout. She told Manley Crosby that the Hinkle boat was to have its decks painted light green rather than buff so she could more readily identify it from the porch of Green Bays during her children's racing. While James would be the person most closely associated with *Fantasy* for the next fifty years, his sister Jean also raced and later bought a Wianno Junior of her own. What's more, Mary Hinkle also sailed and occasionally raced *Fantasy*, winning an event in July 1921.

The Hinkles were but one example of how families of the founding fathers — in the Hinkles' case, it was a founding mother who bought the boat — established a tradition that would be continued seamlessly by those who followed. Fathers and mothers, sons and daughters, brothers and sisters — all more or less adopted their boats into the family. What's more, it was not uncommon for a boat to be purchased by parents primarily for their children, girls as well as boys.

When William Parker Halliday bought his Senior, he used his daughter's initials A. P. H. for the boat's name. Anne Pillow Halliday actively campaigned *A.P.H.* for the next thirteen years and remained involved with the boats and those who sailed them all her life. Commodore Dowse's daughter Margaret sailed the family's *Dione*, which Dowse, classically educated, had named for the Greek goddess. Andrew Adie's daughter Andrea had already learned to sail the family's Class C knockabout named *Dotty* — and won a race in 1914 — even before her father bought the new Crosby one-design. Adie named the boat *Snookums*, then a commonly

used term of endearment applied variously to wives, daughters, and sweethearts. In this case, Snookums probably referred to Andrea.

Outdoors-oriented Abby Staunton Hagerman was active in Camp Fire Girls at home in Kansas City, Missouri, before her father Frank bought her a Wianno Senior when she graduated from Vassar in 1914. Abby's involvement with the boat continued long after she married Morrison Shafroth, a Colorado attorney then serving in the army, in 1917. Frank Hagerman himself, however, apparently had little interest in sailing. When the *Kansas City Star* did a profile on Hagerman in December 1921, he was quite a famous attorney who had by then argued an important case before the Supreme Court. He listed his hobbies only as his library, motoring, and golf. Abby's husband Morrison wasn't an enthusiastic sailor, either, but Abby raced *Commy* — named for her grandfather Freeman Comstock whose nickname in

## Portrait of the Fleet
### First Recorded Race Results of the Wianno Senior (Class P), July 25, 1914

| Place | Owner | Boat Name | Time |
|---|---|---|---|
| 1 | Melville | *Ethyl* | 1 hr 11 min 37 sec |
| 2 | Franklin Robinson | *Bobwhite* | 1 hr 17 min 18 sec |
| 3 | G. H. Fiske | *Maxixe* | 1 hr 20 min 30 sec |
| 4 | H. B. Day | *Wendy* | 1 hr 22 min 42 sec |
| 5 | Miss Hagerman | *Commy* | 1 hr 23 min 03 sec |
| 6 | J. Hinkle | *Fantasy* | 1 hr 24 min 04 sec |
| 7 | W. B. H. Dowse | *Dione* | 1 hr 24 min 28 sec |
| 8 | Redfield | *Scarab* | DNF |

the family was Commy — into the early 1960s. "The Shafroths," remembered Carolyn Rowland, "were good friends of mine and Abby was always a strong competitor."

THE FIRST RACE for the WYC's Wianno Senior (Class P) for which results survive was held on Saturday, July 25, 1914. Eight boats turned out, and the results reproduced on the previous page are based on a brief mention in the *Hyannis Patriot*.

The next race of which there remains a record was started at 3:32 in the afternoon of Saturday, August 15, two weeks after the opening of the Cape Cod Canal and the same day that the Panama Canal opened. Results were reported in the *Barnstable Patriot* and are shown in the table below.

Three more boats showed up for this race than the August 3 affair. One of the newcomers, *Snookums*, is associated with her skipper, Wilton Crosby, rather than her owner. This was unusual in the reporting of race results as skippers were typically aboard only to act as advisors. It is worth noting that this event was held on the same day that Nat Herreshoff came to Wianno to race P. Sawyer's *Oleander* in Class C.

This Class P race, like the one that followed a week later, was contested by eleven boats, not the

| Portrait of the Fleet<br>Race Results of the Wianno Senior (Class P), August 15, 1914 | | | |
|---|---|---|---|
| **Place** | **Owner** | **Boat Name** | **Time** |
| 1 | Franklin Robinson | *Bobwhite* | 1 hr 15 min 30 sec |
| 2 | P. (Percy) Melville | *Ethyl* | 1 hr 16 min 49 sec |
| 3 | T. S. Redfield | *Scarab* | 1 hr 17 min 15 sec |
| 4 | Wilton Crosby* | *Snookums* | 1 hr 17 min 32 sec |
| 5 | J. G. Hinkle | *Fantasy* | 1 hr 17 min 57 sec |
| 6 | W. B. H. Dowse (commodore) | *Dione* | 1 hr 18 min 43 sec |
| 7 | G. H. Fiske | *Maxixe* | 1 hr 19 min 59 sec |
| 8 | H. B. Day | *Wendy* | 1 hr 21 min 7 sec |
| 9 | W. P. Halliday | *A.P.H.* | 1 hr 23 min 25 sec |
| 10 | A. S. Hagerman | *Commy* | 1 hr 23 min 42 sec |
| 11 | N. Dubois | *No. 3* | 1 hr 23 min 47 sec |

*Snookums* was owned by Andrew Adie.

fourteen that *The Rudder* reported had been built. Perhaps the most likely reason for the discrepancy is that not all the boats built in 1914 were sold that year. Sail #8, pictured in *The Rudder* in 1915, has no name on her transom, suggesting she was still in the builder's hands. It is possible, but unlikely, that a boat was purchased by an owner with no interest in racing. Subsequent press reports about the original fleet sometimes put its number at thirteen or eleven, the latter number given to a *Hyannis Patriot* reporter for a story printed on August 28, 1930. The matter remains something of a mystery.

The race held on August 22 was sailed in a breeze that started from the northeast but shifted to the southwest, conditions that were apparently lighter overall than had prevailed on the 15th as the race took almost an hour longer. The results appear in the accompanying table.

The final race of the new knockabout's first season was sailed in a strong southwest breeze, probably over the same course as the previous events, twice around a 4½-mile triangle in Centerville Harbor that ran from the Wianno Pier to Craigville to Colliers Ledge. The first three finishers were Franklin Robinson in *Bobwhite*, Percy Melville in *Ethyl*, and William Fiske in *Maxixe*. The *Barnstable Patriot*

| Portrait of the Fleet<br>Race Results of Wianno Senior (Class P) Race, August 22, 1914 | | | |
|---|---|---|---|
| **Place** | **Owner** | **Boat Name** | **Time** |
| 1 | Percy Melville | *Ethyl* | 2 hr 14 min 35 sec |
| 2 | T. S. Redfield | *Scarab* | 2 hr 16 min 57 sec |
| 3 | J. G. Hinkle | *Fantasy* | 2 hr 17 min 44 sec |
| 4 | G. H. Fiske | *Maxixe* | 2 hr 17 min 54 sec |
| 5 | H. B. Day | *Wendy* | 2 hr 18 min 54 sec |
| 6 | Franklin Robinson | *Bobwhite** | 2 hr 18 min 55 sec |
| 7 | Wilton Crosby | *Snookums* | 2 hr 20 min 35 sec |
| 8 | N. Dubois | *No. 3* | 2 hr 20 min 53 sec |
| 9 | W. B. H. Dowse | *Dione* | 2 hr 21 min 50 sec |
| 10 | W. P. Halliday | *A.P.H.* | 2 hr 22 min |
| 11 | A. S. Hagerman | *Commy* | DNF |

*Although the newspaper printed the name as two words, it is believed it appeared as one word on the transom.

*One of three knock-abouts built in 1915 was #15 Viking.*

article about this event was printed on September 14 and included information that suggests the first year's racing was seeing some evolution. For one thing, an "Open-Skipper's Race" was included as a separate event. The first three finishers were: Manley Crosby in *A.P.H.,* Wilton Crosby in *Snookums*, and William Fiske in *Maxixe*. This is the first evidence that the WYC saw the need for a separate event in which professional skippers took the helm.

The *Patriot* article about the last race of the 1914 season included results for a separate "Ladies' Race." The first three finishers in this event were Elizabeth Cross in *Wendy*, Pauline Fiske in *Maxixe*, and Margaret Dowse in *Dione*. The paper also reported that there were plans already afoot to build ten more Class P knockabouts for the 1915 season. This appears to have been either an attempt by the source to drum up interest, or simply over-optimism.

As things developed, only three new boats were built in 1915, and three of the founding fathers — Robinson, Redfield, and Dubois — sold their yachts after only one year of ownership. What's more, the enthusiastic newspaper coverage of the WYC's races during 1914 ceased entirely the following year, except for a few brief entries reporting that the Class C knockabout *Stranger* owned by Nelson Bearse had dominated her events. James Gaff Hinkle won a fine, new trophy — the Commodore's Trophy — put up by Commodore Dowse, but little else survives from that season.

How much of what must have been going on at the WYC during 1915 affected reporting of racing activities is now unknown. But the race results largely disappeared from the newspaper, and so did Commodore Dowse's new trophy. It went missing, creating a mystery that would persist for nearly a century. One thing is certain, however: As 1915 neared its end, big changes were impending at the WYC.

EDWARD CROSSETT WAS a modest, shy man who, after graduating Phi Beta Kappa from Amherst in 1905, had become involved in the family lumber business and devoted his working life to the industry and to forest conservation. He also had several hobbies to keep himself occupied. He was a skilled amateur photographer, short-wave radio enthusiast, and collector of fine etchings, drawings, and prints. Edward and his wife Elizabeth wintered in Florida, but when they decided to spend summers on the Cape, they chose a property abutting Henry Day's. In November 1915 construction began on what the *Barnstable Patriot* called "one of the largest houses in that locality." When it was completed in June 1916, Crossett named the house Lynwood, the "Lyn" reflecting the name of his newly born third daughter Carolyn. Once settled in at Wianno, he promptly joined the WYC.

In early February 1916, the *Boston Daily Globe* reported that the WYC's executive committee had succeeded in an ambitious effort to purchase "all the property of the Cotocheset Company. It is proposed to change the Wianno Yacht Club into the Wianno Club. The Cotocheset Hotel will be used as its clubhouse and will be the center of the athletic and social activities of the community."

The hotel had long been a fixture in the village thanks in part to its splendid location overlooking Nantucket Sound. At this time, the club executive committee included prominent Boston lawyer E. T. Blodgett as chairman, William Dowse as commodore, H. L. Bearse as vice commodore, Henry Day as treasurer, and members Thomas F. Baxter of West Newton (who had recently purchased a Class P knockabout that he named *Ruth* — sail #17), George S. Baldwin, and William Lloyd Garrison, Jr., whose grandfather, the famous abolitionist, had summered

in Osterville and was among the original trustees of the village library.

An ambitious $50,000 improvement plan was announced under the oversight of Boston architect Horace Frazer, well-known for the many gracious homes he'd built in Brookline. The old Cotocheset Hotel was renovated with twenty-one new rooms equipped with telephones, electric lighting, and steam heat, the work performed by the Daniel (pronounced Dan'l) Brothers, popular Osterville contractors. The new facility (added to the National Register of Historic Places in 1979) opened in July — it cost twice the original budget — and construction of a new golf course became a principal club project that summer. A boardwalk ran from the Wianno Club past the Wianno Yacht Club to the Dowse house.

Precisely how the new-look club(s) would function as an organization was a matter of some discussion. In its July 4, 1916, edition, the *Barnstable Patriot* reported: "The Wianno Club is an extension of the old Wianno Yacht Club, which has been merged into the new organization." Precisely what "merged" really meant represented an obvious source for confusion and potential conflicts.

Some six decades later, in his history of the Wianno Yacht Club, Townsend Hornor, who, like his father, had served as a commodore, addressed the issue of how things developed following the merger. "For the next thirty years, the Yacht Club operated as an active department of the Wianno Club, although it retained its original Charter and, according to our most senior members, 'yachting' remained the dominant Club activity for a very long time…. For several

*Here is the Wianno Club in 1920. The membership had grown considerably since its transformation from the Wianno Yacht Club. By 1917, there were 213 members.*

months following incorporation, they debated whether the new executive officer's title ought to be 'commodore' or 'president....'" Eventually both titles were maintained, but the mechanics of blended clubs focused on different activities would eventually result in another organizational change.

Having been part of the ambitious transformation, William Dowse became president of the Wianno Club but stepped down as commodore of the WYC and was succeeded in that position in 1916 by Edward Crossett. Edward purchased a Class P knockabout from Manley Crosby — sail #22 — that, perhaps

thinking of his daughters, he named *Tomboy.* To promote interest, and to demonstrate that yachting was still the central activity of the Wianno Yacht Club despite the new golf course, tennis courts, billiard room, and ballroom, Crossett donated a new trophy, the Lynwood Cup, awarded to the boat with the season's highest average points total. The first person to win the Lynwood trophy was James Gaff Hinkle, who had clearly emerged as one of the fleet's most gifted sailors.

The table on page 30 shows the results of the 1916 season. Although some of the founding fathers

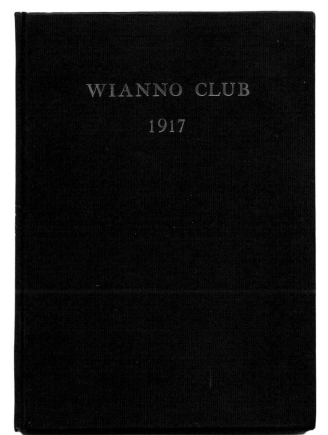

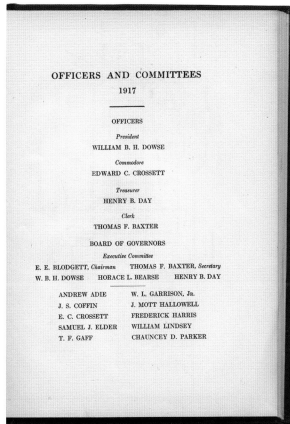

OFFICERS AND COMMITTEES
1917

OFFICERS

*President*
WILLIAM B. H. DOWSE

*Commodore*
EDWARD C. CROSSETT

*Treasurer*
HENRY B. DAY

*Clerk*
THOMAS F. BAXTER

BOARD OF GOVERNORS
*Executive Committee*

E. E. BLODGETT, *Chairman*     THOMAS F. BAXTER, *Secretary*
W. B. H. DOWSE     HORACE L. BEARSE     HENRY B. DAY

| | |
|---|---|
| ANDREW ADIE | W. L. GARRISON, Jr. |
| J. S. COFFIN | J. MOTT HALLOWELL |
| E. C. CROSSETT | FREDERICK HARRIS |
| SAMUEL J. ELDER | WILLIAM LINDSEY |
| T. F. GAFF | CHAUNCEY D. PARKER |

*The opening page of the Wianno Yacht Club's 1917 handbook lists officers and committee members.*

had left, two new members — Baxter and Wells — had been added to the fleet. The full series included twenty-one races. These were held twice weekly, on Wednesdays and Saturdays, along with special events. The season ended on Labor Day.

On April 8, 1917, America entered the Great War. Prior to that, reporting in the *Barnstable Patriot* about the war had been largely detached. There were occasional articles about war events, an ongoing tally of how much each side was spending per day, and a brief entry about blankets and bandages collected in local villages for French wounded, but reporting about the human toll and suffering was absent. By 1918, the war was no longer remote. That June, American forces entered combat at Château-Thierry and Belleau Wood. Joe Daniel, whose brothers Charles and Bob had built Edward Crossett's big house, was "somewhere in France" along with Manley Crosby's

| | | | | | | | |
|---|---|---|---|---|---|---|---|
| Portrait of the Fleet<br>Season Totals for 1916 | | | | | | | |
| **Owner** | **#** | **Boat** | **Points** | **Rank** | **No. of Races** | **Avg. Pts./Race** | **Rank Overall** |
| Day | 2 | *Wendy* | 765.3 | 6 | 19 | 40.3 | 9 |
| Halliday | 4 | *A.P.H.* | 197.3 | 11 | 6 | 32.9 | 11 |
| Hagerman | 5 | *Commy* | 606.3 | 5 | 18 | 44.5 | 7 |
| Adie | 6 | *Snookums* | 1384.4 | 3 | 20 | 69.2 | 3 |
| Fiske | 13 | *Maxixe* | 203.3 | 10 | 4 | 50.3 | 6 |
| Baxter | 17 | *Ruth* | 256.1 | 7 | 7 | 36.6 | 10 |
| Hinkle | 19 | *Fantasy* | 1545.5 | 1 | 20 | 77.2 | 1 |
| Melville | 20 | *Ethyl* | 220.3 | 9 | 5 | 44.0 | 8 |
| Wells | 21 | *Gull* | 226.4 | 8 | 3 | 75.5 | 2 |
| Crossett | 22 | *Tomboy* | 1398.0 | 2 | 21 | 66.6 | 4 |
| Dowse | 23 | *Dione* | 1021.1 | 4 | 18 | 56.7 | 5 |

two oldest sons, Malcolm (Max) and Carroll.

Max was twenty-five years old in 1918 and serving in the 101st U.S. Engineers when he wrote a letter home to his mother on the day before Thanksgiving. The letter was printed in the *Hyannis Patriot*. In it, Max reported that on November 11, his unit had been repairing a road near a French artillery battery when the momentous word arrived that all firing would cease at 11 A.M. Max had been at Verdun when the city was shelled by German big guns and, with the war ended, he wrote Velina: "you can bet we were some happy when they said it was all over." His unit marched one hundred miles in eight days to the rear where Max wrote his letter. When he got back to Osterville, he returned to work with his father and

was involved in the construction of every wooden Wianno Senior save for those built while he was in the Army. He was known fondly to two generations of Wianno Senior owners as "Uncle Max."

The WYC's 1918 season started late, the first race not being held until the last Wednesday in July. After that, however, races were sailed every Wednesday and Saturday through Labor Day. The Class P racing fleet now comprised twelve boats, one more than before the war, but the roster had changed, as seen in the accompanying table. Among the new owners were Ohioan Joel Coffin, who had recently purchased the Lima Locomotive Corporation, and George Talbot's son Fritz, who was a graduate cum laude of Harvard Medical School where he later taught pediatric medicine before becoming first chief of Children's Medical Service at Massachusetts General Hospital.

Introducing the Lynwood Cup was the first but not last of Edward Crossett's efforts to spark competition in the Class P fleet. In 1920, Commodore Crossett unveiled the Long Distance Challenge Trophy, the distance being that from Wianno to Falmouth Heights. The trip back was a separate event contested by the fleet's professional skippers racing for prize money. When Crossett established the rules for this trophy, he stipulated that it would remain in competition unless the same person won it three times. Some years later, when the same person did win the event three times, a small crisis was provoked within the Crossett family.

| WYC Wianno Senior (Class P) Fleet as of August 1918 | | |
|---|---|---|
| 1. | *Snookums* | A. Adie |
| 2. | ***Harriet C*** | J. C. Coffin |
| 3. | *Wendy* | H. B. Day |
| 4. | *Dione* | W. B. H. Dowse |
| 5. | *Commy* | A. S. Hagerman |
| 6. | *A.P.H.* | P. Halliday |
| 7. | *Fantasy* | J. G. Hinkle |
| 8. | ***Which*** | Arthur Gilbert |
| 9. | ***Sylmar*** | George C. Graves |
| 10. | *Ethyl* | P. F. Melville |
| 11. | ***Water Nymph*** | Fritz B. Talbot |
| 12. | ***Buella*** | Rene E. Paine |

*Bold denotes boats appearing for the first time.

# CHAPTER FOUR

# Roaring Twenties

*"Members of the [Crosby] firm said today that the Cape waters are attracting so many and the business at the boatyards is increasing so fast that it seems impossible to keep up with it."*

—Hyannis Patriot, *September 26, 1928*

At the dawn of the 1920s, there began in Osterville a golden age of summers for those fortunate enough to have the resources to build or buy in Wianno or the greater village, join the Wianno Club whose dues in 1922 were $125 (worth about $1,700 in today's money), and purchase a sailboat. Summer people arrived from away to find their homes spruced up and ready for occupancy, thanks to the efforts of local tradesmen, and their boats painted, rigged, and launched at the Crosby yard. Each season, the Melvilles journeyed from Chicago to enjoy their cottage — built by master carpenter Azor Hall — on West Bay.

*This Crosby ad of July 11, 1929, notes the "Famous Wianno One Design Class Knockabouts" and shows the various job titles of the company's officers.*

George Sicard, an 1894 graduate of Yale and later of NYU's law school, lived in Pelham Manor, New York, but had an estate in Centerville on the Bumps River. In 1919, Sicard bought Senior #9 and, nine years later, contracted with Seabury Pearse to build another home on Eel River Road in Osterville, said to cost $30,000.

In 1920, Robert Stewart Kilborne and his wife Katherine began summering at the Wianno Club, journeying to the Cape from their home in western Massachusetts. There, Katherine's father, William Skinner, had first established himself in Northampton after arriving steerage class from England in 1845. This was three years after the world's most famous writer, Charles Dickens, voyaged to America to see the raw but vibrant new country for himself. Out of Dickens's journey came *American Notes* and the novel *Martin Chuzzlewit.* Out of Skinner's journey came a fortune based on vision, hard work, and the manufacture of silk in Williamburg, Massachusetts. In 1921, the Kilbornes bought #43 from Manley Crosby. The boat was purchased primarily for their fourteen-year-old son, Robert Stewart Kilborne, Jr., and named *Unquomonk* for the family's famous mills,

which took their name from the old Algonquin label for a nearby hill and stream.

Norwegian-born Frederic Schaefer, who began an engineering career at a drafting table in Boston and established the very successful Schaefer Equipment Co. in Pittsburgh — a maker of railroad brake equipment — bought a fine summer place in Wianno and purchased Wianno Senior #55, which he named *Dolphin*, in 1924. Rene Paine came down from his Brookline estate and bought a waterfront property in 1918. He immediately purchased Senior #41 that he named *Buella* after his wife, and applied to build and maintain his own pier on Nantucket Sound.

From Baltimore came Mary and Edna Parlett, whose late father, John Fletcher Parlett, had grown up in the family tobacco business and then managed an important part of R. J. Reynolds' operations. The sisters — quiet, private women who enjoyed the garden at their Eel River Road house — arrived in Osterville in the early '20s, and each purchased a Wianno Senior. After they bought a Wianno Junior, they made the boat available to village youngsters, often under the guidance of Joe Daniel's son Mitch. They also became very active Senior competitors. "They were," remembered Carolyn Rowland, "great sports ladies. Mary was the tougher of the two when it came to racing."

In the spring of 1925, the census revealed that the villages in the town of Barnstable were still tiny by today's standards. While Hyannis had a population of 2,294, Osterville then numbered 701 residents. But that was more than Centerville's 484 or Cotuit's 657. That June, however, what the local papers called "Cape

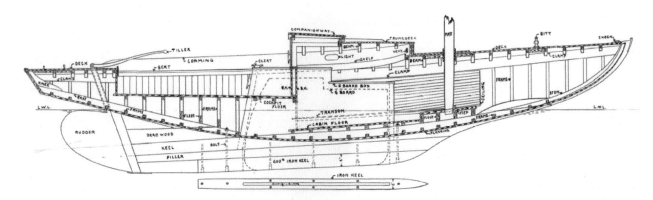

Cod's most important realty transaction in history" occurred at Osterville. Boston developer Ferris W. Norris acquired Grand Island and Dead Neck Beach, and hired landscape architects Olmsted Brothers of Brookline and the Boston engineering firm of Aspinwall and Lincoln to begin laying out "one of the most exclusive summer colonies in the United States." As for the Crosbys, the development of Grand Island had implications that were immediate and profound. The boatbuilders lost their long-standing, local source of oak, pine, and spruce.

Growth was not limited to residential housing development. In Osterville, the time appeared ripe to establish a second yacht club. The Osterville Yacht Club had been inactive for some time before it was revived during an August 1926 meeting hosted at the Crosby Yacht Building & Storage Co. Several WYC members, among them William Halliday, Harry Stimpson, R. M. Roloson, and Dr. A. C. Wilson, also joined the OYC. So did several Crosbys, including Manley and Wilton. WYC Wianno Senior owners competed in OYC races, and the club, less formal than the WYC, had a "cute craft" class, a class for outboard boats, and an "open speed boat" class. That said, the sailing races were as competitive as any others, and top skippers for the Wianno owners such as Fred Scudder, Joe Daniel, and Manley Crosby competed along with James Gaff Hinkle.

Within a year, the club expected its membership to total 150 and work was begun on a clubhouse with a large veranda. "The entire building," reported the *Hyannis Patriot* in May 1927, "is to be up to date in every way.... A large lounging room and a room for the men are some of the features. There is to be also a room for ladies and a card room. This new clubhouse is the first real home the Osterville Yacht Club has had."

There was also expansion of the Crosby family's activities. As the Wianno Senior fleet grew, there was a corresponding need to improve maintenance capabilities. Manley Crosby's nephew Chester — the oldest son of Manley's brother Joseph — recognized the need even as he worked alongside his cousins Max and Carroll and learned to efficiently plank the hulls. "I saw there was a demand for a way to haul out the Seniors to paint and clean them," Chester said in

*Cape Cod Life*'s 1987 article on the Wianno Senior. "In 1926 [at age twenty-one] I put in the first marine railway in Osterville. In succeeding summers I was overwhelmed with the amount of work I got." With one man and his wife Ida to help him, Chester had started what would become Chester A. Crosby & Sons.

IT WAS DURING the mid-1920s that the first and only substantive changes were made to the Wianno Senior's design. *The Rudder*'s 1915 article had noted that "The keel is not a fin, but extends a considerable way under the boat, which enables her to go to windward in shallow water, without letting down the centerboard. It [the deadwood] is cut away somewhat, however, near the rudder, to make easier work for the helmsman when coming into stays [tacking or luffing up]."

In addition to Vaughan D. Bacon's topsides profile and sail plan illustration, *The Rudder* article included two additional drawings, one a full hull profile reminiscent of a construction plan. This drawing (reproduced on page 18) includes the "cut away" portion of the deadwood showing what looks much like a propeller aperture. Whatever the intent of the original keel/deadwood configuration, it apparently was deemed needful of revision.

In 1927, the lowermost portion of the keel that included the iron ballast shoe was extended all the way aft to the rudderpost. The aperture in the deadwood was eliminated and the rudder was made about 8" deeper, extending to the base of the new keel. Board-up draft of 2'6" remained the same as

before. When found agreeable, the revised keel and rudder configuration was made standard in 1928. It is believed that, to maintain the class's one-design nature, all the existing yachts that raced were modified to meet the new standard.

The rig, too, came in for scrutiny. By now, a whole new generation of one-designs had emerged from the drawing boards of Charles Mower, John Alden, Francis Sweisguth, and others. Generally speaking, these boats had the latest in rigs and carried marconi rather than gaff mainsails. The Crosbys reported that the John G. Alden Office had submitted a marconi rig design as early as 1921. The files at Sparkman & Stephens include another proposal drawn by K. Aage Nielsen, but that was likely done between 1936 and 1941.

It is not known whether a proposed marconi rig for the Wianno Senior had something, or anything, to do with the revised keel and rudder, but two marconi-rigged Seniors appeared in 1926. The Mattesons' #64 *Natanis* appears to have been built with a marconi rig. Edward Crossett decided to give the new rig a whirl and rerigged his #22 *Tomboy*. "Well, we tried it," said Carolyn Rowland, "but took it right back out. It didn't have quite the delicacy to windward." Presumably, Carolyn's skipper Joe Daniel, with his deft touch, didn't need much convincing that the Wianno Senior was a better boat with its original rig. By the end of the 1926 season, both #22 and #64 were racing with gaff-rigged mainsails.

Despite the decisions made by both Crossett and Matteson, the 1927 season saw more yachts with marconi rigs. These included #36, #56, #61, #62, and

## Portrait of the Fleet
## 1926 Season Totals (marconi rig included)

| Pos. | # | Boat Name | Owner | Points Total | No. of Races |
|------|-----|-------------------|----------------|--------------|--------------|
| 1 | 47 | *Janabe* | J. M. Hallowell | 1550.2 | 22 |
| 2 | 22 | *Tomboy* (marconi) | E. C. Crossett | 1534.4 | 18 |
| 3 | 37 | *Fiddler* | M. Parlett | 1532.6 | 22 |
| 4 | 40 | *Vashti* | B. White | 1391.2 | 20 |
| 5 | 11 | *Fantasy* | J. Hinkle | 1289.6 | 22 |
| 6 | 33 | *Water Nymph* | F. B. Talbot | 1273.6 | 22 |
| 7 | 28 | *Gull* | E. F. Byrnes | 1230.6 | 18 |
| 8 | 51 | *King Tut* | W. P. Thayer | 1160.8 | 22 |
| 9 | 60 | *Mabel* | H. F. Stimpson | 1113.0 | 22 |
| 10 | 57 | *Second Fiddler* | E. Parlett | 1110.9 | 22 |
| 11 | 44 | *Allegro* | N. Talbot | 1108.5 | 21 |
| 12 | 62 | *Is Zat So* | L. Madden | 953.3 | 21 |
| 13 | 24 | *Mary* | J. F. Syme | 948.1 | 19 |
| 14 | 2 | *Wendy* | H. B. Day | 946.3 | 20 |
| 15 | 13 | *Cockachoice* | N. Foster | 918.4 | 21 |
| 16 | 5 | *Commy* | F. Hagerman | 711.4 | 22 |
| 17 | 50 | *Felyrial* | A. F. du Pont | 682.8 | 12 |
| 18 | 49 | *Peggy M* | F. G. Crane | 659.7 | 10 |
| 19 | 55 | *Dolphin* | F. Schaefer | 602.8 | 13 |
| 20 | 64 | *Natanis* (marconi) | K. Matteson | 480.4 | 14 |
| 21 | 8 | *Sea Dog* | D. Hornor | 471.2 | 12 |
| 22 | 4 | *A.P.H.* | W. P. Halliday | 450.2 | 7 |
| 23 | 36 | *Mimi* | W. K. Sinclair | 423.0 | 8 |
| 24 | 42 | *Arem* | R. Mitchell | 370.5 | 16 |
| 25 | 9 | *Marie* | A. C. Wilson | 320.3 | 7 |
| 26 | 3 | *Alouette* | F. I. Sears | 255.4 | 9 |
| 27 | 6 | *Snookums* | A. Adie | 224.6 | 4 |
| 28 | 35 | | H. Langenberg | 185.2 | 6 |
| 29 | 7 | *Patsy* | J. Tiernan | 90.5 | 6 |
| 30 | 63 | | W. A. C. Miller | 60.2 | 5 |

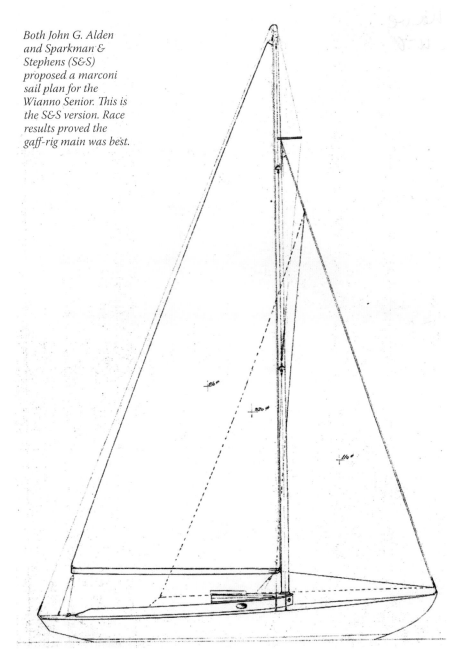

*Both John G. Alden and Sparkman & Stephens (S&S) proposed a marconi sail plan for the Wianno Senior. This is the S&S version. Race results proved the gaff-rig main was best.*

#65, which appears to have been built new with the marconi rig. During the 1927 season, the fleet watched the performance of these boats with curiosity, and the marconi yachts were scored as a separate class.

The earliest surviving race results for these marconi-rigged Wianno Seniors are for an event sailed in late July 1927. Overall, the race was won by James Gaff Hinkle in *Fantasy* in 1 hour 25 minutes. The fastest Senior in the Marconi Class was the Sinclairs' *Mimi* #36, which finished 4 minutes later in 1 hour 29 minutes, followed by the Maddens' #62 *Is Zat So* in 1 hour 29 minutes 15 seconds. Next time out was an early August race sailed in a strong breeze. The Days' gaff-rigged #2 *Wendy* was the first boat to finish in 1 hour 10 minutes. Kent Matteson's #64 *Natanis* was the first of the two marconi yachts entered, finishing in 1 hour 13 minutes 13 seconds. The pattern continued. On August 25, in a strong northeast wind, the fleet set off on a course that involved a beat to the spindle off Hyannis Port and a run home. George Sicard's rerigged Senior #56 was the fastest of the three marconi vessels racing, yet the 1 hour 22 minute 45 second time was 2 minutes and 5 seconds slower than that of the fastest boat, Fritz Talbot's #33 *Water Nymph.*

Comparisons of marconi vs. gaff-rig performance are difficult and, in the end, perhaps have little to teach us. What matters most here is that Manley Crosby's conception of his knockabout as a gaff-rig centerboarder was, despite its excessive weather helm, essentially on target to begin with. Such a cohesive design was not really amenable to, or needful of, so drastic a change as replacing its rig

*A trio of the founding fathers' boats circa 1918. Number 5 was owned by Kansas City, Missouri, attorney Frank Hagerman and sailed for decades by his athletically inclined daughter Abby. To port is James Gaff Hinkle's* Fantasy *carrying its original #19, although that would soon be changed to #11. Sail #6 was first owned by Andrew Adie and often skippered by Wilton Crosby. Faintly visible on #19 and #6 are lazyjacks, included on the boat's sail plan, but dispensed with on #5.*

to "keep up with the times."

Ultimately, within the Senior fleet, fascination with the new rig ended almost as soon as it began. Only one or two of the Seniors continued after 1927 with the marconi sail plan. A rig addition that did become permanent was backstays. These were added in 1928 — according to a *Yachting* article in March 1965, for which the author interviewed the Crosbys — so that a single-luff spinnaker with a hefty 14' pole could be used. This raised the yacht's price by some $90 (about $1,200 in today's money) and increased the challenge to foredeck crew many times over. Newly added backstays reduced headsail sag, permitting a straighter jib luff, which improved the boat's windward performance.

NEAR THE START of 1928, in February, long time WYC member George Talbot died while wintering in St. Stephens, South Carolina. Talbot was seventy-nine years old, and the local newspaper noted that with his passing "expires nearly all of the heads of the old families who located at Wianno during its pioneer days." Dr. Fritz Talbot, the oldest of Talbot's three sons, had become a strong Wianno Senior competitor and was the WYC Commodore at the time of his father's passing.

In March, news reached Osterville that William P. Halliday had died suddenly in Memphis where he'd become chairman of the Memphis Hotel Company and one of the city's leading citizens. Halliday was sixty-three years old. That spring, the club lost three more long-term members including two of the founding fathers. Andrew Adie passed away. So did ex-commodore Dowse who returned from a European trip in April, fell sick and, after seeming to improve, died suddenly at Massachusetts General Hospital at age seventy-six.

Then, in the midst of the 1928 racing season, another of the early summer residents of the village died suddenly. Lawyer James Mott Hallowell had been born in Osterville in 1864 and passed away there sixty-four years later. His son Benjamin then owned #47 *Janabe*, in which he won the Senior Class in that summer's first-ever Edgartown Regatta. Three years later in 1931, James's widow presented the WYC with the James Mott Hallowell Memorial Cup. The cup is awarded annually "to the yacht winning the greatest number of scheduled Club Races sailed under the auspices of the Club including the Fourth of July Race and the Labor Day Race, but excluding all Open and Pre- and Post-Season Races."

In 1929, the WYC got a new commodore, fifty-three-year-old John West Hornor. After pursuing a successful Wall Street career, Hornor had recently retired as a managing partner at the investment banking powerhouse of Dillon, Read & Co. He then devoted himself to various philanthropies and to serving on the boards of several New York hospitals. It was thus a busy retirement but one that permitted Hornor, together with his wife and three sons, John, DeWitt, and Townsend, to spend more time at their Osterville summer home on Eel River Road. Thus began John Hornor's long and colorful stint as commodore, a tenure remembered for its discipline and efficiency.

Like their parents, the young people of that period retained strong memories of Commodore Hornor all their lives. Carolyn Rowland was just starting her sailing career then, and took note of John Hornor's style. "He was a stickler for the rules and he knew them all, and you quickly learned you were expected to know and follow them, too. I think the main thing he wanted the young people to learn was sportsmanship. That was as important as anything to him."

He was also a stickler for having boats participate in races. Anne Halliday remembered that "under Commodore Hornor, all boats were *required* to

*Winter vacation: Here are Manley Crosby, his wife Velina, and son Malcolm in Tarpon Springs, Florida, during the winter of 1927. It looks as if they may be inspecting the local fishing boats.*

show up when he called a race, even on short notice. And they did!"

As Hornor was taking over as commodore, Manley Crosby was completing seven new Wianno Seniors for the 1929 season. Stanley Morton named his new #78 *Seeadler* (Sea Eagle) after the famous World War I raider of Count von Luckner who would later be an opponent of Adolf Hitler. Morton promptly embarked on an active racing career. The Crane family, paper manufacturers in central Massachusetts, purchased #79 and named it after their waterfront summer home in Wianno, *Southlook*. Two of the 1929 boats left Osterville. Henry Gardner took #74 *Firefly* to Hyannis Port and #75 *Senorita* went to West Falmouth. *Curlew*, #76, was purchased by Kenneth D. Steere of Harwich Port, who within a few years, would be the major influence in introducing the Wianno Senior to the waters east of Osterville. *Prodigal Pig*, #13, would remain an integral part of the Batchelder family into the mid-1960s. Long before custom-made, computer-generated Christmas cards became commonplace, the Batchelders created a card that featured a photo of their boat and the message: "The Prodigal Pig — home port, Osterville, Mass. — Master, Batchelder — crew, Batchelder & Batchelder — sets sail for friendly harbors laden with Season's Greetings. Windsor, Connecticut, Christmas, 1937."

The 1929 season saw the introduction of the St. Mary's Island Race, an event that never ventured into Nantucket Sound. Instead, the race began off the WYC pier in West Bay, proceeded through the Seapuit River and around Oyster Harbors into North Bay, and finished off St. Mary's Island. There, a shore gathering was hosted by Nathanael Davis, who owned a home on the island. The race was held through 1934. It was won in both 1929 and 1933 by #37 *Fiddler*, in 1930 and 1932 by #28 *Gull*, in 1931 by #9 *Marie*, and in 1934 by #85 *Venture*.

Foreseeing what at the time appeared to be an "ever-increasing business of building fine yachts," a big new storage building served by five marine railways had been completed at Crosby's in the fall of 1928. That same year, the Wianno Club undertook extensive dredging to improve West Bay and, that June, applied to the State Department of Public Works to "build and maintain a timber pier." In September 1929, an addition was announced "to the huge [Crosby] storage shed, which will be made about 100 feet larger.... Another yacht storage building 120 × 40 feet is to be erected at once...."

In October 1929, the stock market crashed, marking the end of the Roaring Twenties and the beginning of the Great Depression. On the Cape, the Hyannis Trust Company took out a newspaper ad reminding people that "Funds invested in our Savings Department are always available, never depreciate, and insure a good return to the depositor." The *Hyannis Patriot*, like other papers of its time, often published little quips and moral lessons, and in January 1930 saw fit to print this one: "The stock market gambler and the girl who marries an aviator are alike: They both take a flyer."

# CHAPTER FIVE

# Amateurs and Professionals

*"The professionals are not helmsmen but act as crew. They are not allowed to touch the tiller.... The pros may compete in the open races coming back from the Edgartown regatta and going to and from Nantucket regatta."*

— Boston Transcript, *September 9, 1939*

*It's a quiet day at Bass River, perfect for boat work. Seen here is* Valkyrie *with her then-owner Carl Barus. In 1938, Carl bought the boat on Nantucket from Morris Ernst, the New York attorney who successfully defended James Joyce's* Ulysses *against obscenity charges, and became a co-founder of the American Civil Liberties Union (ACLU). Although the boat was originally #7, it was carrying #29 by Ernst's ownership and Barus kept that number. He raced and cruised, going as far as Maine. Not until 1959 did* Valkyrie *again carry sail #7.*

Long before the 1885 formalizing of the Wianno Yacht Club, yacht racing had begun an evolution towards Corinthian (amateur) sailing in which owners skippered and manned their own boats rather than employing a paid captain and crew. On Long Island, the Seawanhaka Corinthian Yacht Club was founded in 1871 with the express purpose

43

of fostering the Corinthian spirit. The Beverly Yacht Club's emphasis on smaller yachts affordable by a growing number of people was another factor driving change. So was the emergence of the various one-design classes.

DESPITE THE WIDESPREAD influence of Corinthian sailing ideals, about half the Wianno Senior fleet had a paid skipper (and in rare instances a paid crew member) aboard. This practice continued from the inception of the class through the 1930s. It is safe to assume that the founding fathers were generally not enthusiastic about letting their children attempt to rig the boats, hoist and trim the big mainsail or, after it was introduced, set and douse the spinnaker on their own. What's more, even many years after the start of the class, not all owners were comfortable about having full responsibility. Many continued the local tradition, established early on, of employing a skipper. Often, a skipper remained in the summer employ of the same boat owner for years. Others, however, sailed for different owners who might hire them for a specific event. In all cases, the protocol was for the paid skipper to serve as an advisor rather than actually taking the tiller. Boats with a paid captain aboard competed in the "Professional Division" while those without were grouped in the "Amateur Division."

Surviving records for the decade 1919–1929 offer insights into how racing was then conducted at the WYC. The season was divided into two primary series, Wednesday and Saturday, with points totals kept separately. Scores were also kept for "Special Races" that included the Long Distance Challenge Trophy together with two others, one of which could have been a women's race, for such events were still being sailed in 1927 and possibly later. "Open Races" were contested by boats with professionals handling the tiller sailing against amateurs and other professionals.

In 1922, point tallies began to be kept for boats sailed by "Amateur Crew" as distinct from those with a professional skipper aboard, and an amateur series of three races became a regular part of the season schedule. On August 30, 1927, the *Globe* reported "The last race of the amateur series, consisting of three races, was sailed off here today in a strong west wind."

The Amateur Series was distinct from the majority of the racing in which the fleet was divided according to boats sailed by amateurs and those with a professional skipper aboard but not handling the tiller. "The boats in the amateur class started first," Carolyn Rowland said, "and five minutes later the skipper class started." One of the first published results of the divisions appeared in the *Globe* for a race sailed on July 13, 1929, when twenty-seven entrants were divided into Divisions A (skipper) and B (amateur). The Steeres finished first in Division B in 1 hour 38 minutes 50 seconds. Channing Wells's #28 *Gull* with a professional aboard, probably Capt. William G. Thompson, finished in 1 hour 35 minutes.

Looking back to a period beginning in 1929 when his father Kenneth David Steere bought #76 *Curlew*, Bruce M. Steere recalled that "the fleet was split into two sections — Amateur and Professional.

About the second year of this arrangement, we caught fire and dominated the Amateur fleet because of two innovations: (1) we bent [raked] the mast forward to reduce weather helm, and (2) we washed off her bottom weekly. The following year the club went back to an A and B Division [but] with Amateurs mixed in with Professionals. The top half of the B Division would move into the A Division for the following race, and the bottom half of the A Division would move back to the B Division."

Division of the fleet was not consistently applied. In September 1931, the Labor Day race attracted the largest fleet of the season — thirty-three boats — and all started at the same time, 10:10 A.M. That year, the Commodore's Cup — then awarded to the yacht with an all-amateur crew sailing in at least two-thirds of the races — was won by Stanley Morton in #78 *Seeadler.* Norman A. MacColl's *Halcyon* finished the season with the highest average score. "Mary MacColl sailed the boat herself," Carolyn Rowland remembered, "and she was always a threat."

Sailing with a professional skipper who knew the area waters and listening to tales of old Osterville as only a local could tell them, provided memories of a lifetime for many in the fleet. Joseph Mattison, Jr. (#84 *Kypris*) never forgot the experience of hiring Joseph Crosby's son Chester for a special skipper's race, probably in 1936. In a recollection that appeared in the class's seventy-fifth anniversary publication, Mattison wrote: "All the way up the windward leg, he kept adjusting. 'Joe, I think we should take in the main a bit. Not quite that much. Just a little. I think maybe we might peak her up a little. Just a little bit

Built in 1914, this Wianno Senior was originally owned by Commodore Dowse and carried sail #23. When sold to Mary Parlett, most likely in 1922, the number was changed to #37 and the name changed from Dione to Fiddler. Here, Mary Parlett (blue jacket) and her sister sail with Joe Daniel's son Mitch at the tiller. The figure facing the camera has yet to be identified.

more, if you don't mind.' He always spoke in that quiet, polite way he had.... I remember Johnny Linehan, sailing #11, got by us and we finished second. I apologized to Chet for the boat's poor performance off the wind. 'I don't care,' he beamed. 'We beat 'em all to windward, didn't we?'"

Chester had begun sailing with Senior owners when he was about sixteen, tending the jib sheets. As he gained experience, he learned that owners often expected the skipper to keep the boat looking sharp. "At one time," he recalled, "we used to shine the brass plates on the tiller as well as the turnbuckles, and the boats looked just wonderful." Chester went on to sail regularly for the Schaefer family in their #55 and the Stimpsons in #60.

Most of the hired skippers were very skillful sailors with an experienced eye for sail trim, tide and wind, and tactics. The Crosbys, of course, were born to it, and Manley, Wilton, Wilbur, Chester, Merrill,

*In its early days — this image is circa 1922 — the Wianno Senior fleet raced without spinnakers, and about half the boats had a paid skipper aboard for guidance. Here we see the boat of one of the class's leading promoters: Henry Day's #2* Wendy. *To port is J. F. Syme's #24* Mary L, *while to starboard is Jack Tiernan's #29 (previously and later #7)* Patsy.

Herbert, and Max all enjoyed success as skippers for a variety of owners. It was Max who oversaw the instruction of Robert Stewart Kilborne, Jr., from the time Stewart began racing at age fourteen in 1920 until he stopped six years later, having won a great many trophies in *Unquomonk* including the 1922 Wianno Yacht Club Championship.

Joseph Burlingame skippered for a number of families. A native of the Cape, Joe grew up playing baseball and sailing and then pursued a career in education, eventually becoming a school principal before moving on to teach math and geography at Milton Academy where he also taught students to build and sail model yachts. Having summers off permitted Joe to skipper for the Wianno fleet, and by 1929, if not earlier, he served as the WYC's yacht master. It fell to him to calculate the season's points and placings, a challenging undertaking.

Fred Scudder, who skippered for Mary Parlett, was among the most highly regarded of the skippers as well as a founder of the Hyannis Yacht Club and an important figure in the business and civic affairs of the town. William Turner sailed with Mary's sister Edna. Captain William Thompson — "Captain Tom" — sailed for both the Wells and Talbot families and was highly regarded by all.

John Linehan, who would become principal of the Hyannis Elementary School and later the Barnstable Middle School, was a popular skipper. Starting in 1949 and continuing until 1970, he influenced a generation of young Wianno Senior sailors as head sailing instructor at the Hyannis Port Yacht Club. Linehan skippered regularly for Jean Hinkle aboard #11 *Fantasy*. The two formed such a strong bond that when John married, Jean gave him the land upon which to build a house. Walter Sherman lived in Hyannis and was Abby Staunton Hagerman's skipper. He stayed with the family for some twenty years, eventually teaching Abby's children to sail aboard the family's two Wianno Juniors, #34 *Sea Horse* and #4 *Pelican*.

In general, the newspaper accounts of the WYC's races did not mention events in which paid professionals handled the tiller, but the Open Races — a series of three events in which boats sailed by a professional competed directly against those sailed by an amateur — were sometimes covered. Usually, the Open events that garnered publicity were those held as part of Independence Day racing. On July 4, 1922, George Sicard's #9 *Suno* won its race, but it was noted that "John Austin is captain of the boat." (Sicard, like a number of the WYC members, owned a cruising boat as well as a Wianno Senior, and Austin also was responsible for delivering the yacht to a variety of destinations.) Capt. William Thompson, sailing #28 *Gull* for Channing Wells on July 4, 1928, placed first. It was Chester Crosby at the helm when H. F. Stimpson's #60 *Malolo* passed twelve boats on the second leg to take first place on July 4, 1931. Twenty seconds behind him was Joe Burlingame at the helm of the MacColls' #41 *Halcyon*.

The WYC did keep records of the Open Series. To cite one year's results, the top three finishers were: (1) Chester Crosby sailing the Stimpsons' #60 *Malolo*; (2) Fred Scudder sailing Mary Parlett's #37 *Fiddler*; and (3) William Turner sailing Edna Parlett's #57 *Second Fiddler*.

The skippers did more than prepare the Seniors and advise the owners. During a picnic in July 1921, Dr. Talbot's then-skipper, William Thompson, rescued a drowning man, the fourth person he had saved. Edward Crossett eventually had one skipper for the family's Wianno Senior and another for his big motor-yacht. Until his death in 1928, Osterville's Preston Wright was employed as captain of Crossett's motor-yacht, which Wright took to the Crossetts' Florida winter home each fall. But it was Joe Daniel, the contractor, who was the Crossett family captain aboard *Tomboy*.

"Well," said Joe Daniel's daughter Nancy during a July 2010 interview, "we all idolized Dad, and the Crossett girls shared our feeling. His opportunity to teach them allowed him to do what he loved."

When Joe Daniel left high school in the tenth grade, he'd already earned a reputation for possessing an extraordinary gift for mathematics. He enrolled at the Massachusetts Nautical School — renamed in 1942 the Massachusetts Maritime Academy — and rose to Master Mariner before he gave up his career at sea to enter the contracting business and raise his family. Edward Crossett jumped at the chance to employ a sailor of Daniel's skills. Chester Crosby once

called Joe Daniel "the best skipper this bay ever knew."

"Dad's greatest rival," said Nancy Daniel, "was Fred Scudder."

After learning the basics aboard her family's Wianno Junior #7 *Bobolink* when she was ten or twelve years old, Crossett's daughter Carolyn moved up to #22 *Tomboy*. "Joe's son Mitch was our jib and spinnaker man," she said. "Joe was skipper, but, as was customary, he never touched the tiller. He would watch the wind and advise. Joe Daniel was a beautiful sailor. I loved him very much."

With Mitch on the foredeck and Joe handling the mainsheet and tactics, Carolyn became a fierce competitor, although her success rather quickly led to a disappointment she remembered all her life. In 1928, the Edgartown Yacht Club invited the Wianno Yacht Club to participate in the EYC's regatta. That year, the final long-distance race to Falmouth was joined by the first long-distance race to Edgartown. In both instances, the race home was a Skipper's Race. The accompanying table shows the results for the first ten finishers in both Skipper's Races.

By 1932, when she was sixteen years old, Carolyn had won the Long Distance trophy twice — her father had also won two of the Wianno-to-Falmouth Heights events — and she did so again that August. The race had been cold and wet, sailed in a strong southwest breeze, and Carolyn had been at the helm for just over 3 hours and 41 minutes. *Tomboy* not only was the first Senior to finish, but beat the fastest Star boat making the journey by 17 minutes, H. F. Stimpson's *Malolo* by 3 minutes, and Jean Hinkle aboard *Fantasy* by 5 minutes. The *Boston Globe* reported on the event, and its headline read: "Miss Crossett Wins Cup Given by Father." But Edward Crossett had other ideas.

"Father didn't think it appropriate for a family member to retire the trophy that he had donated, so I was told I could not accept the cup. I didn't, and the trophy remained in competition until 1946." It was a disappointment that Carolyn never really forgot.

*It is rare to see a photo of a Wianno Senior with her professional skipper at the helm. Here, however, is the Crossetts' #22 Tomboy and skipper Joe Daniel wearing his trademark hat. Daniel was regarded as among the topmost tier of skippers.*

| 1928 Skipper's Race Falmouth-Wianno | | | 1928 Skipper's Race Edgartown-Wianno | | |
|---|---|---|---|---|---|
| Placing | Boat #/Owner | Skipper | Placing | Boat #/Owner | Skipper |
| 1 | 37/M. Parlett | F. Scudder | 1 | 37/M. Parlett | F. Scudder |
| 2 | 60/Stimpson | C. Crosby | 2 | 60/Stimpson | C. Crosby |
| 3 | 22/Crossett | J. Daniel | 3 | 57/E. Parlett | W. Turner |
| 4 | 9/Wilson | M. Crosby | 4 | 47/B. Hallowell | Hallowell |
| 5 | 28/Wells | Thompson | 5 | 68/Wilds | S. Nickerson |
| 6 | 8/Hornor | D. Hall | 6 | 22/Crossett | J. Daniel |
| 7 | 57/E. Parlett | W. Turner | 7 | 11/Hinkle | L. Tallman |
| 8 | 15/Bailey | Unknown | 8 | 61/Madden | Haskell |
| 9 | 2/Day | W. Crosby | 9 | 42/Field | Bearse |
| 10 | 61/Madden | Bearse | 10 | 14/Roloson | Unknown |

# CHAPTER SIX

# An Expanding Fleet

*"Racing at Harwich Port started out as handicap racing. Wiannos did well against the assorted catboats, cutters, and schooners. Our only real competition was a Herreshoff 15 named 'Nancy Jane'."*

—Bruce M. Steere letter to Joseph Hinkle, April 10, 1989

*Up goes the mainsail on #31 Iky at Bass River. Number 31 was built in 1917 and her owner, Irving K. Taylor, was among those hoping to establish interest in the class at a revived Bass River Yacht Club. Here we see #31 (circa early 1920s) trailing a flat-bottomed skiff with an upturned transom to improve performance, while onlookers watch from a moored catboat.*

Initially, few foresaw the scope of what was to come from the stock market crash, but most existing and prospective Wianno Senior owners were, through good fortune, foresight, and breadth of planning, largely insulated from the worst effects. An immediate victim, however, was the Osterville Yacht Club. Its promising renewal came to an abrupt halt. At the end of August 1930, a newspaper announcement reported that the Osterville

Yacht Club would transfer its building to the Wianno Yacht Club. The fine new clubhouse was moved from its waterfront site on Cockachoiset Lane to its current location on Bridge Street. Henry Day had owned the property prior to transferring it to the Wianno Yacht Club in 1927.

"My first recollection of the Wianno Yacht Club," said Townsend "Townie" Hornor in *Cape Cod Life*, "goes back to when the building was coming down the road with a team of horses and wooden rollers from its old location…. My father…bought the building by paying off the Osterville Yacht Club's debts and providing a new set of uniforms for the Osterville Silver Cornet Band." Many OYC members were members of the band, which had been created by Manley Crosby. The new clubhouse, officially opened on July 4, 1931, complemented the new pier built in 1930.

The *Boston Daily Globe* covered the Independence Day opening ceremony, which commenced with a call to attention by a bugler and the hoisting of the flag and then the WYC burgee. Commodore John Hornor then offered brief remarks. He welcomed members of the Osterville Yacht Club, who were automatically enrolled in the WYC. He thanked Frederic Schaefer, owner of #55 *Dolphin*, for his donation to the clubhouse of a watercolor, and Edward Crossett for his donation of a model lighthouse. Following Hornor's remarks, Manley Crosby directed his band "which gave a very creditable performance in view of the fact that before September last there was one-third of its present membership that had never studied any musical instruments."

*Seven years' worth of Wianno Junior results are included on this Hyannis Port Yacht Club plaque. Prominent among the youngsters are Ross Richards's siblings Dudley and Sue, and Edward Kennedy. Ross was among the top sailors produced by the club.*

Despite what had happened in October 1929, the following winter was a busy one at Crosby's and 1930 turned into a banner year for Wianno Senior construction. The Crosby shop turned out eleven new yachts, a figure that would not subsequently be equaled. While the number of competitors racing during the period 1930–1940 would give no indication of economic conditions then prevailing, the number of new Wianno Seniors built during the period is more suggestive of the prevailing economy.

The total number of new boats sold during 1931 and 1932 appears to have equaled the eleven built

## HYANNISPORT YACHT CLUB
### JUNIOR CLASS AUGUST SERIES

| Year | | Boat | Skipper |
|------|------|------|---------|
| 1946 | 1ST. | BETTANOT | D. RICHARDS |
|      | 2ND. | SHORE LEAVE | F. WRIGHT |
|      | 3RD. | ONE MORE | E. KENNEDY |
| 1947 | 1ST. | TENOVUS | E. KENNEDY |
|      | 2ND. | JUDIC | R. ROUNDS |
|      | 3RD. | SEA WINGS | C. & L. SHEPPARD |
| 1948 | 1ST. | SEA WINGS | L. M. SHEPARD |
|      | 2ND. | GANDER | N. MILLIKEN |
|      | 3RD. | PUP | D. RICHARDS |
| 1949 | 1ST. | SEA WINGS | LOUISE SHEPARD |
|      | 2ND. | C. U. LATER | C. M. DuPUY JR. |
|      | 3RD. | JUDIC | R. N. ROUNDS |
| 1950 | 1ST. | SEA WINGS | S. RICHARDS |
|      | 2ND. | TUNA FISH II | F. THUN |
|      | 3RD. | JUDIC | R. ROUNDS |
| 1951 | 1ST. | SEA WINGS | SUE RICHARDS |
|      | 2ND. | GOSLING III | GEORGE CRONIN |
|      | 3RD. | WINDY | LETCHER BENNETT |
| 1952 | 1ST. | WINDY | LETCHER BENNETT |
|      | 2ND. | SEA WINGS | WILLIAM O'NEIL JR. |
|      | 3RD. | GOSLING III | GEORGE CRONIN |

in 1930. The actual number built in each of those two years is not easy to pinpoint because it seems likely that several boats constructed in 1931 weren't sold until the following year. It is believed that three boats were built and sold for the 1933 season. No new Wianno Seniors were launched in 1934 or 1935, two in 1936, none in 1937 or '38, one in 1939, none in 1940, and one boat — #107 — in 1941.

The Great Depression had an impact on boat prices. Kenneth Steere recalled, "We purchased the *Curlew* in the fall of 1928, and at that time the price was $1,500. We ordered the *Venture* in 1929, and Crosby raised the price to $1,800. A year later [Crosby] was trying to get $2,200, but as the Depression continued the price was reduced and by 1932 was back to $1,500. At that time second-hand boats were quoted from $600 to $1,000. By 1934 these had been gradually cleaned up, and at that time Al Johnston sold *Skokie* (#73) for $1,000."

OF THE ELEVEN boats sold in 1930, six left Osterville. Although a scattering of Wianno Seniors had by then made a homeport elsewhere than the Osterville-Wianno neighborhood, the '30s saw formal efforts to expand the fleet. The initial such effort had occurred in 1917. That January *The Rudder* reported: "At Osterville, Cape Cod, the home of the famous Crosby Brothers, more work is in progress than ever before. H. Manley and Wilton Crosby have the following orders...five Wianno 17-foot class one-design knockabouts for South Yarmouth yachtsmen, and two of these boats for Wianno yachtsmen...." This brief magazine entry marks the first published news that

sailors other than those at the WYC had taken an interest in forming a fleet of the new Crosby one-design knockabouts.

The South Yarmouth men were members of the Bass River Yacht Club, first organized in 1896 when several catboats of about 21' on the waterline gathered on Saturdays to race from the river mouth to a couple of marks offshore and back. By the late '90s, the racing had grown to include a variety of boats that needed to be handicapped and a class of one-design flat-bottomed sailing skiffs. Interest had waned by 1910 as the BRYC experienced the ups and downs of membership and interest not unusual in small yacht clubs.

Initially, it seemed as if those involved in the 1917 BRYC Senior effort might get the club going again. Three can be identified: George T. Cobb and *Whisper* #26, Irving K. Taylor and *Iky* #31, and Franklin I. Sears with #3. On July 23, 1917, the *Hyannis Patriot* reported that the South Yarmouth boats were expected to compete with the WYC yachts for an "Open Championship Challenge Cup" to be sailed in August by the Class P knockabouts. While the WYC's 1917 season was a busy one dominated in Class P by James Gaff Hinkle, there is no surviving record of an Open Championship event. By 1922, Sears was racing at the WYC and the other boats had been sold. During the summer of 1926, an informal effort was made to relaunch the BRYC with a scattering of sailboats and motorboats, but it was not until two years later that things got better organized.

On August 30, 1928 the *Hyannis Patriot* published a one-sentence notice: "A meeting will be held

Saturday, September 1st at 5 P.M. at the Old Ship Shops to discuss the problem of reorganizing the B. R. Y. club." The announcement in the *Patriot* was followed a few days later by the meeting itself, held on September 3, 1928.

The man who called this meeting to order was Charles Henry Davis. Big and broad-shouldered, Davis was a South Yarmouth native who had created an independent fortune built on manufacturing and street railways. Although he spent much of his time in New York, he was well known in South Yarmouth for his generosity to residents in need, and also as Cape Cod's leading campaigner for Theodore Roosevelt's Progressive Party. The latter was a passion he shared with Irving K. Taylor, who bought a large estate in South Yarmouth and who was, in 1914, chairman of the Progressive Party in Essex County, New Jersey.

Davis's father Henry had been among those who had initially organized small-boat racing at Bass River, contributing to Charles's lifelong interest in sailing. Charles's membership in the Wianno Yacht Club was one of several, and he also belonged to the Atlantic, Boston, Eastern, Rhode Island, and Royal Canadian Yacht Clubs. At the meeting Davis stressed the need for the BRYC to reach out well beyond a few inner-circle members and make the new club affordable. A $5 membership fee was agreed to. Davis also offered the use of his garage as a club meeting place — he was a serious automobile enthusiast and skilled driver — and even volunteered a section of his riverfront property as the location for a club pier.

Among those joining Davis in relaunching the BRYC was Theodore "Ted" Frothingham, whose father was an attorney then connected to Davis. Ted had graduated from Milton Academy, and spent three years at Harvard before starting the Old Ship Shops boatyard in 1926 with the help of Charles Henry Davis. "He backed me with encouragement and the use of his boathouse," Frothingham wrote. Three or four years later, when Frothingham moved out of Davis's boathouse to a new location up the river, the business, renamed Ship Shops, became, according to Frothingham, "the social headquarters of the Bass River Yacht Club."

During the early 1930s, the BRYC began to grow. A Cape Cod Knockabout Class was established as was a Beetle Cat fleet. In the years before World War II, the Wianno Seniors reappeared and, from a base of six boats, their number would greatly increase in the years after the war. The fleet remains active as the Wianno Senior turns one hundred years old.

SINCE THE SENIORS had first competed at Edgartown in 1928, the Edgartown Yacht Club Regatta had steadily grown in popularity. In 1931, eight years after the first Regatta, 180 yachts showed up to race in nineteen classes. Even Cotuit Skiffs — lively, flat-bottomed, 14′ catboats — made the voyage across Nantucket Sound to take part. The Regatta quickly became an important part of the season for Wianno Senior owners. In 1929, the Falmouth Heights-to-Wianno Long Distance Race was eliminated. It was replaced by the Wianno-to-Edgartown event. In 1931, just three years after the Seniors were first invited to race at Edgartown, thirty-one boats entered. Two years later, the regatta drew even more Wianno Seniors, thirty-six in all.

Early '30s Edgartown Yacht Club records reveal that the Wianno Senior's popularity had begun to spread, if only in a small way. In 1933, while twenty-eight of the Seniors came from the WYC, one arrived from Vineyard Haven, one from Bass River, four from Hyannis Port, one from Quisset, one from Woods Hole, and two from Edgartown. As it happened, the first two finishers in each Division that year were from the WYC. In Division One (with skipper), Greg and Betty Wells in #28 *Gull* placed first and Mary Parlett in #37 *Fiddler* placed second. In the Second Division (amateur), H. and G. Wheeler placed first in #99 *Wiggle* and Jean Kiley in #62 *El Cid* placed second.

Given the enthusiasm of WYC members for the EYC Regatta, it is not surprising that some EYC members took notice. Of the new boats built by Crosbys in 1930, five were purchased by Martha's Vineyard owners, and there was an effort there to establish a Wianno Senior fleet at the Edgartown Yacht Club despite the club's existing *eight* fleets. In its summary of the 1931 season, the EYC race committee reported: "Seventy-nine craft comprised the active racing fleet. In the five knockabout classes were twelve Interclubs, eight Katamas, six Wiannos, seven Edgartown Fifteens and two Navigators of the Junior Yacht Club." Other classes included Catboat, Dory, Sneakbox, Beach Boat, and Skiff. These classes competed in a Saturday Championship Series and Wednesday Series. As of 1931, if not before, Seniors also participated in the club's race to Nantucket, competing for the Orr Cup, named for the EYC's Race Committee Chairman (1925–1969), Alexander M. Orr, who also served as commodore from 1935 to 1937.

Although the EYC noted six Wianno Seniors on its roster, the number of Wianno Seniors actually racing never appears to have included more than three boats. These were Carl and Alex Vietor's #90 *Hobgoblin*, William Brown's #81 *Ariel*, and Francis Danforth's #87 *Eroica*. The Edgartown Seniors carried a "W" on their mainsail above the number. Of the five Seniors purchased by members of the Edgartown Yacht Club in 1930, four had modified cabins. *Eroica*, #87, was one of these. So were #88 *Haze*, #89 *Adios*, and #90 *Hobgoblin*. The cabins of these boats extended 15" aft of the normal position to enclose the centerboard trunk and had two portholes on each side. Whether the change was done at the behest of the customers or was an attempt to broaden the boat's appeal to more cruise-oriented buyers, no more such Seniors were built.

*Eroica,* an extended-cabin Senior that raced, won the Wianno Senior Class in 1931, the 1932 race to Nantucket, and the 1932 Saturday Championship Series and Wednesday Series. The Vietors' #90 *Hobgoblin* and the Browns' #81 *Ariel*, were raced in 1931 and, presumably, 1932. After that, however, no further record of Wianno Senior competition at the EYC appears, except, of course, the big annual Edgartown Yacht Club Regatta.

The Wianno Senior that entered the 1933 Edgartown Regatta from Woods Hole was one of

*Built in 1930 for Francis Danforth of Edgartown, #87* Eroica *was one of the Wianno Seniors to have an extended cabin. Although enjoyed by their owners, the Seniors on Martha's Vineyard did not prosper as a class — their mainsails carried an identifying "W" — at the Edgartown Yacht Club.*

four Seniors then in the Woods Hole Yacht Club's squadron. *Qui Vive* #10 was owned by Franklin A. Park, president of the Singer Sewing Machine Co. Walter O. Luscombe, the son of a prominent Woods Hole businessman, purchased #6, naming it *Bellina*. *Whistle Wing* #12 and #51 *King Tut* were also in the fleet — along with one Lawley and six Herreshoff and S boats. But the Wianno did not prosper as a one-design fleet in Woods Hole, either.

IN 1928, IN THE MIDST of complex but lucrative stock endeavors involving entertainment companies, Joseph P. Kennedy purchased the Hyannis Port cottage he'd been renting since 1926. He promptly began remodeling the Marchant Avenue house, and in June 1929 the *Hyannis Patriot* announced: "What will probably be the first private installation of talking pictures apparatus in New England or the entire country is nearing completion in the summer home of Joseph P. Kennedy, motion picture magnate and financier...."

Kennedy's own interest on the Cape centered on golf — he'd been refused entry to the Cohasset Club only to be welcomed at the Hyannisport Club — but his waterfront house made it natural for his children to take up sailing. Joe Jr. and John became active participants in whatever racing was going on at Hyannis Port during the late '20s. Among the family's fleet were two Wianno Juniors — *Tenovus* (the name reflecting eight children, Joe, and his wife Rose) and, after the birth of Ted, *One More*.

Seeking to improve conditions in its harbor, in October 1930 the Hyannis Civic Association attended a hearing in Boston to discuss with the state a proposed new breakwater. The plan was to build the breakwater from the shore out to the existing breakwater that had been built by the federal government. The idea, according to the *Hyannis Patriot,* was to make "the harbor as fine an anchorage place for small yachts as can be found on the Cape."

By this time, the once-active Hyannis Port Yacht Club had been moribund for years, its last races reported in the newspaper having occurred in 1909. But in 1932, two summer residents from Pittsburgh, William Y. Humphreys who owned a place on Squaw Island, and H. J. Brooks, Jr., joined with Hyannis Port's F. A. Loevy to get the club going again. Humphreys, who owned a big, raised-deck motoryacht named *Halcyon III*, became the first commodore.

This activity, apparently, did not escape Joseph Kennedy's notice. In 1932, he paid a visit to the Crosby Yacht Building and Storage Company where he encountered Wianno Senior #94. "The boat," said Joe Gargan, a Kennedy cousin who spent summers with the Kennedy family at Hyannis Port, "had been built on spec. Joe walked in and bought it." Christened *Victura* — "about to win" — the Wianno Senior was presented as a fifteenth birthday gift to John Fitzgerald Kennedy.

As was customary, Joseph Kennedy hired a skipper to oversee his childrens' sailing activities. Prior to 1933, this man was a Coast Guard Academy graduate and merchant mariner named James A. "Jimmie" MacLean. Subsequently, and over his wife Rose's objections, Kennedy hired thirty-five-year-old John "Eric" Ericson. Ericson was a contrast to

MacLean and to the genteel Osterville captains. According to Leo Damore's *The Cape Cod Years of John Fitzgerald Kennedy*, Ericson "was forceful, loud and coarse, with a colorfully explicit Norwegian accented vocabulary...known as a heavy drinker — once during an Edgartown regatta, it had taken almost the entire village police force to quell him."

The HPYC's initial fleet roster of 1932 included six Wianno Seniors but — in an effort to distinguish the club from its exclusive near-neighbors — left off the word "Wianno" in its official designation. At Hyannis Port, the boat was labeled the "Senior One Design Class." Of these boats, four raced in a series that began on July 18 and concluded on September 10. The results were (1) Frank S. Bissell in *Taravao*, (2) L. F. and C. F. Loutrel in *Pequod*, (3) Whitney Wright

in *Neonym*, and (4) John F. Kennedy in *Victura*. The following year saw a doubling in the number of boats racing, and throughout the remainder of the decade the HPYC Senior fleet generally drew nine to twelve boats each season. The accompanying chart shows the results for the 1935 season.

Several of those in the early HPYC fleet would go on to play influential roles at the club. Gardner Schirmer became well known as an able instructor. "Ted Kennedy and I learned to sail in Wianno Juniors under Gardner," remembered Joe Gargan. William Sinclair — known to most as "Pop" — became a beloved commodore, and his Senior *Mimi* remained in the Sinclair family into the early 1990s, under the care of daughters Dody and Tish and later granddaughter Betsy Loutrel. Betsy recalled that her parents,

*A teenaged John F. Kennedy mans the halyards while his younger brother Ted assists aboard #94* Victura. *Joseph P. Kennedy bought the boat in 1932 as a fifteenth birthday present for Jack, who cherished his Wianno Senior all his life.*

## 1935 Season Rankings for the HPYC Senior One Design Class

| Placing | Owner | Boat Name |
|---|---|---|
| 1 | Ralph A. Anderson | *Rita* |
| 2 | Joseph P. Kennedy | *Victura* |
| 3 | L. F. and C. F. Loutrel | *Pequod* |
| 4 | Eric Swenson | *Green Dragon* |
| 5 | John J. Daly | *Halcyon* |
| 6 | William R. Sinclair | *Mimi* |
| 7 | Frank S. Bissell | *Taravao* |
| 8 | F. G. Schirmer | *Wiki Wiki* |
| 9 | Whitney Wright | *Neonym* |
| 10 | Herbert Merrick | *Water Nymph* |
| 11 | D. M. Humphreys | *Scud* |
| 12 | C. H. Draper | *Shuttle* |

*Here is #36* Mimi, *long owned by W. R. "Pop" Sinclair of the Hyannis Port Yacht Club. "The* Mimi *and sailing were two of my dad's greatest pleasures," said Dody Sinclair Loutrel. "They are ours, too."*

*Built in 1917 and raced with great success by R. Stewart Kilborne, Jr., #43 was later purchased by Lou Loutrel of the Hyannis Port Yacht Club, who named her* Pequod *and became an enthusiastic member of the class.*

like so many involved with the Wianno Senior, had met thanks to the boat, but few would have guessed a romance would blossom out of a protest meeting.

"Mom [Dody] and Dad [Lou Loutrel] met because of a protest between Pop and what he then called 'those Loutrel boys.' I'm not sure who was protesting whom, but I think Pop was in the wrong. My mother tagged along to the protest meeting, and the rest is history. Dad always said she was the first girl he had met who liked to do all the things he did including sailing and racing boats." Lou and Dody Loutrel (and Lou's brother Fran) remained devoted Wianno Senior sailors for many years, and both served as HPYC trustees and officers.

BY THE EARLY 1880S, as the first pioneers were renting or building summer places in Osterville and Wianno, the village of Harwich Port was also seeing growth of seasonal residents. A principal attraction of the village was its "mere" or salt pond overlooked by what, in June 1881, the *Barnstable Patriot* called "one of the most popular, as well as most delightfully situated

Hotels upon the Cape." This hotel was the Sea View House. In a move that now seems incredible, not to mention environmentally impossible, a narrow channel connecting the mere to Nantucket Sound had been filled in and a "trotting track" had been built around the pond. Hotel guests could view the races from their rooms' windows. Artist Charles D. Cahoon, who lived in Harwich, created a painting of one such event.

The sulky track remained until 1887 when the channel was reopened, permitting small boats to access the pond. By 1905, the state had improved the channel considerably, dredging it, lining it with riprap, and building a granite jetty on the western side of the entrance. Now, the infamous midges that had thrived in the brackish pond disappeared and a whole new ecology evolved. A fleet of big, beautiful catboats began making "Wychmere Harbor" its home, and cottages began to dot the area around the pond even as larger houses elsewhere in the village attracted new owners, many from New York. One of them was Kenneth David Steere.

Like Edward Crossett, Kenneth Steere had been born in Iowa. After getting his law degree, and prospering in several business enterprises in Cincinnati and Texas, Steere found himself working in New York where, by the late '20s, he had become a senior partner at Paine-Webber and was living with his wife Grace in a fine house in Bronxville. "He told my grandmother," said Lucy Steere, daughter of Kenneth's youngest son Bruce, "that she was in charge of finding an appropriate summer home where the family could gather, but it should be close enough so he could work all day Friday but be with his sons the next morning. She selected Cape Cod."

Initially, the big house that is now the Ocean Edge resort in Brewster was under consideration, but Grace felt the warmer waters of Nantucket Sound would be more inviting for the family, which had been spending time in Harwich Port since 1922. In 1929 when Kenneth was forty-five, he and Grace purchased a house on Ayer Lane in Harwich Port that they owned until their deaths in 1963.

During the summer of 1929, Kenneth Steere began putting his summer plan into effect. He took the train from New York each Friday evening and arrived in Hyannis in time to race #76 *Curlew* at the WYC with his sons. David was then nearing sixteen years of age and Bruce was ten. Father and sons sailed on their own without a skipper aboard, although Steere had earlier hired Captain Lorenz Doane for $250 to spend a summer teaching David how to sail.

"Captain 'Low' taught me the rudiments of sailing [aboard a Cape Cod Knockabout] and such priceless lore as the medicinal value of chewing tobacco applied to a cut finger," Steere recalled.

"I always admired my father-in-law," said Jan Steere-White who married David Steere in 1958. "He'd get off the night train from New York in the early morning and be picked up to go home and change. Then he'd drive to Wianno with the boys to race. After each race, they'd sit down to see what they could learn from the result."

It did not take Kenneth Steere long to confront the reality that living in Harwich Port and having to drive to Osterville several times a week had decided shortcomings even though, as David Steere remembered, traffic on Route 28 "was very light." In 1930, Steere bought a second Senior — #85 *Venture*. In this boat, the Steeres became regular competitors at the WYC. *Curlew*, meanwhile, lived in Wychmere Harbor, a good learning ground for Bruce, who could soon sail the boat by himself. At the WYC, the Steeres' results, usually appearing under David's name, often included high placings.

"Uncle Dave and my father knew so much about the boat," Lucy Steere remembered. "Uncle Dave experimented for years with sails, ballast, and mast position because he understood the Wianno design from an academic point of view." In 1933, to more conveniently store and care for his Wianno Seniors, Kenneth Steere acquired a piece of waterfront land in the northwest corner of Wychmere Harbor and hired retired shipwright Charles B. Ransome to build a dock and boathouse. There was an east-facing gangway over the marsh grass leading to stairs down to a 10' × 12' float. A marine railway was built and, soon enough, the Steeres' boathouse was

functioning like a little boatyard.

There was now enough interest in sailing around Harwich Port to form a yacht club, and in 1933 a group of seven men got together to do just that. They included Bert R. Andrews, Waldo Brown, Aaron Davis, boatbuilder William D. Lee, Neil Mc-Math, Palmer Putnam, and George Rockwood. Officially known as the Stone Horse (for the Stone Horse lightship) Yacht Club of Harwich, the stated mission was "to help people who go upon the water by encouraging the exercise of courtesy, judgment and skill in the handling of craft...and in general to encourage yachting." The club's fleet included a variety of boats including Norwegian prams, catboats, cutters, a Herreshoff 15, schooners, and the 22', Crocker-designed Stone Horse Junior and Stone Horse Senior. All these boats raced under a handicap system, but a fleet of Sam Crocker–designed Compass Class boats was also initiated.

With a yacht club now literally in his own back yard, it didn't take long for Kenneth Steere to begin thinking about a local Wianno Senior fleet. "He became convinced," said George Rockwood, Jr., whose father was among the SHYC's founders and its second commodore, "that the Wianno Senior was what was needed, not the Stone Horse Junior. So he began convincing other members to buy Wianno Seniors."

An immediate challenge was that the local boatyard, the Lee Shipbuilding Company, was then offering both the Crocker-designed Stone Horse Junior and Senior sailboats. "Our father," Bruce M. Steere recalled, "was a thorn in the side of this group because he began buying up Wiannos that were for sale, refurbishing them, and selling them to residents of Harwich Port at his cost." Jan Steere-White remembered finding among her late father-in-law's papers an invoice for five boats. It is uncertain if these were pre-owned and ready for refurbishing or new boats built on spec that hadn't been sold, but they cost $700 apiece from Crosby's.

Despite the Wianno Senior's known qualities as a seaworthy centerboard boat well adapted to local waters, it took some convincing to get the SHYC fleet going. George Rockwood remembered that a sailing contest was arranged between Dave Steere's Senior and a Stone Horse Junior owned by Palmer Putnam, an MIT graduate whose family owned the New York publishing house G. P. Putnam and Sons. "He'd won a lot of races," said George Rockwood, "and wanted a contest with Dave. This finally occurred around 1936 or 1937, and Dave left him far behind."

Looking back on this period, Bruce Steere remembered that "In due course the Wianno fleet came to be regarded as the senior, most prestigious fleet at Harwich Port." During the late '30s the SHYC's Wianno Senior fleet grew, and within a few years it numbered ten boats racing under what the club called Class A. "Senior racing was really hot and heavy by 1940," said Lawrence "Renny" Damon who grew up with the boats. This initial group of Seniors provided a strong nucleus that would, after World War II, grow into a highly competitive fleet and produce one of the most successful Wianno Senior skippers of his time.

*When Kenneth Steere and his wife Grace bought a summer home in Harwich Port in 1929, they purchased Wianno Senior #76 and named the boat* Curlew.

CHAPTER SEVEN

# Gone with the Wind

*Here, circa 1968, is #85* Venture *sailing off Harwich Port under the command of David Steere with his then wife Jan at the shrouds.* Venture *was bought in 1930 by David's father, Kenneth Steere.*

*"With their father, Ambassador Joseph P. Kennedy, an interested spectator aboard Chester Crosby's 'Bookie', the Wianno Yacht Club Committee boat, the helmsmanship of Jack and Joe Kennedy Jr...boosted the Harvard sailors back into the lead."*

— *Leonard M. Fowle,* Boston Daily Globe, *June 24, 1938*

In 1928, Herbert F. Crosby sat down to talk catboats with a writer for *Motor Boating* magazine named Gregory Mason. Then seventy-five years old, H. F. reflected on how the Cape had changed since his father Horace's boyhood some ninety years earlier. Born in 1826, Horace had grown up during a time long before there were summer

65

visitors or "concrete highways and gift shops along 'em enough for a man to spend a fortune in a couple of miles." The arrival of the first pioneers in Osterville signaled the great changes that Herbert Crosby referred to, changes that wholly remade the life and economy of Cape Cod.

As more summer residents arrived and the Wianno Senior fleet grew, people and boats became interwoven into the fabric of life in different towns and villages. The wealth of the WYC members who summered in Wianno and Osterville, in particular, had continued to work to the village's benefit. When the 1927 season got off to a slow start elsewhere on the Cape, the *Hyannis Patriot* reported that the Daniel Brothers predicted "Wianno [and Osterville] will have a normal season.... Everything is going the same at these places as in years past.... We look for a good, normal season at Wianno."

Just as they had in earlier times when newcomers bought property from Henry Day and engaged local tradesmen to build or enlarge homes, local residents continued to be appreciative of the opportunities derived from the Wianno Senior owners. In 1932, the nineteen skippers then employed by WYC members signed a letter to commodore Hornor expressing their "appreciation for his keen and unprejudiced interest in our local racing. It is our wish that with his co-operation and support, the Wianno Races will continue to grow in popularity and that with his help, the cause of racing will continue to thrive."

The interactions between wealthy summer people and locals could take some unexpected twists that occasionally were reported in the local newspaper. In July 1925 Mrs. Alexis du Pont accompanied her husband to the West Barnstable train station to see him off on the Cape Codder to New York. Somehow she lost a valuable diamond ring, for which she placed a notice in the newspaper. The West Barnstable woman who found and returned the ring received a $300 reward, then worth over a month's wages for a skilled carpenter. In November 1925 the local paper reported that Mary Parlett would pay $50 to send two local girls to a New Hampshire camp the following summer to learn to be Girl Scout patrol leaders.

The Wianno Senior owners could be civic minded in other ways, too. By the late 1920s, while James Gaff Hinkle was living in Chestnut Hill and working as an investment counselor in Boston at Preston Moss, his older sister Jean had taken up residence in Osterville. In 1939, she moved into a residence designed by architect John Barnard that had been added on to Green Bays. By then, Jean was serving as one of three park commissioners in Hyannis. Later, she opened Port Fortune Kennels in Osterville and, starting in 1939, she served on the Barnstable School Committee and also acted as a de facto guidance counselor. "She would bring in many college catalogs and tell the boys and girls," remembered her nephew Jim Hinkle, "that they must 'go over the canal' and go to college."

Whether they called the Cape home or, more typically, initially stayed there only during the summer season, those who experienced Cape Cod life before the development of the mid-1920s recalled

*Today's Wianno Yacht Club's committee boat is named in honor of past-commodore John Hornor, whose decade in the position (1929–1939) was the longest in club history.*

67

that epoch with nostalgia that could border on yearning. Ted Frothingham's parents began taking him to Bass River in 1906, and he never forgot those times. "When you arrived for the vacation, there were barrels and boxes of food that the family had had shipped down from S. S. Pierce in Boston: staples to last until fall," he wrote in his memoir *With a Grain of Salt*. Growing up riding his bike over sand roads to greet his father at the train station; living in a house where a windmill pumped water and there was no electricity; leaving the stable door open so the family horse could watch the sailboats — all these things made a lasting impression on Frothingham who would later become an important figure in the Wianno Senior fleet. "Looking back on life on Cape Cod prior to 1925 seems a dream," he wrote.

In Osterville, for the most privileged, it was a life centered on socializing at the Wianno Club, sailing, and playing golf. The Adies, to the amusement of local boys, were seen with some frequency in the village riding in a coach pulled by four horses, a "coach-and-four." As they would in later years, romances sometimes blossomed between club members, not always with parental approval. R. Stewart Kilborne, Jr.'s marriage at age twenty to nineteen-year-old Barbara Briggs prospered despite initial family objections and the sale of *Unquomonk*. For a time, James Gaff Hinkle dated Andrew Adie's daughter Ann before they both moved on. Elizabeth Wells, whose father Channing owned #28 *Gull*, would marry Heywood Fox, owner of #8 *Sea Dog*.

Of course, those who became involved with boats during that time weren't all Wianno Senior owners or members of the Wianno Club. Richard "Deke" Ulian was only five years old when his father expanded his retail clothing business to Hyannis and rented a cottage in West Yarmouth. Suddenly, Deke found himself transported into a world far removed from any he had previously known, a place where his babysitter would take him sailing and teach him the ropes. "We had a cottage two roads up from the Lewis Bay Yacht Club," he recalled of those times. "The roads were dirt. The sun was hot. The feet were bare."

Ulian carried his boyhood and adolescent memories of watching Cape Cod Knockabout races into adulthood. Many years later, when Ulian acquired Wianno Senior #7, he became friendly with William Halliday's daughter Anne, who was related to the boat's second owner, John Tiernan. "I want to tell you about my cousin Jack," she told Ulian. "He loved his boat. He coiled the lines as neatly as he'd seen done on the Great Lakes vessels he remembered from his boyhood. He actually raced little and sailed little. But that boat was the closest thing to his heart."

ON AUGUST 26, 1930, the Nantucket Yacht Club initiated a new regatta and Wianno Senior owners were among those who voyaged to the island to compete. Courses were laid out with the starting line not far off the harbor's jetties. Each leg was designated, as was then still typical, with the traditional compass point directions, such as north-northwest ¾ west, and the distance in miles. The 1930 race was won by Mary Parlett in #37 *Fiddler*, followed by James R. MacColl in #41 *Halcyon* and Henry S. Stone in #69 *Sunny*. It was a good season for Mary Parlett. Earlier in August,

*The Madden family's #61* Spindrift *races downwind. At the tiller is John Madden. His wife Mary sits opposite on the afterdeck. Seated forward of John is probably his brother Robert. The boat was bought new in 1926 by Michael Lester Madden, the boys' father, and remained in the family until severely damaged in the 1954 hurricane.*

she had also won the 1st Division at the Edgartown Regatta. That year's long-distance skipper's race from Wianno to Edgartown was won by Chester Crosby in Harry Stimpson's #60 *Malolo*, followed by Joe Daniel in the Crossetts' #22 *Tomboy* and Delton C. Hall in the Hornors' #8 *Sea Dog*.

The Nantucket Regatta of 1930 was just one event that inaugurated a busy decade of expanded racing. The development of a fleet next door to Wianno at Hyannis Port resulted in an interclub racing series. Years earlier, members of the WYC had participated in the HPYC's regattas. On September 4, 1908, WYC boats took home several prizes, and William F. Low, the WYC's measurer, acted as one of the judges. But a quite different sort of rivalry emerged in 1935 in the form of team races between the HPYC and WYC. Surviving information suggests that entrants were selected by each club from among its fleet's top three or four highest-scoring boats. If there was doubt that a boat might not be able to participate in all races, one or more backups were also selected. Three boats from each club then faced off during the series with scores tallied for each yacht and cumulatively for each club.

The first of these team races in 1935 involved three yachts from the WYC and four from the HPYC. It was an event that Bruce M. Steere, who was sixteen at the time, never forgot. The last of the event's five races was sailed on August 26 in a Force 5–6 (17–27 mph) west-by-southwest wind, heavy enough that the Wianno contingent thought the race should be canceled as had the first in the series on July 15. But it wasn't. Under the taunting of the Kennedys'

skipper, who was calling them sissies, the Steeres and others proceeded to race.

In a letter written to James Gaff Hinkle in April 1989 when he was seventy, Bruce Steere recalled: "Our secret weapon was a heavy-set fourth crew member named [Howard] Blossom from Osterville. We bent on our flat Ratsey and raced the race of our lives. Dave loved heavy-weather sailing. We were first around the windward mark, and when Joe and Jack rounded behind us, *Victura* was hull down on the horizon. We never heard another peep from the Kennedy professional."

This initial WYC vs. HPYC team race was won by the WYC, 53¾ to 51½. The highest-scoring boat was John Madden's *Spindrift* #61 with 21¼ points followed by the Steeres in #85 *Venture* with 14¼ and the Kennedys in #94 *Victura* with 14. Expectations were always high in the Kennedy family. "He was always saying," remembered Joe Gargan of his uncle Joseph P. Kennedy, "'Try to be number one.' But as long as you were trying, he didn't care. But if he thought otherwise, you'd hear about it. One time when Teddy and I were racing and he was watching from his powerboat, we had a problem with our spinnaker launch and barely won. He said, 'If you're gonna clown around, why bother?'"

Lucy Steere recalled that her grandmother, Grace Steere, was present following one of the HPYC-WYC team races won by David Steere. "She was waiting at the Wianno Yacht Club for her husband and boys to come in from racing. Mr. and Mrs. Kennedy were, likewise, waiting for Jack to come ashore. The results of the race were already known:

# Portrait of the Fleet
## Lineup for the 1936 WYC vs. HPYC Team Races

| Yacht/HPYC | 1st Race | Yacht/WYC |
|---|---|---|
| #43 *Pequod* | | #22 *Tomboy* |
| Louis Loutrel | Captain | J. R. MacColl III |
| Francis Loutrel | | S. Albright |
| Dora Sinclair | | H. Blossom |
| #77 *Rita* | | #62 *El Cid* |
| Frank Syme | Captain | Jock Kiley |
| James Whitehead | | Gordon Wheeler |
| Tom Sinclair | | J. W. Hornor, Jr. |
| #94 *Victura* | | #73 *Vitamin D* |
| Jack Kennedy | Captain | S. Albright |
| Eric Swenson | | H. Cameron Morris |
| Nancy Tenney | | Horton Batchelder |
| **2nd Race** | | |
| #94 *Victura* | | #13 *Prodigal Pig* |
| Jack Kennedy | Captain | S. Albright |
| Eric Swenson | | H. Blossom |
| Nancy Tenney | | Horton Batchelder |
| #36 *Mimi* | | #62 *El Cid* |
| Tom Sinclair | Captain | Jock Kiley |
| Dora Sinclair | | J. W. Hornor, Jr. |
| Alec Wiggin | | Harry A. Wheeler |
| #43 *Pequod* | | #73 *Vitamin D* |
| Louis Loutrel | Captain | F. L. Day |
| Francis Loutrel | | H. Cameron Morris |
| Eleanor Merrick | | J. R. MacColl III |

| Portrait of the Fleet<br>Lineup for the 1936 WYC vs. HPYC Team Races | | |
|---|---|---|
| **3rd Race** | | |
| #94 *Victura* | | #101 *Quip* |
| Jack Kennedy | Captain | S. Albright |
| Frank Bissell | | Mrs. Norman Driscoll |
| Nancy Tanney | | H. Blossom |
| Eric Swenson | | J. R. MacColl III |
| #43 *Pequod* | | #13 *Prodigal Pig* |
| Louis Loutrel | Captain | H. Batchelder |
| Francis Loutrel | | Wolcott Day |
| Tom Sinclair | | Jock Kiley |
| Dora Sinclair | | James A. Waller |
| #77 *Rita* | | #73 *Vitamin D* |
| Frank Syme | Captain | F. L. Day |
| Thayer Syme | | H. Cameron Morris |
| George Cutler | | Robert Gill |
| Alex Wiggin | | George Day |

Steeres first, Kennedy second. When Jack came running up the dock to tell his father how well he did, the ambassador looked Jack in the eye and said that he didn't raise any of his children to come in second, and that when Jack started beating the Steere brothers he would have something to brag about." At the end of the 1935 season, Joseph Kennedy hired a new skipper.

The 1936 team race results appeared in both the *Boston Globe* and *Herald*, which on July 14 reported that *Pequod* had a 30-second margin at the first mark and increased the lead to two minutes over J. R. MacColl's *Tomboy* — he'd bought the Crossetts'

boat — at the finish. The headline for that mention: "Hyannisport Boats Shade Wianno Y.C." The tables on this and the previous page list the skipper and crew of each yacht.

During the prewar years, the HPYC won the interclub trophy known as the "Darlington Challenge Cup" on four occasions: 1936, 1937, 1938, 1939. The WYC triumphed three times: 1935, 1940, and 1941. The chart on page 73 tells the story of one of these events, the 1937 series.

The chart reveals close results between the two clubs, with just a single point separating them. Although not indicated on the chart, one race, on

# Portrait of the Fleet
## 1937 HPYC vs. WYC Team Race Results

| | JULY | AUGUST | AUGUST | AUGUST | AUGUST | | |
|---|---|---|---|---|---|---|---|
| Wind direction | E | | WSW | SSW | SW × W | | |
| Velocity | 12–9 | | 20 knots | 5 knots | 6–9 knots | | |
| Tide | E | | E | W | E | | |
| Weather | Clear | | | Cloudy | Cloudy | | |
| Day | M | M | M | M | M | | |
| Date | 19th | 2nd | 16th | 30th (a.m.) | 30th (p.m.) | Races sailed | Total Points |
| *Victura*   John F. Kennedy (H) | 6¼ | 3 | 6¼ | 3 | 2 | 5 | 20½ |
| *Mimi*   Thos. T. Sinclair (H) | 5 | 4 | | 6¼ | 5 | 4 | 20¼ |
| *El Cid*   J. C. Kiley, Jr. (W) | 4 | 3¼ | 4 | 5 | 3¼ | 5 | 19½ |
| *Ethyl*   Richard Burnes (W) | 3 | 1 | 3 | | | 3 | 7 |
| *Pequod*   C. F. Loutrel (H) | 2 | 2 | | | | 3 | 4 |
| *Jolly Roger*   J. A. Waller (W) | 1 | | | | | 1 | 1 |
| *Quip*   Stuart Albright (W) | | 5 | 5 | | 3 | 4 | 13 |
| *Halcyon*   J. J. Daly (H) | | | 2 | | | 1 | 3 |
| *Fantasy*   Miss Jean Hinkle (W) | | | | 4 | 1 | 2 | 5 |
| *Green Dragon*   Eric Swenson (W) | | | | 2 | 4 | 2 | 6 |
| HPYC | 13½ | 9 | 8¼ | 11¼ | 11 | | 52¼ |
| WYC | 8 | 12¼ | 12 | 9 | 10½ | | 51¼ |

August 23, was postponed by a rainy northeaster. *Fantasy* was, for this series, sailed by Jean with skipper John Linehan.

THE RECORDS OF the WYC for 1938 note that the "Yachting Season was ushered in by 10 Colleges visiting us to engage in an Intercollegiate Yacht Race." The colleges — Harvard, Cornell, Yale, Trinity, Williams, Brown, Penn, MIT, Princeton, and Dartmouth — had sent two teams each to Wianno to compete for the McMillan Cup. This trophy had been established in 1930 by Baltimore architect and accomplished ocean racing sailor William McMillan who, four years later, married Grace G. Roosevelt, a granddaughter of Theodore and cousin of Franklin.

While dinghies were at the core of intercollegiate racing, the McMillan Cup was sailed in larger one-design boats provided by different yacht clubs. It was the WYC's Stuart Albright, then a Dartmouth student, who arranged for the 1938 event to be sailed at Wianno. On June 21, 1938, some sixty college yachtsmen went out to practice in the Wianno Senior knockabouts. The event was covered by the *Boston Globe*'s yachting editor, Leonard M. Fowle, the third generation of his family to work at the paper and a man so devoted to intercollegiate sport that he would later be known as the "father of college sailing."

The 1938 McMillan Cup series was sailed over courses laid out by Chester Crosby and blessed by good weather that prevailed from June 22 to 24. Leonard Fowle, who had graduated from Harvard in 1930, brought an intimate understanding of sailboat racing, the Ivy League, and journalism to his coverage of the series. He recorded the events of each day with exciting reporting like this on June 23: "Williams passed Tech to assume the lead before the Kennedy boys came through with a second and a fourth to give Harvard a point and a quarter advantage over the Purple sailors in the most closely contested series in the 11-year history of the McMillan Cup." (The event had actually begun in 1928 but under another name.) The next day, however, Fowle reported that after Williams's top sailor, future *America*'s Cup skipper Robert N. Bavier, Jr., withdrew a protest, "The Crimson burgee of the Harvard Yacht Club waves at the college yachting masthead for the first time since 1934."

The WYC's record of this event noted that "The young men evidenced advanced seamanship, conducted themselves in exemplary fashion; they all seemed to enjoy the varied racing provided them, and were loud in their appreciation of the hospitality extended to them…." The accompanying chart shows the results as recorded in WYC archives.

THE DECADE 1930–1940 saw a remarkable consistency in the Wianno Senior fleet. In 1930, twenty-seven boats competed in two divisions at the Edgartown Regatta. In 1940, thirty-three boats competed in two divisions in the regatta. Of course, competitors had changed. Mary Parlett, who won Division I at Edgartown in #37 in 1930 didn't compete there a decade later but did finish fourteenth in the Championship Series. In 1940, Division I at Edgartown was won by W. C. Cook in #55 *Saidee*. Among the new faces at Edgartown in 1940, three stalwarts remained:

## Results of 1938 McMillan Cup Sailed aboard Wianno Seniors at WYC

| College | 1st Division Skipper | 2nd Division Skipper | Points | Rank |
|---|---|---|---|---|
| Harvard | Loring Reed and Jack Kennedy | Jack Kennedy | 114½ | 1 |
| Dartmouth | Robert Brown | Stuart Albright | 107 | 2 |
| Williams | Stanley Turner | Robert N. Bavier, Jr. | 106½ | 3 |
| MIT | Herman Hanson | Eric Olsen | 92¼ | 4 |
| Trinity | John C. Kiley, Jr. | Robert C. Madden | 89½ | 5 |
| Cornell | Irwin W. Tyson | Nicol Bessell | 84¼ | 6 |
| Princeton | F. Gardner Cox | John T. Ames, Jr. | 83¾ | 7 |
| Brown | John Mason, Jr. | Ralph L. Fletcher | 74¼ | 8 |
| Yale | Edward Seymour | Gerald Swords | 74 | 9 |
| Pennsylvania | Samuel Merrick | James A. Wallen | 58¼ | 10 |

James Gaff Hinkle finished second in Division I. Abby Hagerman, long-since Mrs. John Shafroth, placed sixth. Edna Parlett, who placed third in Division II in 1930, placed 4th in Division I in 1940.

As the 1930s drew to a close, the *Boston Transcript* sent a staff correspondent to Osterville to report about the winding down of the season at the WYC and the impending departure of members "to their homes from Daytona to Denver." He wrote that "The Wianno [Yacht] Club, sitting white and tidy at the head of West Bay...is satisfied with its 1939 season.... It is true that to a 'furriner' went the much-prized James Mott Hallowell Memorial Cup awarded to the yacht winning the greatest number of regular races. This was won by James A. Waller of Philadelphia who sails the senior class *Jolly Roger*, but he was the only out-of-stater to gain a major trophy.

"Paul Bauder of West Newton, 1938 Dartmouth graduate, took the Lynwood Prize awarded for the highest average score of the season, and also one leg of the Hollow Hill Challenge Trophy awarded to the yacht winning three championship series."

The last prewar team event was held August 20, 1941, and pitted three HPYC boats against three from the WYC. John Kennedy was tops in points, edging out Abby Shafroth in *Commy* 13½ to 12, but the WYC won two of the three races — one a drifter sailed in no more than 5 knots of wind, another in a 5–10-knot southeasterly, and one in a rough 15–20-knot southwesterly — and took home the Darlington Memorial Trophy. This last race of the series, sailed off Wianno, was, for eleven-year-old Joe Gargan — nephew of Joseph P. Kennedy — memorable for what happened afterwards.

| Portrait of the Fleet<br>Edgartown Yacht Club Regatta, 1940 | | |
|---|---|---|
| Division I | | |
| Position | #/Yacht | Owner/Club |
| 1 | 55/*Saidee* | W. C. Cook/WYC |
| 2 | 11/*Fantasy* | J. G. Hinkle/WYC |
| 3 | 25/*Jolly Roger* | J. A. Waller/WYC |
| 4 | 57/*Second Fiddler* | F. Edna Parlett/WYC |
| 5 | 60/*Allecto* | F. E. Platt/WYC |
| 6 | 5/*Commy* | Shafroth/WYC |
| 7 | 61/*Spindrift* | R. C. Madden/WYC |
| 8 | 7/*Valkyrie* | Carl Barus/BRYC |
| 9 | 73/*Vitamin D* | E. K. Morris/WYC |
| 10 | 54/*Winita* | R. E. Chapman/BRYC |
| 11 | 12/*Whistle Wing* | H. M. Kidder/WHYC |
| 12 | 72/*Plover* | A. H. Castonguay/HYC |
| DNF | 8/*Sea Dog* | William Hickey/HYC |
| DNF | 41/*Halcyon* | J. J. Daly/HPYC |
| DNF | 43/*Pequod* | Thayer Brown/HPYC |
| DNF | 48/*Go Getta* | George Day/WYC |

"The *Victura's* sails were in a big canvas bag and when we got back to the house, Jack reached back to pull them out of the family's Chrysler convertible. The next thing I heard was, 'Oh, gosh, I hurt my back! Joey, get those sails.' He went to bed and his grandmother put mustard plasters on his back all night long."

Despite a bad back, which would likely have rendered him 4F and unfit for service, Jack Kennedy entered the Navy (initially the reserve) in the fall of 1941. This was made possible because, while ambassador to England, his father had known Captain Alan Kirk, then naval attaché. With Kirk's help, Kennedy passed his physical in Boston, received his commission, and reported to Kirk at the Naval Intelligence Office in Washington.

ON DECEMBER 1, 1941, while on the way to his Boston office, Henry Brown Day suffered a fatal heart attack at the West Newton train station. Day, the tireless

| Portrait of the Fleet<br>Edgartown Yacht Club Regatta, 1940 | | |
|---|---|---|
| Division II | | |
| Position | #/Yacht | Owner/Club |
| 1 | 101/*Quip* | Mrs. Kenneth Boyd/WYC |
| 2 | 105/*Fire Chief* | R. W. Latham/WYC |
| 3 | 81/*Jivaro* | Paul Bauder, Jr./WYC |
| 4 | 85/*Venture* | Shef van Buren/SHYC |
| 5 | 106/*El Cid II* | J. C. Kiley, Jr./WYC |
| 6 | 82/*Cave Canum* | Philip Carney/WYC |
| 7 | 76/*Hermanos* | A. L. Priddy/BRYC |
| 8 | 99/*Wiggle* | H. and G. Wheeler/WYC |
| 9 | 93/*Wiki Wiki* | Dr. P. P. Henson/HYC |
| 10 | 84/*Kypris* | Marguerite Bodell/WYC |
| 11 | 77/*Segaie* | Jerome Powell/LBYC |
| 12 | 94/*Victura* | J. F. Kennedy/HPYC |
| 13 | 91/*Moby Dick* | R. Gill and W. Taussig/WYC |
| 14 | 78/*Lancer* | J. Bentinck-Smith/WYC |
| 15 | 83/*Nandabid* | David Homan/SHYC |
| 16 | 74/*Firefly* | H. A. Gardner, Jr./WYC |
| Withdrew | 98/*Gammoner* | W. and G. Detweiler/HPYC |

promoter of development at Wianno, devoted owner of #2 *Wendy*, and president of the Wianno Club from 1934 to 1937, was gone. By this time, Day had been a member of the New York Stock Exchange for twenty-seven years and was president of the Day Trust Company, which had been founded in Boston by his father in 1865.

Six days after Day's passing, Pearl Harbor was attacked and the United States entered World War II. On Cape Cod, the newsletter of the BRYC reflected: "It is a very different state of affairs that faces us all this week, from that when our last newsletter was written. In Bass River yesterday afternoon, the air raid siren brought a very clear realization that we all have a very big job ahead, one that we will all be united to accomplish no matter where we are located or

what may be asked of us. The memory of many happy summers at Bass River, and the way of life we all believe in, only makes us more determined to maintain it, to preserve everything that we always have, and always will cherish."

What appears to have been the final effort to hold a Wianno Senior race after Pearl Harbor occurred during the first summer of the war. On July 21, 1942, the WYC sponsored the "First Annual Regatta of the Wianno Senior Class." As it happened, the event had to be hosted by the Hyannis Yacht Club when the original course became unusable because of planned U.S. Army anti-aircraft practice. Eighteen entrants — "skippers and crews to be Corinthian" — from the WYC, BRYC, and SHYC competed. This last race of an era resulted in victory for #73, sailed by new owner Ben Baxter, followed by Dorothy Winship in #31 *Riptide* and Whitney Wright in #80 *Neonym.*

The race report stated that "Immediately following the finish of the event, Official Measurer gave *Noname, Riptide* and *Neonym* a clean bill of health and Yacht #73 will in due season receive the well-earned trophy which it is hoped may in years to come, be treasured as the first permanent award of many Annual Wianno Senior Class Regattas." But a second such event was never held.

During the war, the races that continued at the WYC involved Wianno Juniors. Senior racing at BRYC also ceased, but competitions continued for Cape Cod Knockabouts and Beetles. What's more, recognizing the potential loneliness of young men stationed on the Cape far from home, the BRYC started an "August Sundays Soldiers Series" in which

at least twenty servicemen were invited to sail.

The second week of September 1944 saw a hurricane of such magnitude that it would affect the entire East Coast and come to be called "The Great Atlantic Hurricane." The storm was less intense than the 1938 hurricane that struck New England, but it, too, was deadly. When the hurricane struck Cape Cod, it sank every boat still in the water in Hyannis Port save for the Sinclairs' Wianno Senior #36 *Mimi.* Dody Sinclair later remembered: "In 1944 she was the only boat left afloat in the Hyannis Port harbor, having dragged her mooring and an anchor several hundred feet."

The Sinclairs' boat fared better than a great many homes. It was estimated that forty-one thousand houses were lost to the great storm. One of them was the house built by founding father and one-time WYC commodore W. B. H. Dowse. Many years later, Manley Crosby's oldest grandson Ted reported that along with the house went the garage in which both the family chauffeur and Margaret Dowse had sought shelter. The garage sailed across East Bay and delivered its occupants safely to the marsh. The house was never rebuilt. The family gave the land on which it had stood to the Town of Barnstable. The property has been known ever since as Dowse's Beach.

*The fleet sets off. The Wianno Senior fleet is seen here beating past the committee boat* Bookie, *probably during the early '30s. Shown are Henry Stone's #69* Sunny, *#73 (probably the Johnstons'* Skokie*), #99* Wiggle, *owned by Harry and Gordon Wheeler, and William Scott's #91* Moby Dick. *At the right is #2* Wendy, *owned by the Day family from 1914 through 1939.*

# CHAPTER EIGHT

# Life Begins Anew

*"Proud owners with peeling noses, paint streaked cheeks and blistering hands will heave a sigh of relief and feel that hibernation is now over and life begins anew—and so it does. Yes, the sailors get active."*

— Boris Lauer-Leonardi, Editor, The Rudder, *March 1945*

*This rare, immediate postwar image of the fleet in 1948 shows three of the original 1914 boats. Number 5* Commy *is still being raced by original owner Abby Hagerman, but under her married name Mrs. Morrison Shafroth. Number 12 had had four owners by the time Gardner Jackson of the Wianno Yacht Club acquired her in 1947 and named her* Pegasus. *Number 11* Fantasy *was campaigned as always by James G. Hinkle. Number 55 was built in 1924 and was named* Maxixe II *at the time of this photo.*

Although the WYC's "annual" regatta of 1942 was not repeated during the following years of the war, sailing at the club and elsewhere continued in boats smaller than the Wianno Senior. On the home front, there was a recognized need to maintain some semblance of normalcy as a means of keeping up wartime morale. So, at the WYC as elsewhere, competition continued for youngsters and those not in the service.

The clubhouse was, according to Townsend Hornor, "open evenings for the use of troops stationed along West Bay." Of course, sailing magazines continued to be published during the war years. Covers of *The Rudder* during this era showed a wide variety of boat-related activities. They ranged from Eleanor Roosevelt christening a new barge at Camden, Maine, to sailors painting bottoms, and a Stan Rosenfeld shot of sport fishermen aboard an Elcoette cruiser. Despite gas rationing, those anglers found a way to get out for an afternoon's sport in the Gulf Stream.

Wianno Seniors, however, spent the war years ashore as their skippers entered the service, sometimes in the Army or Air Corps and often in the Coast Guard or the Navy. Jack Kennedy's service aboard PT-109 is doubtless the best known, but it was echoed by many others. However, the experience of one longtime owner, in particular, had a direct impact on the resumption of activity at the WYC after the war. "My father," said Jim Hinkle, "served in the Navy Department in Washington, D.C., negotiating defense contracts with companies in the private sector. His rank was lieutenant commander."

Upon his return to civilian life, James Gaff Hinkle — who had literally grown up with the Wianno Senior, the Wianno Yacht Club, and the Wianno Club — was asked to become commodore in 1946. Few, if any, men would have combined Hinkle's organizational know-how with a deep understanding of club operations. The Wianno Club's expenses were comparatively high and had more to do with the costs of operating what was essentially a fine hotel and golf course than with the WYC's sailing activities. Under

Hinkle's guidance, the Wianno Yacht Club now separated from the Wianno Club. The terms of the arrangement were that the Yacht Club would lease its West Bay property from the Wianno Club and that both would henceforth fly the WYC burgee.

"He wouldn't have taken on the job without the understanding that there would be the split," recalled Hinkle's son Jim. "The lease was to be at the cost of $1 per year."

Having dealt with this important organizational challenge, Hinkle used his Navy experience as he turned his attention to the matter of the club's launch, or lack of it. Hinkle's longtime friend Chester Crosby had, at the beginning of the war, sold his boat *Bookie*, a fixture at the club, which had chartered the vessel for use as a committee boat. What's more, the WYC's old pier would no longer be available to the Yacht Club as a place from which to watch the start of races. (The record is vague on whether the pier was heavily damaged in the '38 or '44 hurricane and then dismantled.) Even had the pier survived, shoaling would have forced the Wianno Senior starting line to be moved.

"With this in mind, and after considerable negotiation," Hinkle wrote in his 1946 report to the WYC's Board of Governors, "the Commodore purchased from the War Shipping Administration Craft Disposal Division a forty-foot Navy type launch for $3,200. The craft was in reasonably good shape, and had a 75 H.P. Buda Diesel engine. [The company had been founded in 1881 in Buda, Illinois.] The engine new costs $3,200 alone."

These Navy 40-footers were substantial, stable,

## First Postwar Season: 1946 WYC Senior Racing

| Event | Top 3 by Yacht #/Name | Owner/Club |
|---|---|---|
| First Wednesday Series | 62/*Rondot*<br>5/*Commy*<br>105/*Fire Chief* | Roland Derosier/W<br>Mrs. Morrison Shafroth/W<br>J. J. Bodell/W |
| Second Wednesday Series | 106/*El Cid II*<br>105/*Fire Chief*<br>5/*Commy* | John C. Kiley, Jr./W<br>J. J. Bodell/W<br>Mrs. Morrison Shafroth/W |
| Sat. Championship Series | 106/*El Cid II*<br>15/*Viking*<br>84/*Kypris* | John C. Kiley, Jr./W<br>Harry L. Bailey/W<br>Joseph Mattison, Jr./W |
| James Mott Hallowell Challenge Trophy | 15/*Viking*<br>5/*Commy*<br>11/*Fantasy* | Harry L. Bailey/W<br>Mrs. Morrison Shafroth/W<br>James G. Hinkle/W |
| Lynwood Trophy | 106/*El Cid II*<br>105/*Fire Chief*<br>62/*Rondot* | John C. Kiley, Jr./W<br>J. J. Bodell/W<br>Roland Derosier/W |
| Independence Day Race | 62/*Rondot*<br>5/*Commy*<br>25/*Jolly Roger* | Roland Derosier/W<br>Mrs. Morrison Shafroth/W<br>James Waller/BR |
| Long Distance Race Challenge Cup | 11/*Fantasy*<br>62/*Rondot*<br>15/*Viking* | James G. Hinkle/W<br>Roland Derosier/W<br>Harry L. Bailey/W |
| Open Race from Edgartown | 105/*Fire Chief*<br>15/*Viking*<br>95/*Beacon* | J. J. Bodell/W<br>Harry L. Bailey/W<br>Albert Rockwood/W |
| Open Race to Nantucket | 15/*Viking*<br>82/*Cave Canum*<br>78/*Lancer* | Harry L. Bailey/W<br>J. P. Carney/W<br>W. Tausigg, Jr./W |
| Open Race from Nantucket | 15/*Viking*<br>84/*Kypris*<br>37/*Fiddler* | Harry L. Bailey/W<br>Joseph Mattison, Jr./W<br>R. W. Scott/W |
| Labor Day Race | 62/*Rondot*<br>25/*Jolly Roger*<br>11/*Fantasy* | Roland Derosier/W<br>James Waller/BR<br>James G. Hinkle/W |
| Edgartown Regatta Winners | 49/*Bettahad* (Div. 1)<br>73/no name/ (Div. 2) | Ross Richards/HP<br>Ben Baxter/HC |

and able boats. Club members brought the launch up from New York and were astonished by how little fuel the diesel burned. Some modifications were undertaken at Crosby Yacht Building & Storage and the big launch now became the club's committee boat. Hinkle's wife Mary, known within the family as "Pie," took one look at the boat, painted Navy gray, said it reminded her of an elephant, and promptly called it *Dumbo* after the title character in the 1941 Walt Disney film. The name stuck.

The following summer, Pie Hinkle persuaded her husband that their sons James Jr. and Joseph should get a taste of the American West. Thus, instead of spending the summer of 1947 racing #11 and serving as WYC commodore, Hinkle found himself in Encampment, Wyoming, at the famous "A Bar A" ranch. It was an interlude that Hinkle never lived down. When he had to step back into the club limelight in 1948 after the untimely death of the new commodore, W. Palmer Letchford, James Gaff Hinkle was known as the "Commodore on Horseback."

IN A CHANGED WORLD, people were eager to restore their lives to remembered routines. The WYC was officially opened on Tuesday, June 25, 1946, and Edward N. Wilkes, Jr., and Norman H. Batchelder, Jr., reported for duty as Yacht Master and assistant Yacht Master. A full slate of races was sailed in 1946, and the Seniors also journeyed to three regattas. The first Wianno Senior race on Saturday, June 29, drew eleven boats, the same number that had raced during the initial season of competition in 1914.

In late July, the Hyannis Yacht Club, which had originally been organized in October 1895 and re-established in 1927, hosted a regatta, and Seniors participated. Soon, the HYC would have its own small group of highly competitive Wianno Senior sailors. A few days later, when the twenty-third Edgartown Yacht Club Regatta was held in August 1946, it attracted two hundred boats, the largest field since 1931. The WYC's first postwar long-distance race to Edgartown was held just ahead of an easterly gale that forced cancellation of the first day of racing at Edgartown. Commodore Hinkle won the Long Distance Race, his third such victory. Since Carolyn Crossett had been asked by her father to decline the cup upon her third win in 1932, it was James Gaff Hinkle who now retired the twenty-six-year-old Long Distance Trophy. (The Hinkle family put the cup back in competition in 1989.)

By now, thirty-two years after they'd been built, only two of the original 1914 yachts — #11 and #5 — were still in the hands of their original owners. While the '30s had seen new boats and new faces, the immediate postwar period saw many boats change hands again as a new generation of Wianno Senior sailors entered the fleet. Sometimes, these owners had connections to those who had previously owned the boat. Others, of course, did not and new Wianno Senior skippers now began to emerge, most on Cape Cod, but several elsewhere, as the composition of the fleet began its postwar evolution.

At the end of the 1946 sailing season, Edward Crossett's daughter Carolyn embarked on a new voyage. On October 27, at Wianno, she married George Rowland, who had served in the naval reserve in the

*Built in 1931 for Ann and Francis Bird of the Wianno Yacht Club, #95 was originally named* Beacon. *The Birds raced only occasionally and subsequent owners appear to have followed suit, using the boat primarily for daysailing and some low-key racing. This image shows #95 in 1956 when she was named* Roweida VII *(soon renamed* Fleetwind*), and owned by William Danforth of the Wianno Yacht Club.*

Pacific during the war. Although Rowland's brother Benjamin had bought Wianno Senior #83 when it was new in 1930 and kept it for six years, George was not a sailor. By the late '30s, Carolyn's own interests had turned to golf, but the Rowlands remained members of the WYC and Carolyn continued to present the Lynwood Trophy for many years.

WHEN JEAN HINKLE was serving on the Hyannis Park Commission in the 1920s, one of her colleagues was Frederic F. Scudder, owner of the local coal company. Born in Osterville in 1892, Scudder served in the Army's transport service in both world wars, held important civic positions, and was a founder of the Hyannis Yacht Club. Like Manley Crosby, Scudder was musically inclined. He possessed a fine bass voice and performed regularly at a variety of venues. In addition to his other gifts, Scudder was an accomplished sailor.

"My dad was one of the better Senior sailors," said Dick Scudder. "He would leave his coal business on race days and get the boat tuned up and ready for the owner to come aboard. He was paid about $25 a day." Fred skippered regularly for Mary Parlett aboard her #37 *Fiddler* and they enjoyed much success. His brother Stuart sailed with Edna Parlett aboard #57 *Second Fiddler*.

Fred Scudder's premature death at age fifty-seven in May 1949, just before the start of the sailing season, was a sad surprise to the Wianno Senior fleet. Now James Gaff Hinkle wrote a letter to Scudder's widow Ethel asking for permission to use her husband's name on a new trophy to be awarded in his

honor. On June 1, 1949, Ethel replied: "I wish to assure you that I gladly give my permission to have the trophy proposed in memory of Fred. It is a wonderful tribute to him and I sincerely appreciate the thought. Wianno Seniors were his first love in boats. Your very kind letter helped so much and was deeply appreciated." The Frederic F. Scudder Memorial Trophy has been the class championship trophy since 1949 and remains the class's premier award. Although the regattas involved have changed over time, the Scudder Cup is still presented to the yacht having the highest average point total in six races sponsored by local yacht clubs on Nantucket Sound over three weekends.

Initially, the Scudder Cup was dominated by sailors from clubs other than the WYC. Hyannis Yacht Club's Ben Baxter, whose restaurant overlooked the harbor, won the Scudder Cup series in 1949, 1950, and 1952 aboard his unnamed #73. Baxter's fourth place at the HYC's 1952 regatta was enough for him to win the Scudder Cup for the third time. That, however, was Baxter's last Scudder Cup victory.

In 1951, another Hyannis sailor, Gardner Schirmer, won the Scudder Cup. Schirmer was a skilled racer and a longtime instructor at the HPYC. His win was followed by William "Pop" Sinclair's in *Mimi* (#36) in 1953. The following year, the Scudder Cup was won by HPYC member Ross Wentworth Richards in #117 *Bettayet*. Ross had learned to race in his Wianno Junior *Bettanot* in the late '30s and soon developed into a highly skilled competitor who was recruited by Tabor Academy. After the BRYC's Allan Priddy won the Scudder Cup in 1956, Richards came back to take it in 1957 and another HPYC sailor, Durban McGraw, won it in 1958 in #109 *Dungolphin*. But it was Richards's 1954 Scudder Cup win that prefigured what, some years later, would be perhaps the most impressive performance in the history of competition for that trophy.

POSTWAR, IN AN EFFORT to ensure uniformity, a Wianno Senior Class Committee was formed and each yacht club with a Wianno Senior fleet appointed a Committee member. These included James Gaff Hinkle from the WYC, Whitney Wright from the HPYC, Dr. Paul Henson from the HYC, Richard E. Lincoln for the BRYC, and LeBaron Church from the SHYC. The BRYC's Allan Priddy was the first Class Chairman. The class recognized the Southern Massachusetts Yacht Racing Association (SMYRA) as the governing authority for its races. On March 15, 1948, the Official Rules and Regulations for the Wianno Senior Class were published and approved by SMYRA. The rules covered equipment requirements, sail dimensions, and limits on modifications to the boats.

Despite the great enthusiasm of WYC members displayed in 1946, participation by Wianno Senior owners in racing declined somewhat during the next few years. The largest WYC fleet that assembled in 1951 numbered fifteen boats, two less than in 1950. The club's 132 members were six fewer than in 1950. At the annual meeting in August 1951, the suggestion was made that the membership committee solicit all new summer residents and ask current members to submit the names of likely prospects. The success of this effort, and others, was modest.

After one new boat was commissioned in 1952, no more were launched until 1962.

At Bass River and at Harwich Port, however, the Senior fleets were growing as existing boats were purchased and brought to their new homes. Between 1947 and 1954, thanks in large part to the enthusiastic leadership of BRYC Commodore Joe Small, seven more Seniors arrived at Bass River, and that number would more than double in subsequent years. In August 1949 the SHYC introduced the Marcus Hall Cup — named in honor of the club's late commodore. The first event was won by David Steere, who retired the cup six years later in 1955 upon his third victory. The only other winners were W. R. Sinclair in 1951 and 1953 and Ben Baxter in 1950 and 1952. In 1954, Archibald Clarke, treasurer of the Stone Horse Yacht Club, sent James Gaff Hinkle a check for $23. The amount represented the one-dollar membership fee in the Wianno Senior Class for each of the Wianno Seniors then registered at the club. Kenneth Steere's enthusiasm for the boat and for promoting a competitive fleet at Stone Horse had paid off.

Recognizing the need for some device that would help bring Wianno Senior owners together and build enthusiasm, Hinkle used his position as chairman of the class association to begin issuing an annual bulletin starting in 1954. Thus began an effort to create a yearly roster of each yacht's current name and owner and the owner's address. In his third class bulletin printed in 1955, Hinkle noted with regret the peculiar decision by the Nantucket Yacht Club to exclude yachts under a certain size from participating in its regatta. The Seniors were among the boats excluded.

"...let it be known," Hinkle responded in Bulletin #3, "that Wianno Seniors have been navigating in Nantucket Sound for forty-one years and under all kinds of weather conditions and never has any one of these boats foundered or overturned. Wianno Seniors have sailed around the Cape many times, up the Maine Coast and are considered entirely seaworthy by all authorities."

Twenty-eight years later, when the Seniors were also excluded from the Figawi race, three owners took it upon themselves to have their own race not merely *to* Nantucket but *around* the island and back to Bass River. "Three beers' worth of thinking," recalled Bill Lawrence, "produced the concept." Anyone familiar with the waters traversed will immediately understand the challenge involved. "Well," said Lawrence who shared the helm of #135 with three family members and finished second to Jim Light's #147 and ahead of Lloyd "Mac" McManus in #158 *Molly*, "it is mighty lonely on the backside of Nantucket at 3:00 A.M!"

Not only were the boats seaworthy, but the seamanship skills and camaraderie developed by Wianno Senior owners often enough became the basis for participation in big-boat ocean racing. James Gaff Hinkle had set a kind of example when he began competing in the Bermuda Race in 1919 but, particularly after World War II, other Wianno sailors followed suit. Among those in the Wianno fleet who became serious ocean racers were David Steere, John Kiley, Joe Mattison, Robert Gill, and Heywood Fox.

"They were all hard-core sailors," said Richard M. "Rick" Burnes. "From 1955 on, my dad [Richard "Bunny" Burnes, Sr.] made fourteen trips across the Atlantic in a 50' ketch and competed in ten or twelve Bermuda Races. The Wiannos were a jumping-off place for ocean racing. They are real ocean boats themselves, certainly more like a big boat than a dinghy."

THE ORIGINAL DESIGN BRIEF for the Wianno Senior, according to the 1915 article in *The Rudder*, specified that the boat "have cruising room for two." The term "cruising room" suggests how different expectations were for some sailors of that era compared to today or, for that matter, to those of fifty years ago. Many years after the fact, designer L. Francis Herreshoff—Nathanael's son—would look back on his cruising experiences as a boy and young man. Francis, who was born in 1890, noted that his early voyages were accomplished without an engine, electricity, or a toilet and that these conveniences were neither expected nor missed.

The first known cruise aboard a Wianno Senior was made in 1915 by seventeen-year-old James Gaff Hinkle, his brother Tony, and cousin Stuart. The three young men left Osterville and completed a circumnavigation of Cape Cod, getting a tow through the year-old Cape Cod Canal. During the '30s, the Hyannis Port Yacht Club set aside the week following the Nantucket Regatta for cruising, and in 1934, three of the club's Senior owners, Frank Bissell (#97), Whitney Wright (#80), and Lou Loutrel (#43), made another Cape circumnavigation.

"We set off at daybreak for Monomoy Point in a light sw wind," Loutrel wrote. "Unfortunately the wind died at sunset and we all fought a head tide

*It is the mid-1970s at Edgartown and #148* Madeline *is trying without much success to fly her spinnaker on a close reach. "We would have been faster without it," remembered Richard M. Burnes, Jr.* Madeline *was built in 1969 and raced by the Burnes family until 1992.*

around Race Point and Woods End arriving in P-town harbor about 1 A.M. — 20 hours underway."

The crews spent a day sightseeing and then made sail for Scituate, hoping to connect with the New York Yacht Club's annual cruise and, at the canal, "hitch a ride astern of some of the big yachts that were being towed by their tenders." Unfortunately, the Wiannos were ignored by the passing fleet and were finally rescued by a 25' catboat from Mattapoisett. "We all felt like Magellan on arrival home!" Loutrel wrote.

In July 1947 Ted Frothingham decided it would be fun to make "an ocean voyage in a Wianno Senior" and, together with two friends, Jim Elliott and Mike Wallner, prepared to sail his #77 *Dimbula* (officially *Dimbula III*) from Bass River to Mount Desert Island. The trio had spent nights aboard during regattas and had cruised Cape waters during the fall after racing had ended, so the idea of sailing to Maine did not seem far-fetched. They equipped *Dimbula* with cabin, running, and compass lighting powered by dry cell batteries, anchors and spare line, tools, clothing and foulweather gear, charts, life preservers, and a portable radio that would serve, more or less, as a radio direction finder.

Much of this voyage was spent in fog and mist. After encountering a whale while drifting in light air on the second day out, *Dimbula* picked up Boston and Portland radio stations and got a crude position fix. Late in the afternoon, they spotted Cashes Ledge buoy, confirming that they were on course and well on the way to Mount Desert. They encountered more fog as the voyage continued, and Ted

*Built in 1917, #26* Whisper *was thirty years old when acquired by Peter Stanford. Here we see #26 in Canadian waters where she cruised in 1954 and 1955. The boat was fitted with an enlarged cabin intended to somewhat increase comfort. Stanford voyaged from Connecticut to Georgia and chronicled his adventure in* Yachting *in 1953. He won the Off Soundings race in 1957.*

Frothingham was in the cabin calculating course and distance when his crew summoned him topside.

In his write-up about this adventure, Frothingham recalled the arrival at their destination like this: "Behind us the fog was like a gray wall, and ahead the whole island of Mount Desert, with its round hills, lay bathed in the most glorious late afternoon colors and shadows. It was exactly like one of Maxfield Parrish's lovely paintings. A sight none of us will ever forget. Just around the point lay Otter Cove, which was to be our anchorage."

When the sailors called home after their seventy-two-hour trip, nobody believed they were in Maine, assuming the Wianno Senior had made it to Provincetown. "It wasn't until we gave them our Bar Harbor telephone number and they called us back that our friends would believe us," Frothingham wrote. The boat stayed in Maine for the next two years, and the voyage home, beating to windward the whole way, took seventeen days. "No wonder," Frothingham remarked, "Maine is spoken of as being *Down* East."

But the round-the-Cape cruises and the trip to Maine were modest in comparison to an ambitious voyage by a returned Navy veteran who had graduated from Harvard in 1949 and received his master's degree from King's College, Cambridge, in 1951. In 1953, Peter Stanford set off with two crewmen to sail #26 *Whisper* from Connecticut to Georgia. Stanford already had gained significant experience cruising aboard his boat because, in 1947, he had sailed her to Nova Scotia and encountered especially rough going on the leg from Mount Desert to Yarmouth.

"We shortened down to triple-reefed main and storm jib," Stanford recalled, "but the boat was overpowered so we bore off to run under bare poles, trailing lines over the stern to frustrate the heavily breaking seas. This was no go—the first big one came aboard, completely filled the cockpit, and gave the cabin house such a smack that I felt it might be cracked…. We brought the vessel to, and I lashed up an improvised sea anchor by frapping the anchor line around the working jib on its club, and lowering the rig over the bow weighted by the anchor. That brought her head around a bit but not enough, for the seas hit the exposed weather bilge, causing the lee rail to dig in in a destabilizing way…. I then took in our storm jib (which I still have as a talisman) and hoisted it on the peak halyard, tacked down and sheeted to the end of the main boom. This brought

her up enough that the seas hit her at an angle which actually straightened the vessel out a bit, bringing her more head to the wind as the seas roared by…. When we got to Yarmouth next day, in calm weather in an oily swell, the fishermen we met coming out wouldn't at first believe that we'd spent the night at sea."

*Whisper* would face an even tougher test on her cruise south in 1953. That winter, the thirty-six-year-old boat underwent a thorough rebuild at Saybrook Marine. No effort was made to keep the boat a one-design. Instead, an enlarged cabin house was built and seated on sturdy beams, and a bridge deck was added to reduce the size of the cockpit. The centerboard was removed and a new keel, 4" deeper than the original, was added to make up for the loss of the board. In his article about the cruise published in *Yachting* in 1954, Stanford described the boat as "essentially a day sailer with a bit of shelter forward." He had five weeks to make the trip to Georgia and back, and his main worries were not the mosquitoes and hurricane that might be encountered but the likelihood of light headwinds and calms.

Like so many cruises, this one included moments of splendor and others of serious challenge. Stanford's Wianno Senior put in impressive runs, sometimes covering 150 miles in a 24-hour period. Seas were encountered that towered half the height of the mast, and the crossing of the bar at Savannah became a truly dangerous adventure. There, *Whisper* suffered a knockdown. "Seeing the sea looming," Stanford remembered, "I closed the hatch, where I'd been piloting, and when I reopened it as she came up, I remember the cabin house emerging like an island

*One of the original 1914 boats and still sailing after World War II, #9 Marie was owned by Wilton Crosby for a time in the early '50s. After he sold the boat, she was lost in the hurricane of 1954.*

in a meadow of broken water everywhere, with the helmsman delighted to find there was still a boat under him (he'd been wearing a lifeline, of course). Below there was only a little mopping up to do where water had squeezed in between the hatch boards under pressure."

They had made it to Savannah in fifteen days.

# CHAPTER NINE

# Changing of the Guard

*"It was a fabulous time and they were wonderful people and for me, who'd never been on a boat, the Wianno Senior provided experiences I could never have anticipated."*

— Lew Gunn, Stone Horse Yacht Club, on getting started in the fleet

*Wianno Senior #73 was twenty-one years old in 1949 when her then-owner Ben Baxter won the first-ever Scudder Cup. He repeated the feat in 1950 and 1952. Baxter never named the boat, but when he passed her on to his niece Connie Moore, she named #73 in his honor — Uncle Benny. Connie enjoyed a successful racing career, and when her brother Stan took over Uncle Benny, he won the Scudder Cup in 1962 and 1966. This shot was taken by Norman Fortier in, it's believed, 1973, the last year Stan owned the boat.*

In his introduction to the fourth annual Class Bulletin in 1956, James Gaff Hinkle wrote: "Despite the fact that races are often held in heavy winds and very rough seas, in all of these forty-two years of racing, no Wianno Senior has ever capsized or swamped. And to the best of our knowledge there have been no fatal accidents during races. There have been some close calls, however, and a word of caution seems appropriate at this time to preserve this fine record." Hinkle reported the new requirement of the Hyannis Port Yacht Club that a life ring with ample line attached be carried on deck.

*When his father James retired the family's #11* Fantasy, *Joe Hinkle bought the newly built #137 in 1966. He named the boat* Fantasy II. *This image was shot circa 1969.*

He also noted he had carried one in the cockpit of *Fantasy* ever since 1914, and had even had one occasion on which to use it.

Such reminders about safety aboard are never amiss, and as the '50s trended on, Hinkle doubtless felt such a remark was appropriate on several levels. For one thing, failure to comply with the HPYC's new life-ring requirement could result in disqualification. For another, the inherent safety of having a professional skipper aboard was now a thing of the distant past as the tradition had ended with the war. What's more, many of the boats were by now, in many cases, old and in need of repair, whether their owners knew it or not. The fleet was also seeing the entry of newcomers who varied in age and experience including, a new generation of young people born before or during the war.

As was the class tradition, there was no distinction between girls and boys, and both had the opportunity to learn what sailing was all about. "I started sailing at age seven in 1947 aboard my dad's Lawley daysailer," said Lee Williams, then Lee Shannon. "He replaced that with a Wianno Junior when I started taking lessons at the Hyannis Port Yacht Club. John Linehan was the instructor and I had just the best time there. He was a school principal and knew how to handle kids. If you misbehaved, you'd be kicked off the pier for three days. He had a lot to do with me taking it for granted that the girls could do the same thing as the boys. He said, 'Don't let the boys bully you.'"

Soon enough, Lee was racing in the Junior fleet every Wednesday and Saturday and continued until the boats were lost in 1954 to Hurricane Carol. At the Blue Hill Meteorological Observatory, a 135-mile-per-hour gust was recorded and the hurricane toppled the spire at Boston's Old North Church where the famous lanterns had hung on the eve of the American Revolution. By the time she reached her late teens, Lee had gained significant experience — the Juniors were replaced by challenging Uffa Fox-designed, 15' fiberglass Albacores — but the Wianno Senior "seemed like a total dream to me. I used to watch them coming in with the setting sun behind them, and they were just so pretty. I was enamored with them without actually knowing much about them." That changed when George Winthrop Moore, the father of her friend Connie Moore, bought a Wianno Senior.

Win Moore was a Hyannis businessman whose primary sporting interest was golf, not sailing. As had so often been the case in the class, when Moore bought #73, it was for his children. In 1956, at age sixteen, Connie took over #73, which her cousin's uncle, Ben Baxter, had sailed to Scudder Cup victories in 1949, 1950, and 1952. Baxter, who had purchased a Navy landing craft to ferry work trucks to and from Nantucket and Martha's Vineyard, had retired the Senior to a shed where it remained until 1956.

Hauling the twenty-eight-year-old boat out of its shed was a big step for Connie Moore. At age nine, she had started sailing under the watchful eye of Francis "Poppa" Hammatt at the Quanset Sailing Camp in Orleans. Campers learned to sail in Spaulding Dunbar-designed Bay Birds on Pleasant Bay. When Connie was eleven, her father organized a sailing program at the Hyannis Yacht Club with high-school teacher Mac MacSwan as the instructor. There, Connie progressed to Beetle Cats and Cape Cod Knockabouts. All this provided a solid foundation for moving to the Senior and inviting her friend Lee Shannon to help learn the boat.

"I never really raced with Connie on #73," Lee remembered; "however, we practiced tactics on it as we prepared for other competitions. Most notably, she had me learn to set and fly a spinnaker. She would be at the helm and I would set the chute by myself. We experimented with all sorts of ways to set the chute — 'rotten cotton' twine, buckets, and plastic bags. We had a lot of fun, although I feel exhausted now just thinking about it. We sailed in many competitions in the late '50s, and we won the Prosser Cup (Southern Massachusetts Women's Championship) and did fairly well at the Nationals as well."

Whatever the future success Lee and Connie would experience, there were challenges to be surmounted in getting #73 into shape. "It took a few years to put the boat back into racing condition," Connie recalled of #73. "Uncle Ben went with us each time to help us learn about the Senior. During our first season, after a Scudder Cup race, he kept asking me if the tiller seemed light. After the third time he asked, he put his hand on the tiller and immediately went for the stern of the boat. He looked over the transom and said some words I won't repeat. Half the rudder was missing."

Worse was to come. The following year, 1957, #73 — now named *Uncle Benny* — was attempting to round a channel marker at the Bass River Scudder Cup event. "We were forced down on the marker," Connie said, "and somehow the marker didn't move out of our way in time, so it rolled right under the boat. On the way into the harbor, the boat was not acting right. We had lost the iron keel, the whole piece. The next season, after the keel had been replaced, I finally won a prize on my own and my father always referred to it as the $1,000 trophy!"

By 1960, Connie's brother Stan had assumed increased responsibility for #73 and in 1962 took over the boat when his sister married and left the Cape. Moore had won his first race at the HPYC in 1950 at age eight, and by the time he began crewing for his sister aboard #73 he already had the foundation on which to build a solid racing career. "In my early years," Moore said, "all I remember is pumping bilges in old #73. That had to be done at least three times a week and five times when racing. But then I also began sailing the downwind leg while my sister handled the others."

Moore learned that he didn't care much for sailing but loved racing, an affection developed initially under the tutelage of his uncle. "I owe all to previous Scudder Cup champion Ben Baxter," Moore said. "He taught me the currents, tides, and how to race a Wianno Senior." Moore's sailing skills were further developed thanks to tutelage from a skipper remembered by all who sailed against him as the HPYC's top sailor. "Ross Richards was ten years older than me and he was also my mentor," Moore said. At age twenty, Stan Moore won the Scudder Cup in 1962 and did so again in 1966.

By the time Moore won his second Scudder Cup, #73 was in need of significant repair. Although he had long since learned exactly how much to rake the mast and generally set up the boat, Moore knew it was time to move on. He bought a new Wianno Senior in 1973, #173, which he named *Stanley Steamer*. "I set up the new boat like the old one and it took three years to win a race," he said. "I couldn't get the helm right." By 1977, however, with some help from one of the fleet's most analytical sailors, Moore was again back in form, and won that year's Scudder Cup. "I spent time tuning up with Jack Fallon," Moore said, "and finally realized my main was too baggy. We kept moving the mast until it was just right. If I couldn't get it right, Jack would tell me. He knew the boats as well as Ben Baxter."

John T. "Jack" Fallon had grown up street-smart in Roslindale, and the family was well connected in both Boston politics and business, but Jack was no newcomer to Cape Cod. His grandparents had a home at Old Silver Beach in Falmouth where Jack learned to sail aboard Cape Cod Knockabouts, and his mother summered in Maushop Village at Popponesset. There, during summers, Fallon — whose father had died in a flu epidemic when Jack was two years old in 1926 — worked at the Inn before joining the Navy. After his discharge, Fallon entered the commercial real estate business in Boston, beginning a venture that would include, among other things, development of the Prudential Center. It wasn't long before Fallon's success allowed him to indulge his competitive desire to race sailboats.

"Jack and I married in 1949," said Antoinette "Toni" Fallon, "and we gave up golf for sailing." When he looked back on the start of his highly successful and sometimes contentious racing career in the Wianno Senior fleet, Fallon recalled in a *WoodenBoat* article published in 1989: "I always had a yearning for silver...we built shelves for trophies in my study before we built our [Weston] house, before we got the Wianno." With encouragement from his ever-enthusiastic friend Ross Richards, in 1951 Fallon purchased Wianno Senior #120 and later acquired a license plate that read W120.

The boat Fallon bought was named *Marna*, an acronym of her original owners' first names, Marjorie and Nate Hunt of Hyannis Port. Not willing to challenge the old belief that it's bad luck to change a boat's name, #120 remained *Marna* after Fallon bought her. *Marna* was a nearly new boat, as the Hunts' initial plans had changed and Fallon purchased her a year after she'd been built. "Jack was

*Two of the top boats of their era sail in close company. Ross Richards (Hyannis Port Yacht Club) skippers #141* Bettawin *while Jack Fallon (Wianno Yacht Club) sails #120* Marna.

building a new house in Weston," Ted Crosby remembered, "and I went up to see it. He showed me this big boulder in the cellar and said it was going to cost $5,000 to remove it. We were looking at it and then he said, 'Well, I'll buy the boat instead.'"

Fallon's first few years with *Marna* remain something of a mystery as the boat appears in no surviving race results. "I simply enjoyed the boat for the first few months I owned her," Fallon wrote in *WoodenBoat*, "then I decided it was time to find out what racing was all about.... After a while, Roland Derosier, who had been very successful with #62, agreed to crew with me and began teaching me the

ins and outs of the Wianno." The earliest surviving record of *Marna*'s racing career under Jack Fallon is that of the 1956 Edgartown Yacht Club Regatta. In a race sailed in a light and variable southeast wind, the Priddys aboard #76 *Hermanos* came first, followed by Connie Moore in #73 *Uncle Benny* and Rodger Nordblom in #91 *Robwind*. Fallon finished last of the fourteen boats.

AT THE HEIGHT of the 1955 racing season for the Senior fleet, Edward Clark Crossett died in Santa Barbara, California, at age seventy-three. While older members of the WYC knew Crossett as a staunch

*Still the skipper — this portrait shows H. Manley Crosby near the end of his life.*

*Built in 1931, #91 was acquired by Rodger Nordblom in 1954. Rod changed the boat's name from* Moby Dick *to* Robwind *and campaigned her for twenty years under the burgee of the Stone Horse Yacht Club. This image shows #91 in 1969.*

competitor and for his guidance of the club during its critical expansion period, his professional interests had made him an important figure in the wood products, paper, and lumber manufacturing businesses. But it was Crossett's passion for art, for learning, and for photography that may have had the most far-reaching impact on others. Edward Crossett took some of the early photos of Wianno Seniors and he passed on a passion for photography to his daughter Carolyn. He left a major part of his art collection to his alma mater, Amherst, and endowed his daughter Carolyn's college, Bennington, with the funds to

build and maintain the Edward Clark Crossett library, which opened in 1959.

In January 1959 Horace Manley Crosby died at his house in Osterville. He was eighty-eight years old. Manley's nephew Chester, who had begun working in the shop as a boy, remembered his uncle in F. Winston Williams's 1987 "Warriors of Wianno" article in *Cape Cod Life*. "He was a wonderful man, and I have fond memories of him because he had a way of handling men." In its obituary, the *Barnstable Patriot* devoted a paragraph to Manley's musical accomplishments, noting he'd founded the Osterville Silver Cornet Band fifty years earlier and the Excelsior Band before that (probably not long after his return to the village from Brooklyn). While the newspaper account noted that Manley had designed a great many boats, only one was mentioned by name. It was the Wianno Senior.

The passing of H. Manley Crosby was recognized as an important, even historic event for the Wianno Senior Class, and discussion began about how best to commemorate Manley's importance to present and future Wianno Senior sailors. On August 16, 1960, James Gaff Hinkle wrote a letter to sixty-two-year-old Wilton Crosby, the third of Manley's four sons. "I have been to N. C. Wood & Son and have ordered a trophy to be designated as the H. Manley Crosby Memorial Trophy," Hinkle noted. "In view of the fact that the Scudder Trophy is a large and rather unattractive loving cup, I thought it appropriate to have for your prize a Revere bowl of fairly good size — about 13 inches across the top — and replicas thereof about 4 inches across. They are of plated silver

100

and, I think, very distinctive."

The trophy was established to reward the yacht that scored the second-highest average points resulting from competition in all inter-club races for Wianno Seniors approved by SMYRA. Essentially, the trophy became the one awarded to the boat finishing with the second-highest point total in the Scudder Cup competition. Hinkle initially ordered three replica trophies to get things started and asked Wilton for his approval of the plan. Wilton responded promptly, saying, "We are delighted with your selection of the Revere bowl, also the engraving is just the way we would like it."

During the first six years of competition for the H. Manley Crosby Memorial Trophy, only two skippers won it. David Steere triumphed four times. The other winner in that period—in 1961 and 1963—was Jack Fallon. In 1957, after his initial disappointing results, Fallon began a concerted, even all-consuming effort to bolster his racing skills. Fallon improved steadily, and in 1959, he won the Scudder Cup, the Long Distance Race to Edgartown, the Edgartown Regatta, and the Ocean Race Trophy.

"He got good by sailing every day from dawn to dusk," said Pam Fallon Jagla, who began accompanying her father aboard *Marna* when she was six years old in 1956. "Only when it was starting to get dark off Popponesset would he head for home. He always studied the wind and the water and he knew the depths over every shoal and where the eddies would form. He learned to predict wind shifts well before they happened. And he asked everyone if they wanted to get their boat and go out and practice. It

wouldn't matter if it was John Kiley or Dr. Currie or the Edmondses or the Kennedys. So we'd have 'brushes' with all these other boats as a way of improving, and he'd always say that if you want to do something well, then practice."

Fallon also became an attentive boat tuner and kept meticulous records. He experimented with jib lead placement and re-stepped the mast time and again — seeking just the right rake — before the start of the season. He painstakingly adjusted the forestay and the shrouds and studied how varying the tension affected the boat. All these settings were recorded in notebooks. So was the setup of the boat for each race along with the race conditions. Eddie Gallagher, a protégé of John Linehan, who went on to skipper a Wianno Senior named *Watch Out* in the early '60s, recalled that "Jack Fallon tank-tested a Wianno Senior hull at MIT to gauge balance and centerboard angles."

All this attention to detail gave Fallon what to others could appear an innate understanding of the Wianno Senior, but it was, in reality, an understanding based on patient study and analysis. Some years later, when Marblehead sailmaker Bruce Dyson began racing aboard *Marna* and observing Jack, he concluded that Fallon was a "good helmsman but a *great* boat preparer."

Little or nothing escaped Fallon's attention. During a period when he served on the board at Eastern Airlines, he learned of a durable new paint that was being used on the airplanes. He told the Crosbys about it and brought some to Osterville. The resulting hard and glossy finish marked an early use of

*A silverware-bedecked #120* Marna *at rest. At the bow is crewman Hugh MacColl standing next to "Toni" Fallon. Skipper Jack Fallon is just abaft the mast next to Ted Crosby.*

Awlgrip, and others soon began asking for it. "It was good," said Ted Crosby, "as long as the boat didn't rub against a piling, because the touch-up was hard to match."

Preparations for each season began while *Marna* was still in the shed at Crosby's. "We practically lived in the boatyard," said Pam. "He would sit with Teddy and Malcolm [Crosby] and ask questions and learn about the boat. One year, he was in the boat shed all by himself and had jacked up the boat to paint the bottom, and something happened and the boat crushed his fingers. He had to wait until someone came in and found him." This accident did nothing to diminish Fallon's enthusiasm.

"THE PAST SEASON was one of the most active in recent years in inter-club competition," wrote James Gaff Hinkle in his introduction to Class Bulletin #10 in 1961. "More yachts were recorded as starting than in many years past, beginning with the first event which was the long distance race sponsored by the Wianno Yacht Club from Wianno to Edgartown and ending with the final competition at the Hyannis Port Regatta for the Commodore Sinclair Trophy in which 32 starters were listed. This augurs well for the revived interest in the class."

That increased interest was aided as Crosby's received orders for several Seniors to be built during the winter of 1962, the first new construction in a

decade. These new yachts included #123, #124, #125, #126, and #127. Later, reflecting on how these new boats performed during the 1962 season, James Gaff Hinkle noted: "Although the new yachts were excellent performers, they did not outclass even some of the oldest yachts in commission which speaks well for the permanence and duration of these boats."

Coincidentally or not, this increased interest in the Wianno Senior occurred shortly after the election of John F. Kennedy as the thirty-fifth president of the United States. With Kennedy's entry into the White House, the Wianno Senior became, in essence, the nation's "first boat." A headline in the May 21, 1961, issue of the *Boston Globe* asked: "Will President Kennedy Compete at Wianno?" After Kennedy's election, a close watch was kept on the waterfront to see if the president might decide to go sailing. On July 20, 1963, the *Boston Globe*'s yachting writer John Ahern reported from Edgartown that "The nation's number one sailboat came out to race Friday afternoon and all over Nantucket Sound young yachtsmen could be heard exclaiming: 'I saw him.'"

What they saw, however, was not the president. It was instead the junior senator from Massachusetts, Ted Kennedy, at *Victura*'s helm. Reporter Ahern clearly done some background work and ferreted out a bit of information about Wianno Senior #94. "*Victura*, famous as she is, is not one of the better Wiannos and she may be one of the worst. Her sails are old and if there is a spinnaker in the sail locker, it saw no action Friday.

"Yet Teddy was close to Dave Steere's *Venture* every inch of the way on the close reach down to East Chop and on the run and reach back to the harbor. Also on the way back, *Victura* successfully held off the bid of Jack Fallon's *Marna*, a good boat well sailed."

Perhaps *Victura*'s glory days were over, but #94 had enjoyed considerable success in the prewar inter-club races between the WYC and HPYC and was a good heavy-air performer. Jack Kennedy's last race win, however, appears to have occurred in 1949 — the year he began his campaign for statewide office — at the Edgartown Yacht Club Regatta. It was a big field with the boats divided into two divisions. Joe Gargan was aboard *Victura* along with Ted Kennedy and Jack's friend Torbert "Torby" Macdonald. Macdonald had been a Kennedy roommate at Harvard, captain of the football team, and, like Jack, he also served as a PT boat skipper. After the war, he graduated from Harvard Law School and served in Congress where, in 1967, he became known as the "father of public broadcasting."

"Jack and Torby were late to get aboard," remembered Gargan of this race. "They came running down the pier in their swim suits and tee-shirts and jumped aboard. We had a couple of Harvard sweatshirts with hoods that Torby and I put on, but Jack stayed in his tee-shirt.

"The start was downwind and at the turning mark, *Victura* was last of the Division II boats. While the fleet beat to windward towards Cape Poge, Jack said, 'What the heck, they're going that way, we'll go towards Falmouth.' We sailed for about an hour in the wind, cold, and fog, and we were shivering in those soaking sweatshirts and Macdonald was singing

*It is August 7, 1960, and John F. Kennedy — newly nominated as the Democratic presidential candidate — is seen here with Jackie Kennedy aboard* Victura *in Hyannis Harbor.*

'Roll Me Over in the Clover.' Then we saw a boat headed toward the finish and heard the gun. I yelled, 'I can't believe we're second in Second Division.' But then we got a gun ourselves and learned we were first in Division II and second in Division One. Well, that boat was heavy, and I think it was great in heavy air and Jack was a great helmsman."

Jack Kennedy's promising life came perilously close to being cut short as Gargan steered *Victura* back into Edgartown Harbor. "He always loved to toss a line off the stern and be towed behind the boat," Gargan said. "He was doing this while we sailed up the harbor, but all of a sudden, a powerboat came charging up and there was no way they would see him, and I thought, 'They're gonna kill him.' It was a close call."

Gargan was also aboard *Victura* during what turned out to be President Kennedy's last sail late in the summer of 1963. He'd gotten the okay from the president to take out a doctor friend for a brief sail. "Doctor Kearsley was learning how to work the jib-sheets when the Coast Guard and the Hyannis police boat came out and told us that President Kennedy would like me to bring *Victura* to the pier so he can go for a sail." The president boarded the boat together with Jackie and top aide Kenneth O'Donnell. With Joe Gargan and his friend in the cockpit, Jack Kennedy steered *Victura* out to the spindle marker off Hyannis Port, turned around, and sailed home.

"Richard Kearsley got quite a kick out of this," Gargan remembered. "When we got ashore, he said, 'That was fantastic. You invite me to go sailing with you, and I wind up sailing with the president of the United States.'"

NOT EVERYONE WHO joined the Wianno Senior fleet and went on to an impressive racing career grew up on the Cape, came from a sailing family, or had previous experience with boats. While Jack Fallon, Dave Steere, Stan Moore, and other Wianno Senior stalwarts were hotly contesting the various races in 1960, a tall and athletic Canadian who'd barely set foot on a Cape Cod beach was taking sailing lessons from an eight-year-old at the Stone Horse Yacht Club.

Lewis James Hamilton Gunn, known to all as "Lew," was born in Edinburgh, Scotland, in 1918 and, after his family moved to Canada, Lew's passion for the demanding game of cricket took him to the highest levels of the sport. "I had never even been near salt water until I was about forty-two years old," he recalled. But in 1939, Gunn had left Toronto where he was connected to the Board of Trade, to take a job as an inspector at the Remington Arms factory in Bridgeport, Connecticut, which was then producing munitions for Great Britain. During his years in Bridgeport, Gunn met and married Sally Curtiss whose family rented a summer place in Dennisport. Postwar, Gunn's business and cricket activities kept him very busy, but eventually, in 1960, he finally visited the Cape. After a long drive from Toronto to Dennisport, Lew asked, "What do we do now?" The answer was "Oh, we go to the beach."

Lew Gunn's first day at a Cape Cod beach is etched firmly in his memory. "I sat down on my towel. After a while, sand crept up my bathing suit. A young man went by in a 13' skiff. I yelled, 'I'll give you $125 for your boat.' He brought it to the beach. That is how my sailing career began."

Mostly, Gunn found himself racing against teenagers. He was starting from a knowledge base that was essentially zero. Early on, when one of his young sailing teachers told him to take down the spinnaker as they were approaching the leeward mark, the term "leeward" was entirely new to him. Yet, Gunn was highly competitive. What's more, he wanted to show what a staunch Canadian cricket champion could do in a sailboat race. He began thinking of himself as an "invader" who would soon be winning races in America. As he learned the ropes, rules, and tactics, Gunn noticed the "big boat" of the SHYC fleet, the Wianno Senior. He was impressed by the boat's purposeful look and abundant rigging.

"I said to myself that before I could think of buying a Wianno Senior, I had to start winning in the Bullseye," Gunn remembered. "I learned pretty quickly and was winning races in two or three years."

Gunn's first sail aboard a Wianno Senior was a demonstration with Bill Crosby at the helm. "It was a windy day and we went around Grand Island," he remembered. "The boat felt huge and powerful after my Bullseye and it was very scary." Gunn's eight-year-old son Elliott — who would later crew for his dad — was aboard, and he remembers that sail as frightening. "The water was so close to the deck and we kicked up a huge wake," he remembered. "I was put ashore so the sales pitch demonstration could continue."

Elliott's father had a different reaction to his first sail aboard a Wianno Senior. "The thing was," Gunn remembered, "I loved it."

In 1965, Gunn bought newly built #134 for

*A champion Canadian cricket player before he turned to sailing, the Stone Horse Yacht Club's Lew Gunn won three consecutive Scudder Cups starting in 1978 and became the first Wianno Senior skipper to have competed in both wooden and fiberglass models. He preferred the former. This photo was taken in August 2011.*

The skiff's transom said Buzzards Bay on it, words that fascinated Gunn. "Buzzards Bay." He decided to see what Buzzards Bay looked like, and drove off the Cape and eventually to Cape Cod Shipbuilding, the long-established shop that, postwar, had become an early and successful pioneer of fiberglass construction. The proprietor at Cape Cod Shipbuilding was E. L. Goodwin, an engaging man well-known to several generations of small-boat sailors. Among the new boats on display were a Bullseye and a Cape Cod Mercury. "The Mercury cost less so I bought it," Gunn said. "Then I saw the kids sailing Bullseyes at Stone Horse, so I traded the Mercury for one of those."

*Lew Gunn's #134* Invader *reaches quickly through the Nantucket Sound chop in 1973. "The cross-cut main is old-school," said long-time competitor Kevin Cain. "The photo is a throwback to the days we sailed Olympic and Gold Cup Courses. While she looks to be overpowered, the reaches were often very tight and if you let the main out to flatten the boat, you would often drag your boom in the water. Nowadays the courses are generally windward/leeward and such a reach is unusual."*

$5,000. He had the boat painted what would become his signature color, a dark blue that was a different shade than the Kennedys' *Victura*. "Jack Fallon was an inspiration to me and to the Wianno Class," he said. "Fallon, Steere, Stan Moore, and Frank Lloyd were top sailors, and it became my ambition to beat the living daylights out of them."

Gunn now began practicing and racing *Invader*. "I got wild about it," he said. "I loved it. I'd fly down from Toronto every weekend and race." Within a few years, Gunn was highly competitive in SHYC Wianno Senior races, but it's unlikely that anyone in the fleet could have anticipated what the future held for the cricket-playing invader from Toronto.

IN 1964, THE WIANNO Senior celebrated its fiftieth anniversary. In the Class Bulletin issued that spring, James Gaff Hinkle noted the anniversary caused him to remember the oldest boats in the fleet and some of the men who had been responsible for establishing the class. "The earliest years bring up names like *Wendy* #2, *A.P.H.* #4, *Commy* #5, *Snookums* #6, *Sea Dog* #8, *Fantasy* #11, *Maxixe* #13, *Viking* #15; Commodore W. B. H. Dowse, Max, Elli, Wilbur, and Manley Crosby, Uncle Bill, Al Sherman, Fred Scudder and many others...."

By now, Hinkle himself was revered in the fleet as a perfect gentleman of the old school. "He always raced," remembered Jan Steere-White, "sitting straight up and wearing a tan linen sport coat. For bad weather, he had an old-fashioned yellow slicker."

The fiftieth was a significant milestone, and as if to demonstrate the boat's ongoing appeal and the lure of the class itself, three more new Seniors were launched. They included #129 for Dr. W. Lawrence Wilde of the WYC, #130 for J. W. and David Scarbrough of the SHYC, and #131 for Dr. Joseph A. Valatka of Scituate. Another boat was ordered in 1964 for delivery in 1965; it was #132 for Attorney General Robert Kennedy of the HPYC. When he attended a party held at the Crosby yard to celebrate the fiftieth anniversary, the *Boston Globe*'s Frank Falacci was surprised to learn that "it simply did not occur to any Crosby that the firm might capitalize handsomely by this news [of a new boat for the attorney general]." Yet, for the Crosbys, there would have been nothing to differentiate their approach to the owner of #132 from any other customer. All were treated with equal courtesy and respect.

*"We didn't come close to winning the race," recalled David Scarbrough of the 1964 Edgartown Yacht Club Regatta, "but the downwind leg was our sole moment of glory. I still remember Ted Kennedy going by us upwind." Scarbrough's #130* Manana *was a new boat when this was taken. David is at the helm. Bink Garrison is standing and handling the spinnaker sheet and guy. Jack Maloney is seated just ahead of David.*

The season began with an invitation series of tune-up races sponsored by class stalwarts George Edmonds and Bob Lenk. Later that season, James Gaff Hinkle noted that the addition of new boats to the fleet in both 1963 and 1964 "sharpened the competition markedly."

Although the normal slate of races was scheduled for the 1964 season, a celebratory "Wianno Senior Class 50th Anniversary Regatta" was also planned. The Regatta replaced the WYC's Light Ship Race and was sponsored by the Crosby Yacht Building & Storage Company. A unique aspect of the event was that two separate divisions were formed, Division One for boats in racing trim and Division Two for boats used for daysailing and modest cruising. Spinnakers would not be used by Division Two boats and they would sail a different course started at a different time.

The *Cape Cod Standard Times'* Dorothy I. Crossley covered the event, and she introduced it writing that "The same solid guts that made one Wianno sailor President pitted men and boats last week against the elements, as the late John F. Kennedy's former competitors celebrated a half century of Wianno Senior racing at the Wianno Yacht Club." The Anniversary Regatta generated great interest, and forty-five owners signed up. In Division I, thirty-three boats registered while Division II drew twelve boats. In both cases, the onset of dirty weather had an impact on the actual number of participants, and only thirty boats made the starting line in Division I and seven in Division II. The accompanying chart shows the results for the top boats in each Division.

The fiftieth season of racing was dominated by Dave Steere in #85 and Jack Fallon in #120, with longtime racer Lou Loutrel (#36) and Stan Moore (#73) and newcomers Peter and Tim O'Keeffe (#127) beginning to make their presence felt. The 1964 Scudder Cup was won by Jack Fallon with a score of 494 out of a possible 500. That year's report to the Class Committee noted that "Thanks to the fifty-year-old no. #11 *Fantasy* [Hinkle], the fleet was spared from a clean sweep by Fallon although he came in just behind #11 at the Stone Horse Regatta. Number 85 *Venture* [skippered by David Steere] won the Crosby Memorial Trophy."

*Fantasy's* days were numbered. A parted

| Portrait of the Fleet<br>Wianno Senior 50th-Anniversary Regatta, August 1964 | |
| --- | --- |
| **Division I — Boats in Racing Trim** | **Division II — Boats in Non-Racing Trim** |
| 1st: #120 *Marna*, Jack Fallon | 1st: #48 *Bessie II*, Bruce Hammatt |
| 2nd: #83 *Sovereign IV*, Harrison Bridge | 2nd: #7 *Valkyrie*, Doug Higham |
| 3rd: #123 *Kialoa*, Mary Mattison | 3rd: #95 *Fleetwind*, Manter-Hall School |
| 4th: #91 *Robwind*, Rodger Nordblom | |

One of three new Wianno Seniors built during the class's fiftieth-anniversary year in 1964, #129 was originally owned on Cape Cod before she was purchased in 1989, moved to Maine, and renamed *Tradition*.

shroud required a more complicated repair than at first seemed necessary. Then James Gaff Hinkle entered a Harwich-Bass River race that was sailed in what Pam Fallon Jagla remembered as "the windiest day I was on a Senior. I would say it was blowing 35–40 and the salt spray off the waves created a fog. We had our heavy weather main and jib. We won the race by 40 minutes. We expected to see my mother in our motorboat at the finish, but she was not to be seen. Instead, she was down close to the beach at Bass River towing *Fantasy* out of shallow water before she beached. She had lost her keel on the windward leg. She was towed to the Priddy Boat Yard for repair."

James Gaff Hinkle had a decision to make. "He always said he would either scuttle the boat on Horse Shoe Shoal or give her to Mystic," said Jim Hinkle, Jr. "He chose the latter."

Mystic used the boat for a time, but *Fantasy* leaked too much to be viable either for sailing or as an in-water display. Hinkle had the boat returned to Osterville, where she was fully restored. "All the men at Crosby's worked to make her ship-shape," said Jim, Jr. Today, a century after she was built, *Fantasy* is stored at Mystic Museum's Rossie Mill Building, where she is available for study by anyone interested in a prime example of one of America's oldest and most enduring one-design classes.

In 1965, James Gaff Hinkle's younger son Joe — known as Jodie to many in the fleet — placed an order for the family's second new Wianno Senior. They named her *Fantasy II*.

# Chapter Ten

# Arms Race

*"If we continue to allow sailmakers to 'stretch' the legal limits on sail dimensions and skippers to pay up for new expensive gear, we will continue to lose the one-design nature of the fleet."*

—*letter of HPYC Rear Commodore and Race Committee Chairman, Lawrence Singmaster to John "Jack" Fallon, March 1977*

For almost fifty years since its inception as a one-design in 1914, the Wianno Senior Class had experienced little or nothing in terms of challenges to what was or was not legal. Beginning at some point in the prewar era and in effect by the 1930s, racers were required to sign a Class Conformity Certificate attesting that their boats met all Class Rules and Regulations. These required that the boat had 600 pounds of inside ballast (including an outboard motor's weight, if carried),

113

*Circa 1969, Ross Richards leads the way downwind in #141* Bettawin *followed by the O'Keeffes in #127* Rapparee *and #87* Alert, *built in 1930 but significantly upgraded under John and Anthony Correa. "We are using Hood mitre-cut mainsails," said Tim O'Keeffe. "It was clearly superior and remained so for most of the '70s."*

a 30- to 40-pound anchor, bucket and boathook, oar and oarlock, compass, and several other items. There was no specific mention at all regarding the size and measurements of the main and jib, or the $90 single-luff spinnaker introduced in 1928.

This benign compliance with rules didn't really change in the immediate postwar era. Right through the mid- to late 1950s, there seemed little difference in the level of competition from earlier times. There had always been some within the fleet able to spend more money on their boats than others, but that wasn't unique to the Wianno Senior nor did more money invariably mean triumph over the more skillful. "The shoestring budget guys always have a difficult time, and their learning curve is normally much longer," said James "Jimmy" Bartlett whose mother, a lifelong sailor, had urged him to learn to sail at age twelve in 1956 at Bass River under the tutelage of Ted Frothingham. "But you learn if you stick with it. It is being out there that matters."

By the mid-'60s, however, it would take more than "being out there" to consistently compete in the topmost echelon of the fleet, and the matter of how to keep the Wianno Senior a true one-design class had become a serious challenge. Every aspect of the boat was now demanding of scrutiny, including the uniformity, or lack of it, of the hull itself. In February 1965, James Gaff Hinkle addressed the issue in a letter to the Class Committee. "We are all aware that the boats are built to a mould and not to marine engineering specifications and that there may be some minor variations from time to time in the hulls as the old moulds become destroyed and discarded and new moulds prepared. I think this is unavoidable, but I doubt it is a deterrent to the continuing and extraordinary life of this Class. I think our main concern now lies with the specifications covering the sails."

In the years before World War II, sails were built of Egyptian cotton to drawings on file at Ratsey & Lapthorn on City Island, New York, and at Crosby's. Postwar, cotton sails became a thing of the past as new synthetic fabrics were developed that greatly improved performance, and owners also began experimenting with gadgets to better control and adjust sail trim. For the Wianno Senior Class Committee, a variety of issues soon developed regarding everything from how sails should be measured to, in the case of the spinnaker, their construction methods.

The rule regarding sail size stated: "Sails of any make or nature will be allowed provided that: (a) they conform to the standard sail plan as drawn by the Crosby Yacht Building and Storage Company dated December 1936, amended in December 1961." This wording was soon revealed for what it was, either inadequate to the task or just about right depending upon one's interpretation. Jibs with zippered luffs were used by some owners but not others. The balloon spinnaker that, after a trial in 1958, replaced the old single-luff spinnaker became another item of concern, as explained in an April 30, 1964, letter from James Gaff Hinkle to David Steere.

"Bill Crosby indicated to me that some persons were considering introducing a wire in the luff of the spinnaker for better reaching results. This was excluded years ago in the old-type spinnaker and it was thought the parachute automatically eliminated it; but this does not seem to be the case, and I think it should not be allowed."

Throughout the spring of 1964 Hinkle, Dave Steere, and the Class Committee became involved in all sorts of details relating to sails and such rigging details as the specification of the running backstays. Nothing was simple. When Hinkle proposed changing the wording "Sails shall not exceed the following measurements" to "Sails shall conform to the following measurements," Steere noted, "We have operated to maximum sail dimensions since the class was organized, and the proposed change of this regulation would require all sails to conform to maximum specifications would make obsolete sails that did not reach maximum dimensions and would cause an undue financial hardship on the class."

The debate soon became perhaps the most important topic of discussion throughout the fleet. In February 1965, Samuel Hartwell, then commodore of the HPYC, wrote Hinkle approving proposed rules and amendments but noting: "I think this is a one-design only by grace of general consent of the owners and your Committee. Nothing can be done about hull building…. On the other hand there is far too much gadgetry, particularly with respect to sails. I not only think zipper sails should be outlawed, but that a single sail maker should be chosen, standard specifications decided upon, a limit set on number of sails purchasable and at what intervals. This at least would standardize the motive power. Perhaps also a limit in degree from the vertical for rake of the mast. There is nothing new in these notions, the International One Design Class has successfully observed such regulations for years, and happily, too."

Hyannis Port was not alone in its concern. In October 1966 Robert E. Lenk, owner of #70, wrote Hinkle: "I brought up the infringements, or rumors thereof, only to point up what I consider a necessity in one-design racing — strong enforcement of the rules. I believe that we are quite lax in this area for no one wishes to point an accusing finger. Possibly we could overcome this by automatically inspecting all boats and sails once or twice a season by a committee. If this is too much or can't be done, then all the rules in the world cannot be effective against anyone desiring to violate them."

Sensible as Hartwell's and Lenk's comments were, it would take some two decades before the key measures they recommended were adopted. Instead, the Class entered a period that lasted from roughly 1964 to 1985 and became known as the time of the "arms race" or the "the sail wars." Jack Fallon fired the opening shots.

"Dad brought Ted Hood down from Marblehead," remembered Pam Fallon Jagla. "He'd show up at the house in his Top-Siders looking every inch the yachtsman, and they'd take the boat out."

Fifteen years earlier, Frederick E. "Ted" Hood had left Wentworth Institute before his senior year and opened a small sail loft above Maddie's, a popular and often noisy bar on State Street in Marblehead. From that modest beginning, with the help of his father Stedman, Hood had grown into perhaps the most recognized sailmaker in the country. This success was built upon the Hoods' proprietary Dacron cloth woven on their own looms and Hood's innate gifts as a sailor. As the laconic Ted Hood and outspoken Jack Fallon sailed together aboard *Marna*, Fallon was not shy in offering suggestions about how Hood could improve his sails, which were in widespread use throughout the Senior fleet.

"They'd go out for a day and Dad would tell Hood what was wrong with the jib, for example," said Fallon's daughter Pam. "He and Hood would then argue, and they'd come in and Dad would take the sail and mark it up with black Magic Marker, and it often turned out his ideas were good ones."

Of course, the Class Committee was aware of what was going on and Hinkle understood what was at stake. In December 1966 Hinkle received a letter from Frank B. Jewett, Jr., a successful racing sailor from Vineyard Haven involved with SMYRA. Part of the letter discussed sails and how the Rhodes 19 fleet was addressing the one-design issue. "Uniform sails are the most important single factor in ensuring equal performance capability in one-design boats," Jewett wrote. He further noted how the fleet planned to ensure affordable, identical sails and that a thirteen-page set of specifications had been needed. Hinkle remarked: "Apply this to our Wianno Senior sails and guess what the outcome would be!"

In the fall of 1965, there was consensus that a Hood jib be tested outside of competition to see if one could be developed that would better balance the boat and permit all masts to stand plumb. But there was no rush, and possible approval for such a sail was not even contemplated before 1968 when the Fall Bulletin noted that "there is a growing feeling among the contestants that some limitation should be put on the number of sets of sails that can be used in any season. This problem could be explored during the winter and made the subject of some ruling by the Committee for next year or sometime in the near future."

Jack Fallon, meanwhile, wasn't waiting for any new sail specifications rules. He was using his new Hood sails in his "brushes" with other Wianno skippers, some of whom, naturally, wanted to acquire their own versions. But the Hood-modified sails were just a starting point and Fallon looked elsewhere for ideas, for anything that would create a faster sail.

Fallon, the Roslindale High School graduate, soon began working with Jerome "Gerry" Milgram who, in 1961 and 1962, had received three degrees from MIT including a master's in Naval Architecture and Marine Engineering. Milgram, who sailed on the MIT team and later raced Thistles with considerable success, had written his master's thesis on sail aerodynamics that included new ideas for cutting sail panels to achieve the desired shapes.

"The shape," said Milgram, "came from aerodynamic theory and my computer program that showed how each cloth panel was to be cut to achieve the computed shape. Some practical experience was an essential addition, of course."

The jibs developed by Milgram for the Wianno Senior in the early to mid-'60s were cross-cut with seams glued and sewn. They were built in Milgram's Somerville loft of Howe and Bainbridge "Yarn Tempered Cloth." "I think we were just fortunate that our style of sailmaking led to very fast jibs right out of the box," said Milgram. "We just had to guess on the amount of jibstay sag."

The mainsail, too, came in for scrutiny and, starting in 1968, another Marblehead sailmaker, Bruce Dyson, began working with Fallon and others in the class. "Jack and I came up with what we thought should be the shape," Dyson said. "He said he wanted it to be light so as not to affect the heeling, and we wound up creating a light-air and heavy-air main. Jack also had an old mitre-cut main, and we figured out a vang to bend the boom and help shape the sail and get more power. He left the boat in the water until January, and I'd come down with my sewing machine. We made five experimental mains before we came up with one we liked."

The challenge of finding a sailcloth better than Hood's, which was proprietary, remained. One way to address the issue was to take a Hood main and re-cut it. "George and Sally Edmonds bought two new Hood mains and gave them to me to take apart," Dyson recalled. Still, using the best non-Hood sailcloth available to him, Dyson created a light-air and a heavy-air main, the latter cut flatter and requiring that the peak not be dropped so much as wind increased. These sails, said Dyson, "dominated."

Looking back on the 1968 season, James Gaff Hinkle reported there had been "no controversial points raised as to measurements and equipment; but there is a growing feeling among the contestants that some limitation should be put on the number of sails that can be used in any season. That same fall, on October 30, 1968, at age seventy, Hinkle ended his fifteen-year tenure as chairman of the Wianno Senior Class Committee. He informed his fellow committee members and Samuel Rogers, president of SMYRA, that "the time has come to give some of the enthusiastic younger racing owners of these boats an opportunity to take their turn on this Committee."

Hinkle's service had been both long and devoted, and his final year at the helm was clouded by the assassination on June 5, 1968, of Robert F. Kennedy, owner of #132 *Resolute*. "A heavy pall hangs over it all from Harwich Port to Wianno," wrote John Ahern in the *Globe* on August 18. He quoted HPYC sailing instructor John Linehan: "You can feel the gloom. There's not the zest and desire to go out and compete."

*Here is #140 swelling up and awaiting her mast. Built in 1968 when the class "arms race" was well underway, #140 was owned by Wianno Yacht Club member Alton Churbuck, who cared little for racing but enjoyed the boat for twenty-four years. Restored by Marcus Sherman at Hyannis, the boat is now called* Spirit *and is owned by Richard Egan, longtime proprietor of Crosby Yacht Yard.*

Hinkle's resignation prompted Dave Steere—who replaced him as chairman—to write: "You have been actively associated with this fleet from its beginning and under your leadership, the class has prospered and grown. One of the races which stands out most in my mind took place in the '30s when *Venture* and *Fantasy* practically match-raced all the way over from Wianno to Edgartown only to arrive before the Committee boat could set up the finish line. Perhaps someday we will again have fleets as large as we had in those days."

As for the sailors who won the Scudder Cup during the earlier years of the sail wars, from 1968 to 1976, Fallon won four times with an impressive crew that often included Bruce Dyson, Gil McManus, and John J. "Donnie" McNamara, holder of two national championships in the 210 class (1951 and 1955) and winner of an Olympic bronze medal at Tokyo aboard 5.5-Meters in 1964. George Edmonds, Jr., won the Scudder Cup twice during the period, Dave Steere once, and Boardman Lloyd once. In 1969, a Scudder Cup performance was turned in by a sailor whose natural ability seemed equal to the task of overcoming world-class crews and the latest sails. That year, Ross Richards won every race of the Scudder Series, a feat that has yet to be equaled. (Because only one race was sailed at Edgartown, five races rather than the usual six comprised that year's series.) As always, the competition had been of high caliber. Stan Moore (#73 *Uncle Benny*) placed second, Robert Gill (#117 *Phebe*) third, Stephen Morris (#124 *The Junk*) fourth, and Lew Gunn (#134 *Invader*) fifth.

"Ross," said Stan Moore who had won the Scudder Cup seven years earlier, "was in my opinion a notch better than all of us."

It was an opinion widely shared in the fleet. "The whole Richards family," said longtime Wianno Senior sailor and 1998 Scudder Cup winner Peter O'Keeffe, "was exceptional. This included his sister Sue and his brother Dudley who became a world-class figure skater only to die in the 1961 plane crash in Brussels that took the lives of the U.S. Figure Skating team. Ross always knew which side of the course to be on, how to look for wind, how the tide would affect the boat and the race. He left me in the dust." In 1973, when Ross died, the Ross Richards Memorial Trophy was introduced, awarded to the boat with the third highest points total in the Scudder Cup series.

Even as the Scudder Cup Series maintained its status, the WYC vs. HPYC team races, popular events that had begun before the war, ended in 1965. According to John Kiley's best recollection, "Things had become very contentious. There were a lot of pre-law students and engineers who were racing. In the last series, there may or may not have been a collision, but people thought the risk was too serious and repairs would be expensive. But the races were a big thrill for me as a teenager. Once I was assigned [by the WYC team] to control Senator Kennedy, and

*Always the gentleman, James Gaff Hinkle sailed his #11 Fantasy for fifty years and devoted himself both to the Wianno Yacht Club and the Wianno Senior Class.*

I remember that he got more and more ticked off."

Although the team racing ended, the matter of what was legal in terms of the boats themselves — apart from the sails — remained an ongoing topic. In November 1966 Bill Crosby wrote James Gaff Hinkle that it was his intention "to continue pointing out infractions as well as calling attention to any requested changes that do not fall within rule limitations. I have noticed changes in boats stored and cared for in the Harwich Port, Bass River, and Hyannis areas. Without a question many of these people are doing their own modifications."

Ross Richards, unlike some owners before

*Ross Richards remains widely recognized as perhaps the most gifted skipper produced by the Hyannis Port Yacht Club.*

*Two Hyannis Port Yacht Club skippers return from a day of racing. Ross Richards walks beside Ted Kennedy who campaigned his boat despite back troubles.*

and after, had approached the Class Committee about a change he was hoping to make in the new boat he was having built. In 1967, two years before his perfect Scudder Cup performance, Richards asked the committee for permission to use a manganese-bronze keel. Although the keel would be made in the same mold as the iron keel and weigh the same 600 pounds, Richards's request was turned down.

Prior to the 1968 season, Ted Kennedy wrote the committee to suggest that a fifth crew member, under the age of twelve, be permitted aboard during races. Although nobody could argue with the positive aspects of kids sailing with parents, other considerations suggested that the measure not be adopted. "The general consensus," James Gaff Hinkle wrote Stan Moore that March, "seems to be that if any change were made in the maximum number of crews, it should be done only by special permission of the race committee of a specific yacht club for a particular club race and, certainly, not for any inter-club competition."

Still more topics arose. In 1972 it was voted that no adjustments be allowed to the traveler as some had desired. The possible need to fiberglass leaky wooden hulls rather than undertake expensive rebuilds also cropped up, suggesting to Bill Crosby that a "maximum weight limitation would have to be established." The use of boom vangs raised the issue of repair costs involving broken frames likely caused by the stress imposed by the vang. In the 1977 Class Bulletin, the committee banned vangs, noting that "We know some of you have strong feelings that the

*At the time, circa 1970, the tall gas-operated buoy was a familiar sight at Edgartown, and downwind starts were sometimes a feature of the racing. Here (l-r) are #136 Cirrus (Edmonds family), #147 Intuition (Robert Glenworth and Peter Ream), #143 Pertelote (Francis Lloyd), and #142 Cheerful (Fulham family).*

boom vang improves the performance of the boat and it would be hard to argue against this, but an overview would indicate that we try to find out the underlying cause of the damage."

The matter of what to do about sails that might not be illegal according to the rules but whose development and purchase by a relatively small number of the wealthier sailors remained an ongoing and controversial issue. Brownie Swartwood, an attorney who owned a summer home in Cotuit and later went on to become a judge, put the matter into perspective. Swartwood had bought a new Senior in 1975 but soon came to believe it was "unfair [that] there were guys buying sails during the season when others couldn't really afford to do so. George Edmonds understood this and thought everyone should have the same sail and equal opportunity. I thought it was important to keeping the fleet alive."

In March 1977 Lawrence Singmaster, who was then rear commodore and race committee chairman

at the HPYC, sent a frank letter to Jack Fallon, who was by then chairman of the Class Committee. Singmaster wrote: "In the past few years, there has been increasing concern about the exact specifications of 'legal' sails and racing equipment. The recent Dyson jibs are an example of differing views as to what is legitimate in the fleet and what is not. Also, we have been informed that a few boats are employing new and in some cases costly gear that has not been approved by the committee.... There is a feeling that 'the rich get richer and poor are getting poorer'.... In short, we think a clarification of all rules pertaining to our boats, gear, racing, etc. is in order."

But the clarifications for which Singmaster and others were clamoring would take another eight years before they began becoming reality. The "rich get richer" sentiment, however, was not limited entirely to the matter of how many and what sort of sails one could buy. The great wealth of the founding fathers and its concentration in the Wianno neighborhood appears to never have stifled growth of the fleet. Not everyone could afford to live in Wianno, or Osterville, and some of those who could, such as Joseph P. Kennedy and Kenneth Steere, bought elsewhere for a variety of reasons. By the postwar generation, Osterville tended to be home to very successful business people while Cotuit, for example, attracted professionals in varying fields and those in the arts. "There was a little bit of the Cotuit vs. Wianno business," remembered Brownie Swartwood. "It was a generational thing that, at its extreme, would have people thinking of the other place as 'over there.'"

Given the evolving class, ethnic, and religious consciousness prevalent in American society during the Wianno Senior Class's century of existence, it would be naïve to think that some examples of exclusionary thinking did not exist at the WYC. Yet, such matters, while certainly uncomfortable for those involved, were successfully dealt with and the class itself might best be described as a meritocracy that recognized being a "sailor" as the primary qualification for hoisting the Wianno Senior burgee.

THE WIANNO SENIOR had always exerted an appeal to sailors who lived elsewhere than Osterville and the other towns or villages on the south shore of Cape Cod with established fleets. As the years trended on, Seniors found homes at Martha's Vineyard, Nantucket, Woods Hole, Falmouth, and elsewhere. This dispersion, while never really large in terms of numbers, continues to this day. Often these boats were thoroughly enjoyed for daysailing or modest overnight cruises but, even as the "arms race" era was unfolding on the Cape, an enthusiastic but comparatively low-key fleet was forming on Boston's South Shore in Scituate.

The prime mover behind this activity was a popular local pediatrician named Dr. Herbert N. Blanchard. Blanchard, who'd been born in Allston in 1916, graduated from Boston University's Medical School in 1941 and promptly entered the army. He received a bronze star for his service during the crucial Battle of the Bulge in 1944. Blanchard was thirty-eight years old in 1954 when he bought #93 *Shangri-La*, and Crosby's had it trucked to Scituate for $65 on a cradle that cost $10.

*George Edmonds guides #136* Cirrus *on a breezy reach.*

For Herb Blanchard, the Wianno Senior was both a joy and an escape from the pressures of his practice. He sailed a long season — launching in early May and not hauling until Thanksgiving — often with his family and especially his daughter Martha Ellen. Martha remembered that "As a small home-town GP, my father seemed to be on call twenty-four hours a day except for every Thursday when he was sailing on *Shangri-La* away from all telephones. Sometimes, though, the harbormaster came out to alert him if there was an emergency or a baby awaiting delivery."

Eventually, Blanchard's enthusiasm for the Senior proved infectious, and more boats found a homeport in Scituate. "Doc Blanchard was the leader," remembered Herb Towle, a Cohasset electrical contractor who owned #8 *Sea Dog*. "He was just a great guy."

Ann Baird, who together with her husband Cameron acquired another old Senior, #41 *Halcyon*, said that "Dr. Blanchard would get us all together. He truly loved the Wianno and we elected him president of our Scituate Wianno Association. Howard E. North was the Secretary. We belonged to a wonderful little club, the Satuit Boat Club. It was all people who loved to sail, not motor."

In June 1966 Herb Blanchard sent James Gaff Hinkle a brief letter in which he reported that "For the past several years, five or six Wiannos have been racing regularly out of Scituate. Last year being our most fruitful season with six Wiannos racing every other Sunday." He added that three additional boats had entered the fleet for the 1966 season and that "Great interest has been expressed by other people in our group and several are planning to purchase a Wianno Senior."

Racing in the fleet was said to be competitive but informal. "There was one event," remembered Ann Baird, "after which the loser could pick any boat and then we'd all swap for the next race,"

The boats were equipped with sails made by the local loft, Mattern Sails. Bob Vogel remembered his old #16 *Mistral* as the "fastest boat in the Scituate fleet." He replaced several planks, recaulked, refastened about a third of the bottom, and changed the hull's color from light to dark blue. "Even with the work done," he said, "the boat needed a full-time bilge pump."

Although several of the nine Scituate boats were old and required a lot of pumping, Dr. Joseph Valatka committed to a new Senior in 1964 when he purchased #131 *Zurba*. He kept the boat for over a decade. The effort to build and maintain an active Senior fleet at Scituate ended when Herb Blanchard, suffering from arthritis, scaled back his sailing before selling his *Shangri-La* in 1985. Said Ann Baird, "The life went out of the association after Herb Blanchard stopped." But the bonds forged by the boat remained strong and continue to the present day.

AMONG THE THINGS THAT James Gaff Hinkle found most satisfying when he prepared each year's Class Bulletin was passing on news of new Wianno Seniors to be built during the coming winter. In December 1965 he noted that "We are happy to hear that the Crosby Yacht Building & Storage Company will build two or three new Senior class yachts." Any new boat

*It's launching day, 1962, at Scituate Harbor for #16* Mistral. *Built in 1915,* Mistral *was owned by Dave Hall and Ed Craig from 1961 to 1975 and then flew the burgee of the Satuit Boat Club.*

is likely to profoundly affect the lives of its owners, often in ways that could never be imagined. Certainly Wianno Senior #135 soon fell into that category. The boat was bought in part as a gift from Fred Williams's father, Fred Sr., that celebrated Fred's graduation from Georgetown University in 1963 and his impending graduation from Boston College Law School.

The brief correspondence between Bill Crosby and Fred Williams, Sr., has about it a certain courtly, respectful tone that reflected the Crosbys' seemingly inborn sense of how to address their customers. "You can be assured we will build you a fine boat," Crosby wrote when he sent Williams the contract, "one having not only good racing capabilities, but also the safety and comfort of a family daysailer."

In January, after Fred Sr. visited the yard to view progress on #135, Crosby wrote that "Uncle Max

mentions your interest in a teak cockpit floor, such as we are now putting in one of the boats. These floors are narrow layed, edge-grain teak, being caulked and payed with a black compound…. Sometime in the not too far off future I should go over with your son just what he has in mind for racing equipment."

Soon enough, Fred was on the water in his new *Hoya*, named for Georgetown's sports teams. Soon enough, too, Fred was looking for reliable crew. In 1966, someone told Fred Williams that he might want to contact Lee Shannon about crewing aboard his Wianno Senior. "He didn't know I was a girl," Lee remembered of their first meeting. But Fred was impressed enough with Lee's handling of the tiller that he assigned himself foredeck duties, and they raced on courses usually devised by Ross Richards that started at the Hyannis coal pier and went to one or another government mark.

As always, the Senior proved an able matchmaker, and in 1966 Fred and Lee were married, one more of the many couples brought together by the boat.

*Here is a portion of the Scituate Wianno Senior fleet in 1974: (l–r)* Live Yankee *13a/13, then owned by Paul Twohig;* #80 Sunshine, *then owned by Dick Farrell;* #93 Shangri-La, *owned by Dr. Herb Blanchard.*

CHAPTER ELEVEN

# Winds of Change

*"My father and his brothers could see where the boating industry was heading. They decided to get out with what they could."*

— Ted Crosby

*Built in 1930 for an Edgartown yachtsman, #87* Alert *was owned by John and Tony Correa when this image was captured in 1957 or 1958. Here* Alert, *crewed by Tony, Dennis Reilly, and John Creed, leads #92* Varuna, *owned by "Chan" Hughes of the Stone Horse Yacht Club. The boats fly the single-luff spinnaker set on a 14' pole.*

There could be no doubt about it, the boats were getting old. What's more, they'd been getting old for a long time. In November 1966 one of the Seniors in the Bass River fleet, #87 *Alert*, then thirty-six years old, suffered a broken mast. *Alert* was owned by two brothers, John and Anthony "Tony" Correa, both devoted to their boat and the class. Bill Crosby noted what had happened in a cautionary letter to Jim Hinkle. "The Correa boat pulled a ½" turnbuckle apart, seems hard to believe! The threaded portion pulled directly out of the turnbuckle barrel. I suppose after years of salt, and perhaps un-lubricated adjusting, threads lose their depth with resultant sloppiness occurring. As there are many old boats still going, all should receive close inspection by yard and owner on a regular basis."

Bruce Hammatt had his #48's hull completely fiberglassed. Although Hammatt primarily daysailed the boat on Pleasant Bay, he was concerned whether fiberglassing might exclude his participation from official races. (He was permitted to compete at the 50th Anniversary Regatta's special celebratory, unofficial race "for boats not in racing trim." Hammatt won the race; see Chapter Nine.) Lou Loutrel had already had success with fiberglassing a Kings Cruiser in Ohio and wrote James Gaff Hinkle supporting the idea of fiberglassing a Wianno Senior. Jack Fallon expressed his support as well while noting, as had Bill Crosby, that the issue of the added weight needed to be well understood. Committee member Stan Moore recommended disqualification of any fiberglassed boats until the effect on weight and performance could be judged. (Loutrel eventually took his #36 *Mimi*, built in 1917, to Allan Vaitses in Mattapoisett and had Vaitses fiberglass the Senior using the methods he had pioneered. But by then, *Mimi*'s racing days had ended.)

In February 1967 Bill Crosby shared his experience of fiberglassing with James Gaff Hinkle, saying "a first-class job will probably add some 300 pounds to the hull and more if decks are included…. If weight alone is the main objection then I would think you could live with the few glassed hulls now sailing. I say this as I believe there are weight differences already in the fleet among the wood boats. Off hand, I would say *Victura* would be heavier than *Fantasy II*, especially by mid-season. As to the difference, I do not know, but it might be substantial if the old boat also had a dozen sister frames installed."

Nobody knew better than Bill Crosby and his brothers the condition of the older Wianno Seniors. "Many of the old boats are in need of rejuvenation, as their fastenings have deteriorated, wood may have decayed and worms more than likely have been busily engaged in filling their endless appetites," Crosby wrote Hinkle.

By the mid-'60s, the subject of fiberglassing leaky hulls was a frequent topic of conversation.

Discussion of the feasibility of fiberglassing the hull or bottom and whether such action was in keeping with the letter of the rules would continue for the next eighteen years. In fact, there was no really good way to resolve the matter until the one ultimately decided upon. For the Crosbys, however, the growing impact of fiberglass boats on the marine trade in general and their business in particular was a matter that needed to be dealt with.

"They didn't want anything to do with fiberglass," said Ted Crosby. "In 1972, my father [Horace Manley II known as "Bunk"] was sixty-five and he was the youngest of the boys. Max was seventy-nine. Uncle Bill [Wilton] was seventy-four. They decided it was time to get out. I was hunting in Vermont in the latter part of November that year when the old man called and said I better be there the next morning because they were signing papers."

Thus ended Crosby family ownership of Crosby Yacht Building & Storage Company, an extraordinary business whose history and culture had continued uninterrupted since the time of C. Worthington (1823–1898) and Horace S. Crosby (1826–1894). The new owner, Bill Wood, changed the company name to Crosby Yacht, Inc., and became a dealer for Uniflite, a Bellingham, Washington, pioneer of fiberglass boats built with fire-retardant resins. "The parking lot was full of fiberglass boats," Ted Crosby remembered.

ON OCTOBER 8, 1975, James Gaff Hinkle died at Green Bays in the same house in which he'd been born. The "Commodore on Horseback," known to all in the fleet as "Mr. Hinkle," was seventy-seven years old. "I would

*Brad Crosby plies his trade. Here, Brad is at work truing the sheer clamp.*

best describe my dad as a modest person but a strong individual," said Jim Hinkle, Jr. "I believe he started the Wianno Senior Class Committee, though he probably believed the best committee was a committee of one. It was always a labor of love for him. But his greatest love was being on the water on his own."

With the passing of James Gaff Hinkle, Jack Fallon became chairman of the Wianno Senior Class Committee. The committee members in 1975 included George Edmonds (WYC), Boardman "Boardy" Lloyd (BRYC), David Steere and William Kimball (SHYC), Stanley Moore (HYC), and Wilton Crosby, Jr. The

Spring Bulletin of 1977 revealed that the committee was still dealing with familiar issues. "The so-called Dyson Jib was again thoroughly reviewed and its dimensions again ratified as being within the specifications found in your enclosed Rules."

A new wrinkle was Fallon's advice to the fleet on ways to make themselves and their boats more competitive. He cautioned against a tight leech as being "extremely damaging to the performance of the boat, whether it be a light sail or heavy sail. It will show up with your inability to point competitively and on the helm." He also noted the importance of mast rake to achieving boat balance, and the condition of the bottom.

In 1976, the year that boats #170, #171, #172, and #173 were built, word also began to spread in Osterville that the new owner of Crosby Yacht was facing business problems. The early to mid-1970s had seen steep inflation, enormously high interest rates, and rising gasoline prices that, coupled with a shortage, resulted in long waiting lines at gas stations. Whatever the nature of the problems faced by the yard, the business was sold again. On June 13, 1977, a press release was issued. "Crosby Yacht, Inc. of Osterville, Massachusetts, recently announced that Richard B. Egan has acquired ownership and management of its facilities. Operations will be continued under the new name of Crosby Yacht Yard, Inc."

ALTHOUGH NO ONE foresaw it at the time, the launching of four new boats in 1976 would mark the last Wianno Seniors to be built for a decade, and the class entered what were essentially uncharted waters.

John Kiley, who had literally grown up with the boats — starting with Bob Gill aboard #117 before receiving #114 as a splendid birthday present from his grandparents at age fourteen in 1964 — remembered the period well.

"Starting from about 1976 and continuing until 1986, it was a time of uncertainty, although people might not have thought about it. There was the transition after the initial sale of the yard by Manley's sons, and there was the sense that new life had to be injected."

Not only was the absence of new boats a concern, but maintenance costs were climbing. Preparing and campaigning even a newer boat at the highest level represented a significant annual expense. George Largay remembered the routine. "Bottom preparation could be very expensive. But if one person really got into it, then you had to also. Then, you'd find you needed to keep up with innovations one year after the other. Then there were breakdowns. We broke one mast, two booms, and at least one gaff. You could go through them like matchsticks! And if you had a failure, you had to get it fixed in 24 hours to make the next race. The expenses defied the imagination."

Nobody was more aware of the challenge than the Class Committee. By the spring of 1982, the committee had examined a "development center board" built at Crosby's of plywood sheathed with fiberglass. Rudders and hatches of similar construction were discussed, but there was no vote to authorize any such components. Instead, the commitment was made to creating a fiberglass Wianno Senior.

"There was growing concern," remembered Carter "Bink" Bacon, then a young attorney and Wianno Senior owner who joined the committee in 1983 and became its hard-working secretary, "that construction of wooden boats was not going to be resumed. The newest boats were eight years old, and Crosby was quoting ever-higher prices to build a new one. David Steere, as the new chairman, thought we needed to 'do something' and he organized a meeting of owners at which he proposed the switch to fiberglass. He brought in Bill Harding, who had successfully managed to convert the Herreshoff 12½ one-design to the fiberglass version called the Doughdish, to explain the idea. People were sold."

In April 1983, in response to a query from Lew Gunn, Steere explained that "The fiberglass version will have to be constructed with the same specific gravity throughout the hull as the wooden boat. Shortly we will develop specifications for construction…and the first fiberglass Wianno will be launched in August or September of this year. I have given Crosby Yacht Yard an order for that first boat should it be built."

The time frame Steere referred to soon proved optimistic as a variety of financial, technical, and legal matters arose. On December 6, 1984, Boardy Lloyd wrote Jack Fallon to tell him the nonprofit Osterville Historical Society had approved the idea of sponsoring the fiberglass mold — the only stipulation was that the boat look exactly like the wooden Senior and have the same wooden spars and trim — and that both he and Bink Bacon had been working on the legal aspects.

The challenge of converting from traditional plank-on-frame construction to fiberglass was daunting. How could one guarantee that the fiberglass version would emerge with the same displacement and weight distribution, be structurally up to the rigors it would face, and offer the same sailing characteristics as the wooden boats? These were issues that David Steere addressed by bringing in naval architect Olin Stephens.

Then seventy-five years old, Stephens had behind him a fascinating career. It included ocean-racing wins aboard the famous *Dorade* and *Stormy Weather* (both of which he had designed) in the early '30s, the design of pre- and postwar *America*'s Cup

*Good friends and fierce competitors, John "Jack" Fallon (left) and David Steere pose for the camera, circa 1970. Both men were devoted to the class and served as chairmen. Steere grew up aboard wooden Wianno Seniors starting in 1929 and later became the guiding force behind the fiberglass version. He also served as commodore of the Stone Horse Yacht Club.*

yachts, and even the design during the war of the military's DUKW "Duck." Steere had been a Yale undergrad (class of '37) when he first met Stephens and asked the designer to create a new rowing shell. Later, Stephens designed the second of Steere's *Yankee Girl* ocean racers, an aluminum 51-footer built by Palmer-Johnson, which competed successfully on the international ocean-racing circuit. (The yacht made headlines when she placed second rather than first in the 1971 Admiral's Cup after passing a confusingly located buoy on the wrong side.)

Given the variations between the wooden boats, which had been built over a sixty-two-year period on several different molds, it was decided that no single Wianno Senior would suffice as the basis for the fiberglass version. Instead, five of the most recent yachts were hauled, weighed — they weighed within 100 pounds of each other — and measured at Crosby Yacht. The selected yachts were #161, #163, #164, #166, and #168, all built in 1974 and 1975.

The lines were taken using digital equipment by a representative of the United States Yacht Racing Union (USYRU). At Sparkman & Stephens (S&S), Alan Gilbert, a senior member of the design staff, led the Wianno Senior fiberglass project. Using the lines of the various boats, a single composite was created that best represented a "typical" Wianno Senior. In July 1985 Boardy Lloyd sent a memorandum to "Skippers, Crew and Friends of the Wianno Senior Class" and to his fellow members of the BRYC. In this document, Lloyd noted the Class Committee's concerns for the future of the class if the construction of new

boats was not resumed, and he described what was being done to address the matter.

"In order to make it economically possible to build a new Wianno at a competitive price, the Committee has proposed the idea of raising funds [$85,000–$100,000 was the estimated amount] which would be tax deductible, for the Osterville Historical Society, which would use those funds to engineer and construct a mold for the fiberglass hull…. The cost of maintenance will be sharply reduced, and the continuance of a vital racing class will preserve and should even increase the values of the wooden boats."

As always, the devil lay in the details. With David Steere leading the way, Bink Bacon now began drawing up the legal documents that outlined the roles of all involved in the project including Crosby Yacht, Sparkman & Stephens, the Osterville Historical Society, the proposed mold builder — North End Marine in Rockland, Maine — and the Class Committee itself. Once agreement had been reached, hull #118 was trucked to Rockland for reference purposes, and the process commenced in Rockland of converting the lines into fiberglass hull and deck molds. S&S, meanwhile, had tackled the engineering involved in creating a laminate schedule — the number and type of fiberglass layers used in various parts of the hull. When all these issues were resolved, a hull and deck were molded and shipped to Osterville where, in April 1986, assembly and finishing of Wianno Senior #176 began at Crosby Yacht.

In addition to formally announcing its decision

*Number 176* Lovely Lady *was the first fiberglass Wianno Senior to be completed at Crosby Yacht in 1986. Other than a maiden voyage to Martha's Vineyard, the boat has spent her life on Canandaigua Lake. "Some dry rot in our wooden #154 caused by a box fashioned to conceal a Porta Potti®, and yearly caulking and soaking up, encouraged the idea of buying the first fiberglass hull," said Christine Brown, whose father Bruce Brown purchased the boat. "We have belonged to the Canandaigua Yacht Club since 1964, and the boat is very competitive in our PHRF races."*

*Here is #168 Buckeye reaching for home past the Bass River Breakwater on Thanksgiving Day, 2000. Built in 1975 and among the last wooden Wianno Seniors, #168 earned a reputation as "the driest Senior in the fleet" according to Dr. Brooke Seckel, who purchased her in 1992. Brooke maintains the boat himself and reported that when launched for the 2013 season, she needed no pumping. Fondest memories include "winning the first race I ever entered, the 1993 Malcolm 'Max' Crosby Trophy race, family picnic sails, and easing the main on a reach so my children Tommy and Laura could take turns lying in the 'hammock' between the boom and the belly of the mainsail." On board: Dr. Brooke, Tommy and Laura Seckel, and Matt Fitzsimmons.*

to develop a fiberglass boat, the Wianno Senior Class Committee decided upon an organizational change in the spring of 1985. The change involved formation of a new class association. The association would, according to the committee, "be organized along the lines of a yacht club with two classes of membership, those who owned or represented Wianno Seniors, who would be voting members, and other friends of the class, who would be non-voting members but entitled to attend all meetings and receive all correspondence." The association would have a Board of Governors who also served on the Class Committee and would be responsible for the adoption of rules.

This organizational change was intended to open up the rules-making process and democratize it. Although the arms race would continue, the first step towards returning both the yacht's equipment and sails to the true one-design nature adopted by other classes was taken in 1986. The rules culminated roughly two years of intense collaboration by Bink Bacon, George Edmonds, Boardman Lloyd, and others. The detail was such that a preliminary draft submitted by Bacon in October 1984 was eleven single-spaced pages long.

In addition to spelling out such matters as how sails were to be measured, the permissible tapering of the board and rudder, the fiberglassing of keel, garboards, and decks, and other matters, the committee voted that sails for use in Scudder Cup races would be measured and stamped by the class association. Bit by bit, the new class governance took further steps to bring the Wianno Senior back to its original conception as a one-design yacht. Certain go-fast hardware was either ruled permissible or made illegal. While nobody would expect a boat of the Wianno Senior's type and size to ever be inexpensive to own and campaign — especially if the cost is judged over the span of a limited number of race weekends — everyone now had a better sense of what to plan for. The moves also represented a start towards eliminating the two-tier structure that HPYC Rear Commodore Singmaster had noted in his 1977 letter stressing that those who could afford multiple highly evolved sails enjoyed an advantage over those who could not. Yet, it was only a start. It would be a long time yet before the one-design goal was more fully realized.

AMONG THE FIRST THREE fiberglass Seniors launched was Lew Gunn's. Now, as the fleet prepared for the 1986 season, the question on everyone's mind was this: Had all the work resulted in what had been promised, a fiberglass Wianno Senior that would have no advantage or disadvantage by comparison to a wooden one?

# CHAPTER TWELVE

# A Big Cruise and the Big Question Answered

*"Yes, some were apprehensive, but we had to make a 'glass boat and see how it performs."*

— Don Law, The Register *(Barnstable), October 9, 1986*

Despite all the technical and administrative challenges faced by the class during the early 1970s to mid-1980s, the passed-along love for the Wianno Senior from one generation to the next continued unabated. The feelings instilled by having a Senior in the family tended to be a potent mixture of excitement, enthusiasm, and lingering nostalgia. This could make for a powerful brew of emotions that were not always easy to articulate and that might erupt when one least expected it. Sometimes, passed-down love of the Wianno Senior could result in quite extraordinary adventures.

"My mother started sailing early," said Bob Orr, whose mother's maiden name was Dorothy "Dot" Winship. "She belonged to the Hyannis Port Yacht Club, which was a short drive from where she spent much of her growing-up years on Long Beach Road in Centerville."

Dot's father was Walter Winship, the latest in that family to manage one of the oldest continuing businesses in Boston, W. W. Winship Luggage, which had been founded in 1776. Although Walter Winship spent summers at a family compound on Buzzards Bay in Wareham, his daughter grew up mostly in Centerville with her grandparents. (Her mother, Florence Bearse Winship, died five days after giving birth to Dorothy and her twin sister Florence, known as "Toss.")

When she was twenty-four years old in 1939, Dot became owner of #31, built in 1917 and a gift to her from, it is believed, her maternal grandfather Percy Bearse. Dot named the boat *Riptide*, and her Senior racing career commenced in 1939 in a HPYC fleet that then numbered some eleven boats including those owned by the Loutrels, Sinclairs, Wrights, Dalys, Bissells, Kennedys, Gardners, Hensons, Swensons, and Browns.

"We think," said Chas Orr, Dot's middle son, "that John Linehan was on the boat when my mother was racing. He skippered for a number of people and was an expert sailor."

Dot's last season with the boat was 1941 and it was later sold. Another Senior entered the family, however. Dot's father purchased #12 *Pegasus,* one of the original 1914 boats, which he moored at Onset and stored on his property in Wareham. During the war, Dot married Dr. Robert Orr and although her new husband was not a sailor, she never lost her interest in the sport.

"One summer when my older brother Bob was sixteen and I was around thirteen," said Chas Orr, "my mother convinced my grandfather, who was then in his mid-to-late seventies, to give us #12 in the hope of fixing it up and racing it. We joined the Wianno Yacht Club and set about rebuilding the boat."

The rebuild was accomplished with the aid of family friend and fellow WYC member Geoffrey Roberts in whose Beetle Cat Bob had learned to race. Roberts had what Chas remembered as "a phenomenal workshop at his mansion on Main Street in Osterville complete with a marine railway on the Centerville River. He walked us through the entire process. We stripped the decks and found rotten deckbeams. We refastened the entire boat with bronze screws."

The boat still had cotton sails, which made her uncompetitive. "When we started racing," Chas remembered, "we'd finish so far behind we were lucky if the committee boat was still there." Bob Orr remembered that "Jack Fallon came aboard and gave me some tips including 'Your sails aren't anything to write home about.' My father took me to Ted Hood who made a beautiful set of new sails, and we were competitive after that."

When Bob Orr went off to college in 1961, #12 sat idle and was later sold. "It was a sad day when we said good-bye to *Pegasus,*" Chas remembered. But the good-bye to #12 was not a good-bye to the Wianno Senior. Thirteen years after old *Pegasus* left the Orr

*Built in 1931, #92 passed through the hands of six owners before the Orrs purchased her. Here, circa 1972, she sails as* Varuna *under the ownership of Don Wright.*

family, twenty-eight-year-old Chas found himself living on a houseboat north of Sausalito but dreaming, of all things, about Wianno Seniors. Secretly, he began planning an incredible voyage that would take him from Cape Cod through the Panama Canal and finally to California. What could be better than a stiff-sailing Wianno Senior on San Francisco Bay? One day, Chas called his younger brother in Centerville. He asked Nelson Winship Orr — known to all as "Ship" — if he would like to go partners in a Wianno Senior. A week later, twenty-four-year-old Ship called to say he'd found just the boat.

"I loaded my truck and headed east for Cape Cod and our new sailboat," Chas wrote later.

Built in 1931, #92 was the newest Senior ever owned by an Orr or a Winship, but she was over forty years old and needed work. In September 1974 the brothers hauled their new boat and began reconditioning her. They stripped the hull, recaulked as necessary, and repainted her in a nontraditional but highly visible color scheme of International Orange

*Number #92 underwent extensive preparation by Ship and Chas Orr before they headed south. Here, Ship is at work wooding the hull in preparation for a new bright orange paint job.*

topsides, beige decks and boot top, and a dark red bottom. "We took a lot of flak over the orange paint, but the end product was stunning and drew praise from even the most skeptical," Chas Orr noted. What they didn't know was that, in very rough going, the garboard planks would leak in the vicinity of the centerboard trunk and require them to spend exhausting time at the bilge pump.

The brothers equipped the boat with berth cushions, sleeping bags, a Coleman lantern, a 5½-horsepower British Seagull, an Avon dinghy, and bright orange jumpsuit wet-weather gear contributed by their parents. Dot also had a burgee made for the revamped Senior. On it was a rat rowing a red dinghy, an image that reflected the boat's new name, *River Rat*. "We were in Nantucket on a cruise in the '50s," said Chas, "and there was a club there called the Wharf Rats with a burgee. My mother decided to make a burgee similar to that of the Wharf Rat flags. It symbolized all of us little kids who spent all our time on Long Beach out exploring in little rowboats. They used to call us River Rats."

Several days were spent stowing everything and adjusting the inside ballast so the bow was at its normal height, and finally, at 1500 hours on October 6, 1974, *River Rat* was towed out of the Centerville River to begin her voyage. "As soon as we headed out past the breakwater," Chas later wrote in his memoir of *River Rat*'s cruise, "it became apparent that this was going to be a wet trip."

By now, Chas had scaled back his ambition regarding how far the cruise would go. It was decided to make the destination Sanibel Island, three miles off Fort Myers, Florida, where Robert and Dot Orr had recently built a house. The brothers made it to Falmouth by 1830 hours on their first day. There, the Coleman lantern flickered out when they couldn't find the fuel can. When they woke up the next morning, it was blowing so hard they reefed the sail — a rare event — before heading to Lake Tashmoo. That trip resulted in having to retrieve the lost Avon and repair damage to the outboard bracket, which had to be rewelded. A northeast breeze the next day took *River Rat* all the way to Block Island.

The adventure of a lifetime for two young men was now well underway and it entailed all the challenges one might expect, and more. Much of the trip south was done in temperatures that often fell into the 30s. Sometimes, ice formed on *River Rat's* beige deck. Even south of Chincoteague, it was so cold that numb fingers could barely tie the reef pennants. Then, in 15' seas in Great Machipongo Bay, a wave ripped the jib fittings off the foredeck and the mainsail attachments out of their grommets. It was one of those times when you're too busy to be scared. Ashore, the kindness of a stranger enabled Ship and Chas to get a hot meal and shower at the Cape Charles Air Force Station. They made the needed repairs and pressed on.

The boat's shallow draft was always an advantage, yet several groundings occurred and getting afloat again with the help of powerboats occasionally resulted in quite difficult situations. The Seagull outboard — an antique even when brand new — smoked, died, overheated, even caught fire once, yet managed to push the boat ahead. Shots were heard close by in the Great Dismal Swamp, and while the brothers told themselves the shots were from an errant hunter, it later became likely that the "hunter" luckily had a bad aim. The boom broke twice. The second break forced *River Rat* to enter the inlet at St. Simons, Georgia, close-reaching under spinnaker, and battle her way against the peak of the ebb current to safety.

The brothers pressed on past the farthest point reached by Peter Stanford on his epic cruise south in the early '50s. In Florida, tardy bridge tenders created situations that could have dismasted the boat. South of Cape Canaveral, a Columbia 24 and a big yawl entered into impromptu races with the Senior and both fell behind. Approaching Fort Lauderdale, thoughtless power boaters created dangerous wakes and the outboard's prop hit a floating coconut, breaking the sheer spring. In December 1975 *River Rat* arrived at sandy Sanibel Island, where the local paper did a story about the Orr brothers and their unusual adventure.

Despite all they'd been through, #92 had brought them safely to their destination. In the process, Chas and Ship Orr made the longest-ever voyage by a Wianno Senior.

AFTER METHODICALLY BUT aggressively deepening both his understanding of boat dynamics and helmsmanship, Lew Gunn won his first Wianno Senior race at the SHYC in 1968. Five years later, he sold #134 *Invader* to fellow SHYC member and friend William Kimball, who was seeking to upgrade from his existing Senior. In 1975, Lew purchased his second new Wianno Senior, #169, which he also named

*Invader*. Now, Gunn began winning important, inter-club events. "We'd have won the Scudder Cup in 1977," he said, "but we reported ourselves to the race committee who hadn't seen the foul we committed when we hit another boat at the start of a race." In 1978, however, no such foul kept *Invader* from winning the Scudder Cup, a victory repeated in 1979 and 1980.

Gunn attributed much of his success to his ability to concentrate intensely for as long as necessary. Following Jack Fallon's lead, he kept records of how the boat was set up for each race, the weather conditions, and the results. He observed the emphasis that skippers, including Jack Fallon, Dave Steere, Boardy and Francis Lloyd, and George Edmonds, placed on building a consistent, skilled crew. Gunn's crew included very able SHYC sailors, among them Bill O'Connor, Randy Greene, Trey Hallowell, Kevin Gilbain, Mark Robinson, and Peter Sullivan.

"He wanted a good crew so he could just sail the boat," Robinson said. "You can't just walk on and race a Wianno Senior. You have to know how to set it up for 10 knots of wind or 17, how to adjust everything. We'd set up the peak outhaul so there were two or three fingers' space between the sail and the outhaul fitting, but we'd drop it down to tighten or loosen as needed. We used white tape on the halyards to mark where to ease the peak 5" or 6" depending on conditions and point of sail. Things like that. He didn't want to worry about setting the chute. That was the foredeck crew job. I was twenty-five years plus with him. We'd be out there doing our thing, and he'd be at the helm concentrating, and

he'd always be asking the same question: 'Are we going fast?'"

Peter Sullivan recalled, "Lew was diligent. We'd practice for hours on end. And he developed knowledge about each place we would be racing. We'd get there three hours early and go look at the outer markers to watch the current. Of course tide charts would be checked."

After his third straight Scudder Cup win in 1980, Gunn's cricket-bred sporting sense suggested to him it might not be the best thing for the class for him to keep winning its crowning event. "I didn't compete as I should have after that," he said, "and switched my focus to J/24's. I saw you could race those at Key West in the winter. I got totally immersed in the Js, and at one point I was ranked fiftieth in the world and I was very proud of that."

The three Scudder Cups and his fascination with the J/24 led Gunn to sell #169, something that seemed like a good idea at the time. At a cocktail party, he met WYC member George Largay who then co-owned with his brother Richard #126, a boat he called a "complete dog. It leaked like crazy, and the kind of maintenance needed to keep it in top race trim was fantastically expensive." Well aware of the success Gunn had enjoyed, Largay made an offer and acquired a boat he still refers to as "magnificent."

The unintended consequence of this sale was that the wives of both men were upset. Gunn's second wife Janet was unhappy that the boat she loved and regularly crewed aboard was sold without her being consulted. Largay's wife Sheila — sister of longtime racer John Kiley — was unhappy that her husband now owned *two* Seniors. These were neither the first nor last examples of marital disagreement caused by the sale of a Wianno Senior.

After several years' immersion in the J/24, however, the peculiar magic exerted by the Wianno Senior reasserted itself while Gunn was racing at Edgartown. He happened to witness the Wianno fleet entering the harbor with the late-afternoon sunlight glowing in their spinnakers. "Well," he said, "they were just so beautiful. I guess I just couldn't leave it alone." At the start of the Scudder Cup series in July 1986, Lew Gunn once again found himself at the tiller of a Wianno Senior, a *fiberglass* Wianno Senior #174 named, as always, *Invader*, and asking his crew his familiar and insistent question — "are we going fast?"

That year's Scudder Cup commenced with the measurement of some two hundred sails over a six-week period. Some, mostly spinnakers, had to be re-cut to comply with the measurement rules. As for the fiberglass boats, S&S had judged them identical in all respects — weight, shape, and righting moment — to the wooden models that had been measured. "The biggest difference," said Gunn, who was among the first in the fleet to get intimate with both versions, "was the sound as the boat moved through the water. But as far as performance, no difference. I detected a slight difference in 'touch,' the feel on the helm."

That July, a thirty-boat fleet assembled at Edgartown to kick off the Scudder Cup series. In his summary of the series the following month, Boardy Lloyd noted: "No. 174 (skippered by Lewis Gunn, a former winner of the Series)…performed on the same level as the wooden boats and, but for a disqualification in one race, would have been among the top finishers." Instead, the final results showed that a wooden boat had triumphed and that Gunn's latest *Invader*, after a disqualification, placed seventh. The following year, in 1987, Gunn placed third.

Such results from one of the fleet's strongest competitors confirmed the engineering concept for the fiberglass boat and the conviction of its champion David Steere that a skipper in the Wianno Senior fleet didn't win by having the fastest boat but through mastering the many and variable factors involved in yacht racing and knowing one's boat inside-out. Steere himself had the chance to witness the fiberglass-wood competition before he died on March 21, 1987. In its epitaph, the Board of Governors noted: "David was unquestionably the principal cheerleader, benefactor and organizer of the effort to produce the exquisite reproduction of the wooden Wianno Senior. Together with his brother Bruce, he provided over a quarter of the financing necessary to engineer the new boat and build the tooling for its production…."

The following year, Lew Gunn's fiberglass Senior finished eighth, two places behind George Largay who was still sailing #169, the boat he'd bought from Lew. Not until 1998 would a fiberglass yacht — #177 *Rapparee* sailed by Peter O'Keeffe with his brother Tim as mainsheet trimmer, Hank Cassidy flying the chute and alternating on the jib with John Dale who also watched the wind and other boats — win the Scudder Cup.

In 1998, Lew Gunn finished second in #161, a boat he and co-owner Bill O'Connor had bought

from Bruce Steere. Gunn was glad to be back at the helm of a wooden Senior and found that he felt more comfortable than he did with the fiberglass model. In one of the more novel efforts to potentially confuse competitors, this latest *Invader* was painted blue on one side and white on the other. "Bill and I joked the starboard blue half was mine while the port-side white half was his," Gunn said. "I'm not sure the senior members of the fleet appreciated our sense of humor."

Peter O'Keeffe remembered competing against the blue and white boat. "Sometimes," he recalled, "you'd look up expecting to see the same boats you had just seen but suddenly there'd be a different color boat and you'd wonder — where the heck did that come from!"

BY THE MID-1970S, the Osterville that the pioneers had known was still there, only different. The Dowse house was long gone, of course, but many of the big old homes built in Henry Day's time on Sea View and on Wianno Avenue remained. Carolyn Rowland's girlhood home remained and so did the du Ponts' house on its magnificent venue in Oyster Harbors. 'Tween Waters, the gracious house sold so many years earlier by founding father Franklin Robinson to William Parker Halliday — who had named it — still stood on Eel River Road with West Bay in front and Aunt Tempy's Pond behind. Halliday had sold the big, shingle home to John Hornor, and after the ex-commodore's death at age ninety-four in 1970, the house was owned by his younger son Townsend. Known to all as "Townie," Townsend Hornor's devotion to the class and to Osterville continued the

pattern set by his father, and 'Tween Waters was the essential base for his many and varied activities.

In short, the village still possessed all its inherent charm. It was, and remains, unusual by any measure. "A friend's mother said there were really only two places to live in the summer," Don Law remembered of the time he and his wife Sara Molyneaux began their search for a summer home, "Padanaram and Osterville. We thought Padanaram was nice, but then I met an Osterville realtor around 1975. We rented there [before moving to Cotuit] and then we wanted to sail and explore."

Law's business as a Boston concert promoter brought him into contact with a great many people, one of whom was Ted Kennedy, and the two men became involved in producing a benefit show. That led to an invitation for Don and Sara to go sailing aboard a Wianno Senior, a boat he'd first seen during his growing up years in Westport, Connecticut, where a Senior was moored in the harbor.

"I had crewed aboard Atlantics [the Starling Burgess 30'7" one-design that debuted in 1928] and others, but I didn't really care about racing," Law said. "At the time, a great attraction of the Senior was the shallow draft. I realized you could go all the way up Nantucket Harbor. We were really just interested in sailing and exploring. Ultimately, I thought the Senior was a pretty boat and that I should buy one. Bill Crosby mentioned that Bill Danforth's boat was available."

Built in 1962, Danforth's Wianno Senior #125 was named *Fleetwind II* but when Law bought the yacht in 1977, he changed the name briefly to *Kakini* then later to *Cochenoe*. The name worked on two

*"One of the windiest ever," is how George Largay remembered the 1996 Edgartown Yacht Club Regatta. Here, George helms #169, the boat he bought from Lew Gunn. Just forward of Largay is George Grimes. To port are George's brother Richard and Peter Brauer.*

levels. "When I was a kid in Connecticut," Don said, "we kids used to go to Cochenoe Island, and it had always had a certain magic. It was also the name of John Eliot's first Indian language translator, and I liked the idea that Cochenoe, the man, served as a bridge between cultures much the way sailing craft have over the ages." (In 1631, John Eliot emigrated to the Massachusetts Bay Colony and became involved in proselytizing among the native tribes and translating and printing the New Testament in Algonquin.)

"The Wianno Senior was," Sara quipped, "a big step up from his Sunfish." Now, Don and Sara began sailing their new boat to Nantucket and Martha's Vineyard. "I had 3" foam mattresses made for the cabin seats and we'd take sheets, pillows, lamp and Coleman stove, and camp out," Sara said. "We'd tell ourselves it was luxurious if a bit cramped." For a young couple the arrangement worked. "I had a little motor to put on the transom if we were really in need," said Don. "We had a Navy-surplus inflatable. The boat has a wonderful, large cockpit. We fished and swam and sailed. We were close to the sea. We learned the boat."

*Cochenoe*'s explorations of local waters taught a great many lessons. For one thing, Don learned about the currents in challenging Nantucket Sound, knowledge that would serve him well in the years ahead. Getting the best out of the Wianno Senior, however, was a challenge. "It's not an easy boat to learn to sail," he recalled of his early years. "It's a heavy, gaff-rigged boat and it was a learning experience, but it would teach you all sorts of lessons."

One of those lessons was to hang on. "Once,

when I was coming across the Sound from Succonesset, I was sailing poorly, sitting on the rail, and a sea came past and I got kicked right out into the water."

Law's racing career began a few years after he'd bought his boat when he attended a lunch at Boston's once famous but now defunct Locke-Ober restaurant hosted by the ever-gracious George Edmonds. "There was great fear about the fleet disappearing in the face of the J/24 fleet on Nantucket Sound," he remembered. "In the end, the J/24 fleet never took hold, but nobody could foresee that. The word 'death knell' was heard."

Law and Sara began competing in the early '80s. "I started and was not very competitive. I didn't have good boat speed."

*Cochenoe*'s general setup had been fine for cruising, but the boat needed upgrading before it could begin racing seriously in the intensely competitive fleet. Deke Ulian, owner of one of the class's original 1914 boats, #7 *Tirza*, offered assistance. "We set up the boat's rig and tuned it. We installed new hardware, jib leads, sail tracks, cam cleats — the works. Presto, we finished middle of the fleet. Sara took to the foredeck like a duck to water. Don was a quick learner, great questioner, and talented helmsman."

Now, Law went to work learning more about tactics and assembling a crew that would help make *Cochenoe* a boat to be reckoned with. "I had Kevin Cain and Oggie Pesek," Law said, "two guys with a good bit of experience who helped my learning curve. Oggie was really great in the 'engineroom.' He knew

*Here is* Rapparee, *at the 2003 Wianno Yacht Club Regatta. Tim O'Keeffe remembered: "*Rapparee *finished second in the race, which secured the Ross W. Richards Memorial Trophy. It was a picture-perfect day with bright sun, a southwesterly breeze, and relatively smooth water in the lee of the Popponesset shore. My brother Pete — owner and skipper — is on the far right at the helm with a red hat. I am in the red jacket — tactician and foredeck. Hank Cassidy — jib and spinnaker trimmer — has on a blue jacket. John Dale — mainsail trimmer — wears yellow."*

what would make a Senior go, took a scientific approach. Kevin was great tactically, and my wife did the foredeck and was great at it. When we first started dating, I promised Sara to begin horseback riding and she promised to learn to sail. She more than fulfilled her end, and I never could stand getting on a horse."

Sara said she still thinks of Don, Oggie, and Kevin as the "fab three." Andrew "Oggie" Pesek's grandparents had built a summer house in Wianno and he had learned to sail at the WYC. He got his first Senior experience aboard #124 *Fayerweather* as mainsheet trimmer when it was owned by Penn Edmonds. Taking an accidental elbow in the eye from the skipper didn't daunt his enthusiasm. At age ten in 1972, Kevin Cain began learning the Senior aboard #7 *Tirza*. Then, from age twelve to fourteen — in 1974 and 1975 — Kevin crewed aboard Jack Fallon's *Marna* and he raced with Pam Fallon for a summer after that.

Among those rotating as crew aboard #125 was the always-in-demand John Kiley, who combined an understanding of boat design with his own extensive Wianno Senior experience and a significant Wianno Senior gene pool inherited from his parents and grandparents. "I am one of the fortunate to have crewed with them," Kiley said. So was John McDonough whose father Alan owned at that time #158 *Molly*. John had begun crewing aboard Ulian's #7 *Tirza* when he was seven or eight years old.

"John," said Deke Ulian, "became a master at doping out wind shifts, best in the fleet at that, I think, with a natural sixth sense. One day, I think this may have been 1993, I gave the *Cochenoe* crew a ride out to their boat in my Whaler in Wychmere Harbor prior to the final Scudder Cup race. They were trailing the lead boats going into the last race. I was egging them on. I said, 'The wind is going to scramble and you guys are going to win it.' Just after the start came a 180-degree wind shift from nearly a flat calm. They won the race and the cup."

As he transitioned from laid-back knockabout cruiser to racer — painting *Cochenoe*'s bottom with Pettit Super Slick and wet-sanding to produce a slippery finish — Law remained his engaging and personable self. "Everybody," said Oggie, "adored him. And he made the best sandwiches! The core crew was consistent and he was tenacious. He kept the boat in top shape with the best sails. He would buy a sail, try it for ten minutes, and say, 'No, don't like 'em.' Even then, the sails were a small percentage of what he did to get good. He kept a meticulous log of settings. It was surgical."

When he discovered that his boat's mast had "taken a set" so that the sail could not be shaped identically on both tacks, Law replaced it with another. Law's log indicated to him that, among other things, 75 percent of Scudder Cup races were sailed in winds of 10 knots or less, something that might have surprised some in the fleet. He knew exactly how *Cochenoe* should be set up for those conditions as well as heavier air. Of course, light air was no cause to become less cautious. Once, in light air at Edgartown, Law looked up to find his wife had disappeared from the bow. A moment later, Sara was pulling herself aboard asking, "Did anyone even see me?" After each season, Law reviewed his log entries, studying weather

*Rough ride at Edgartown:* Cochenoe *battles steep seas in 30 knots of wind. "This was a day when I put all my faith in Don, Kevin, and Oggie to not take undue chances and see us through," remembered Sara Molyneaux of the 1996 event. "I could not see anything during this race because seawater streamed in and out of my eyes so fast. I'll never forget heading for a large orange inflatable mark that never seemed to get close enough to round. We finally realized it was adrift!" The race was ultimately canceled.*

trends, boat setup, the effect of tides.

What all this meant from a practical standpoint was that once Don Law got serious about racing, he and his crew won the Scudder Cup in 1984. They won it again in 1985. They won it again in 1986, the seminal year when the fiberglass boat entered the fleet in the guise of Gunn's latest *Invader. Cochenoe* won it again in 1987.

"Even the best could have an off-summer," said Oggie Pesek. "But Don was always there."

Modest and not prone to talk much about how he so often managed to be "there," Law attributed much of his success not only to his crew but to what he had learned during his years of spartan cruising with his wife. "You have to develop a feel," he said. "That was an advantage of cruising in Nantucket Sound. It taught you to get the most out of the boat. Time in the boat teaches when you are fast and when you are not."

Law's time in the boat would see his success continue for another decade. After winning the 2008 Scudder Cup, he more or less "retired" as a serious competitor in the Wianno Senior fleet.

AMONG THOSE WHO quickly recognized Don Law as one of the fleet's toughest competitors was a boat-shop owner from Harwich named Karl Anderson. As a youngster, Anderson had begun sailing at the East Dennis Yacht Club, and he eventually became a winning skipper in all manner of classes including the Widgeon, Turnabout, Cape Cod Knockabout, Rhodes 18, and J/24. After opening Karl's Boat Shop in the spring of 1983 — "Call Karl Today…Sail Faster

Tomorrow" — it didn't take Anderson long to recognize the potential of the Wianno Senior.

"It was the best competition on Cape Cod at the time, and it still is," he said. What's more, the local Senior owners represented, among other things, a potentially good source of maintenance business. Anderson started crewing on Labor Day weekend in 1985 aboard Jimmy Bartlett's #156 *Never Miss*. Bartlett had long experience racing big boats, and over two decades in the Senior. "The unique thing about Wiannos," Bartlett said, "is that for this little corner of the world, it's the best-designed, four-person boat. It just works for the local conditions."

But that Labor Day weekend found Bartlett without his usual crew of youngsters, who had headed back to school. He convinced a big-boat friend named Dave Magowan to come over from Cotuit and called Wianno Senior sailor Rick Bishop as well. Bishop said he could come and that he could probably "grab" Karl Anderson. "I had casually known Karl for awhile," Bartlett said, "and certainly knew *of* him. As the crews gathered at the Bass River Yacht Club, I was very coy about answering the questions as to who was crewing for me. Rick, Karl, and Dave were actually hiding behind the bushes and jumped out at close to the last minute to shove off to #156.

"The highlight of the day was on the second beat of three when passing #143 [the Lloyds' yellow *Pertelote*, a multi-time Scudder Cup winner], Rick looked at Karl — who was on his very first Senior ride — and said: 'You don't know how good it is to see that yellow boat go out the back.' We won that race and Karl, of course, was to see many

After many winning
seasons, skipper
Don Law began
crewing aboard his
#125 Cochenoe, *letting
his own devoted crew
and, sometimes, a
friend, take the tiller.
Here,* Cochenoe *awaits
the results of a Bass
River race in 2006. (l–r)
Sara Molyneaux, John
McDonough, Don Law,
and John Kiley at
the helm.*

For the 2003 season, #125 sailed under the command of Oggie Pesek. Here, Cochenoe sprints upwind with Bill and Ellie Lawrence's #135 Kobold *in Satur-day's Scudder Cup race at Osterville. The following day's race had to be canceled because of high winds. That year, #125 placed seventh in Scudder Cup standings and was lost in the December fire at Crosby's.* Kobold, *built in 1965, was retired after the 2004 season.*

154

boats 'go out the back.'"

After three years' experience with *Never Miss*, Anderson put together a team that included Henry Dane, Rick Bishop, Ian McNiece, and Chris Cooney to purchase #142, then named *Eight Ball*, from Bob Churchill of the BRYC. "We all chipped in to raise the $8,000 for the boat," Anderson said, "but since it was my idea, I was skipper, although later we rotated."

Now, Anderson began applying his extensive experience in other classes to the Wianno Senior, a task that he found was not entirely straightforward. "What we learned from other boats was to prepare well and think through all aspects of the boat. From the beginning, we tried to sail the boat with less helm. Initially we moved the jib tracks in. Then later on, we had a fuller jib that improved balance. I worked on developing sails with Bruce Dyson and Tom Olsen, as was permissible at the time."

It was a steep learning curve that saw Anderson and his crew having to develop quickly in races dominated often by Don Law, John Fallon, Peter O'Keeffe, Burt McManus, and Alden Edmonds. In his first season, 1989, Anderson and company finished second to *Cochenoe* for the Scudder Cup. But in 1990, they won what would be the first of three Scudder Cups. The success didn't stop Anderson from willingly helping others.

Like most who entered the class, Anderson soon learned it had its own unique spirit and way of bringing people together. "He will help anybody," said Oggie Pesek. "He'd hop on our boat and tune it up a half-hour before a Scudder Cup race." As had happened with other sailors since the early days at

the Wianno Yacht Club, Anderson met his wife Mei-An at the get-together following a Wianno Senior race, in this case a Scudder Cup event at Hyannis.

The #142 "syndicate" continued to race the boat hard, finally retiring *Eight Ball* in 2000 when it became unseaworthy. Anderson later transferred #142's rig to his newly built #188 — *Pieces of 8* — and the fiberglass hull allowed him to take his boat tuning up another notch. "It was just amazing," said Joe Lotuff, who is as passionate and attentive to every detail of setting up a Senior, "to see Karl in #188, to see that boat go."

As for #142, it seemed the old yacht was destined to end her days undercover in a barn. But then, thirty-five years after the Wianno Senior that originally had been named *Cheerful* was launched, something happened that would entirely alter her fate.

# CHAPTER THIRTEEN

# A New Beginning

*"The Wianno Senior is a
gigantic part of our lives.
It is why we are
who we are."*

— *Anthony "Tony" Correa, former owner of #87* Alert

Conditions for the 1987 Edgartown Yacht Club Regatta were familiar—windy. Here #120 Marna beats her way into it. Marna placed third in Friday's race (won by Lew Gunn in #174) and fourth on Saturday (won by Ted Kennedy in #194 Victura). (r–l) John Fallon, Jr., Edward Rowland, Steve Ulian, Scott deGrasse.

Nineteen-eighty-nine proved to be a banner year for the Wianno Senior Class. It had now been seventy-five years since the founding fathers at the WYC had agreed to purchase a Class P knockabout, and a fine celebration was planned. That April, recognizing the need to encourage preservation of older boats, the Class Committee voted to "approve on a case by case basis, upon written request, the use of alternative construction methods and materials, such as the West System and fiberglassing the hull…."

| Special 75th Anniversary Awards | | | |
|---|---|---|---|
| **Award** | **Boat #/Name** | **Boat Owner** | **Remarks** |
| Oldest Boat | 7/*Tirza* | Richard Ulian | Only original 1914 boat to participate |
| Traveled the Longest Distance | 51/*Corsair* | Henry Young | Trucked from Lake Minnetonka, Minnesota |
| Best Amateur Restoration<br>   Honorable Mention | 80/*Ardent*<br>121/*Argo* | Philip Holbrook<br>Dr. Dana Weeder | |
| Best Costumes<br>   Honorable Mention | 127/*Rapparee*<br>143/*Pertelote* | Peter O'Keeffe and crew<br>Lloyd family | |
| Senior Skipper | 36/*Mimi* | Dorothy Sinclair Loutrel and<br>Louis F. Loutrel | Recognized Loutrels' more than fifty years of continuous participation |
| Historical Preservation Award | 137/*Fantasy II* | Joseph D. Hinkle | For his leading role in preserving class history through an historical exhibit and as editor of the 75th-Anniversary Book |

To commemorate the anniversary, a great many yachts were spruced up to compete in that year's Scudder Cup, and one race saw forty-one Wianno Seniors at the starting line. The weekend of July 29 drew fifty-eight of the boats to a celebratory regatta, and at a dinner that evening special awards were presented that signified the appreciation of the fleet for the very special place their boats held in people's lives and for the efforts of those who had come before.

The big turnout for the 1989 season once again raised the long-standing issue of how the class should handle the matter of sails. The following August, a two-question questionnaire was mailed to Wianno Senior owners. It asked: (1) Would you like to see any changes in the rule governing jibsheets and related hardware? (2) Would you like to see any changes in the rules governing Wianno Senior sails? The responses to these two questions were various and, in some instances, lengthy and heated, but the general tenor was "No" to Question 1 and "Yes" to Question 2.

On December 20, 1990, the Wianno Senior Class Committee issued its decision in a letter addressed to Scudder Cup participants. In essence, this letter finally summed up years of discussion and argument on all sides of the issue. It noted the inherent complexities in attempting to define what was and what was not permissible regarding something as inherently complex as a sail, an object made of fabrics subject to manufacturing variables that could be built in seemingly endless ways.

"After listening to almost every skipper in the fleet," the Class Committee's letter explained, "meeting with a half-dozen experienced sail-makers and

| Portrait of the Fleet<br>1989: 75th Anniversary Race Results | | |
|---|---|---|
| **Event/Date** | **Winner(s)/Boat Name** | **Presenter** |
| Max Crosby Race/June 17 | Donald F. Law, Jr./*Cochenoe* | George Cronin, Commodore, WYC |
| Edward Crossett Trophy (Wianno-Edgartown)/July 20 | Oggie Pesek/*Cochenoe*<br>Joseph D. Hinkle/*Fantasy II* | Joseph D. Hinkle, WYC |
| Edgartown YC Regatta/July 21 | Thomas H. O'Toole/*Scarlet*<br>Donald F. Law, Jr./*Cochenoe*<br>Lloyd B. McManus/*Chanzia* | |
| Edgartown YC Regatta/July 22 | Donald F. Law, Jr./*Cochenoe*<br>John Pratt/*Turmoil Too*<br>Karl Anderson/*Eight Ball* | |
| Ocean Race Trophy/July 29 | Donald F. Law, Jr./*Cochenoe*<br>John Pratt/*Turmoil Too*<br>Karl Anderson/*Eight Ball* | George Cronin, Commodore, WYC |
| Cruising Canvas Race/July 29 | Donald F. Law, Jr./*Cochenoe*<br>Thomas H. O'Toole/*Scarlet*<br>Lewis J. H. Gunn/*Sea Lyon* | George Cronin, Commodore, WYC |
| W. R. Sinclair Bowl/July 30 | Bruce Hammatt/*Avocet*<br>Louis F. Loutrel, Jr./*Mimi*<br>Wilton B. Crosby/*Shenanigans* | Peter O'Keeffe, Commodore, HPYC |
| Cruising Canvas Race | John T. Fallon, Jr./*Marna*<br>Karl Anderson/*Eight Ball*<br>George Largay/*Eowyn* | George Cronin, Commodore, WYC |
| Stone Horse YC Bowl/Aug. 5 | Bruce Hammatt/*Avocet*<br>Katherine Kittredge/*Hazel Coe*<br>James Light/*Intuition* | Lewis J. H. Gunn, SHYC |
| Bass River Challenge Cup/Aug. 6 | John T. Fallon, Jr./*Marna*<br>John Pratt/*Turmoil Too*<br>Lloyd B. McManus, Jr./*Chanzia* | James Bartlett, BRYC |
| **Scudder Cup**<br>F. Manley Crosby Trophy (2nd overall)<br>Ross Richards Memorial Trophy(3rd overall)<br>4th overall<br>5th overall | Donald F. Law, Jr./*Cochenoe*<br>Karl Anderson/*Eight Ball*<br>John T. Fallon, Jr./*Marna*<br>Thomas H. O'Toole, *Scarlet*<br>John Pratt/*Turmoil Too* | |

cloth manufacturers and drafting one proposed rule after another, the Committee is satisfied that the best course for the Wianno Senior is to adopt uniform sail rules."

The letter stressed that eliminating experimentation in design and selection had downsides but that permitting the continued practice also could be "demoralizing to those who do not have the time or money to keep up with the race to find a better sail." The essence of the message was that "Beginning with 1991, the Class will order sails to be built in quantity by the same sail maker and owners will randomly select their new sails. The details of the new rules will be based upon the experience of the Marblehead, Massachusetts, International One Design fleet, which has lived successfully with a similar rule for the past twenty-five years."

In 1991, the stricter controls enacted specified that Norm Cressy or Doyle Sailmakers of Marblehead were authorized to supply spinnakers to approved dimensions. Limits on sail purchases were enacted of one new mainsail, one new jib, and two new spinnakers. In 1994, it was required that all the mainsails be built by Thomas Olsen. By 1996, all jibs came from Doyle. Looking back on the "sail wars" era in a 2013 interview, sailmaker Bruce Dyson who had developed his highly effective jibs in concert with Jack Fallon and Karl Anderson, reflected that the class "went from a development sail plan to a strict one-design. What was good for me as a sailmaker was not good for the class."

For most, if not all, the sail decision was too long in coming. In June 1991 long-time class member

Rodger Nordblom wrote Bink Bacon immediately after learning of the one-design sail rule. "I believe this has been long overdue and should make the whole fleet more competitive in time," he said.

A significant rift within the social fabric of the class had been opened during the ongoing sail controversy that would be remembered by some for years to come. But Bink Bacon doubtless spoke for the majority when he looked back on the whole affair. "In my opinion," he said, "uniform sails were the 'gold standard' for the true believers in the one-design concept."

In fact, the effort to both keep and improve the Wianno Senior's one-design nature in terms of everything from backstay specifications, weight, deck hardware, and sails would continue in the years ahead. To deal with these matters, at the October 2003 Wianno Senior Class Committee meeting it was decided that an Advisory Panel be established to "review the current one-design rules, consider the sail handling, equipment and techniques currently in use on existing boats and provide the Class Committee with recommendations for changes to the One Design Rules." The Advisory Panel included Don Law, Karl Anderson, Joe Lotuff, John Fallon, and Oggie Pesek working under Boardman Lloyd, chairman of the Subcommittee on Rules and Measurements. As it set to work, the Advisory Panel did so with the direction that it was "to bear in mind that the Wianno Senior is a 'vintage class' and there is a strong desire to maintain the boat's traditional look and feel."

Ultimately, it was the one-sail rule and the fiberglass boat that were the groundwork for the fleet

It's Edgartown, 1973, and photographer Norman Fortier has caught Richard "Deke" Ulian's old #7 Tirza on a run with the Shields Class in the distance. Recalling that event, Deke remembered: "The sails look like the same set of Hard sails I bought in a misapplied attempt to beat the Hood sails most of the winners were using. The main had a tight leech that dragged us back for ten years."

as it looked to the future. Years later, reflecting on the eventual effect of the sail rule change, George Largay summed it up like this. "With the one-sail rule and fiberglass, the boats are much more equal and the sportsmanship is at a high level. The spirit of the class, the camaraderie is much higher today than it was in the past. The competition is very tough but the overtly hostile nature that could develop in past years is gone."

Ironically enough, in 1991, the first year the one-sail rule was implemented, the Scudder Cup was won by Jack Fallon's son, John Jr. John, like his sister Pam, had grown up with the boats and he had started crewing aboard *Marna* at around age thirteen in 1975, just before his father's last Scudder Cup

Sometimes, race preparation means scampering up the mast to deal with rigging issues. Here, during the Hyannis Port Yacht Club Scudder Cup event in 2011, Ryan Lentell tends to the rigging of #190 Golden Summer. *Pat Lentell is in the cockpit.*

*The boat of the president: John F. Kennedy's #94* Victura *is displayed seasonally at the John F. Kennedy Presidential Library and Museum. For years, the boat has been carefully maintained and painted by Malcolm Crosby.*

triumph in 1976. During the ensuing years, as John gained more experience, the chances for conflict aboard #120, never far in the background anyway, grew. "He didn't care for my comments," John recalled, "and I don't really blame him. But he was slowing down and had some vision problems that had developed in the aftermath of his accident."

The accident, perhaps the most serious to befall a Wianno Senior sailor, had occurred several years earlier when Jack Fallon was struck on the head by another boat's boom as it jibed. Pam Fallon saw her father knocked overboard and it was fortunate that Don McNamara was crewing that day, for he was able to get the semiconscious skipper back into the cockpit and wrap him in the spinnaker. "We sailed right ashore and they had an ambulance waiting," Pam remembered. Eventually, eye surgery was needed.

After his father's retirement from active racing of *Marna*, John took over. "When the concept of one-design sails came," he said, "I was always in support of it."

THE NIGHT OF DECEMBER 10, 2003, came with mild temperatures and a light easterly breeze. There was nothing to suggest anything unusual would occur in Osterville, and people were going about their pre-holidays business as usual. But then, at 9:30, something happened of such import that everyone within the Wianno Senior fleet at the time remembers where they were when they heard the news.

"I was playing paddle tennis at the Wianno Club on Sea View Avenue with John Kiley," John Fallon recalled. "As soon as I got home I got a call from John saying the boatyard was on fire."

Toni Fallon's #199
Heritage *was ordered
even as the devastating
boatyard fire destroyed
the Fallon family's #120.
Here #199 surges
downwind past the
Southwest Rock off
Hyannis Port.*

*Here is* Owl *ghosting along at a foggy Eggemoggin Reach Regatta, circa 1996. Aboard are skipper Dick Taylor, crewman John Roberts, and Robin Lincoln, taking a break from her own Senior,* Saltworks. *Taylor used* Owl *primarily for cruising. Among his adventures was a 1990 forty-nine-day, 1,200-mile voyage to Maine and Nova Scotia. "In any port I visited," he remembered after his boat was destroyed in the 2003 Crosby boatyard fire, "Owl was always the center of attention."*

The boatyard was Crosby Yacht. Bill Crosby's son Britton, himself a firefighter, saw the flames from his house close by on Crosby Circle. He grabbed his camera, and began shooting photographs of what was quickly growing into a five-alarm fire. As boat sheds succumbed entirely to flames, ever more fire apparatus arrived and the battle soon involved some two-dozen trucks and rescue vehicles, the Hyannis fire boat, and over a hundred firefighters. John Fallon hurried over to the Oyster Harbors Marine fuel dock and saw that what was known as "the big shed" housing many Wianno Seniors was among those engulfed in orange-yellow fire. Flames billowed high into the night sky.

The Fallons' *Marna* was among the boats being reduced to ashes before the eyes of shocked onlookers. "I was standing with the Egans [Crosby Yacht proprietor Dick Egan and his son Greg] watching the fire," John Fallon said. "I turned to Dick and said, 'This is a terrible tragedy, but will you put us in for a new Senior? Put it in for my mom." He began calling other members in the fleet.

"I was home in Cambridge," Oggie Pesek remembered, "when John Fallon called me from the dock at Oyster Harbors Marine. He said: 'They're all gone.' Which made no sense to me at first."

Once he understood, and after immediately conferring with his in-laws, George and Sally Edmonds, owners of #136 *Cirrus*, Pesek placed a call

*This image of #142* Cheerful *was made in 1969 during the boat's second season. At the helm is John Fulham III. John Cooper-Mullin is handling the spinnaker sheet.*

*"Ralph Lincoln has very generously allowed us to campaign Odin," said Ben Blum, seen here at the tiller. "Over a dozen Bass River sailors under age thirty and several juniors have had the opportunity to race and enjoy this very unique class thanks to Ralph." Here, Ben sails with his brothers Chris and A. J. (red jacket) and F. J. Perfas to leeward. The young men all assisted in the restoration of #162, a wooden Senior originally owned by Rod Nordblom.*

to Shaw Yacht in Rockland, Maine. A decade earlier, Pesek and Don Law had arranged the transfer of the Wianno Senior molds from the original supplier to Shaw, and then arranged for the needed mold repairs. Now, even as the fire was consuming *Cirrus*, Pesek left a message on Shaw Yacht's answering machine. "We need a new boat. Consider this a firm order. Deposit to follow."

The next morning, Pesek drove straight to Osterville to see the damage for himself. Could it be as bad as John Fallon had said? Maybe the ballast shoe could be used on the Edmonds family's new Wianno Senior? It would have been hard then for anyone who hadn't actually witnessed the blaze to grasp the true extent of the damage. Bits of charred shingles, carried on the wind, were found in Cotuit. Only the skill of the firefighters abetted by reasonably calm weather, the favorable wind direction, and slush-covered ground had permitted the saving of

nearby homes. When he got to the boatyard, Pesek learned the truth. Some 40,000 square feet of boat storage sheds had been destroyed.

Oggie Pesek picked his way through the debris until he came to where *Cirrus* had been carefully stored for the winter. "In the case of #136," he said, "I could see that the cast iron ballast had cracked at the hard corners inside the centerboard slot, so it was junk, too. What a depressing sight."

When it was all over, during the following days, a passer-by might have seen a sturdy-looking figure in leather boots walking slowly through what had once been the "big shed." Every now and then, the figure could be seen to bend over and lift something from out of the acrid-smelling black ash and the charred bits of oak and mahogany. Slowly, carefully, Malcolm Crosby gathered up what was left of the boats so many had loved, their bronze hardware, or what remained of it. Malcolm put what he could find of each boat's fittings into a white paper paint bucket. Although there was nothing to indicate which boat was which, Malcolm remembered them all. "I knew where each one had been," he said. He wrote the boat's number on each bucket and, later, he presented each one to its skipper.

"That," said George Largay, "was the loveliest, the most sensitive thing. I keep the bucket on a shelf at home. "It's all I'll ever have of that boat."

ONLY ONE OF THE twenty-one Seniors had been covered by insurance. Of the Kennedy family's boats, two were lost. They were Ethel Kennedy's #132, and Eunice Shriver's #139. The late President's Wianno

jointly owned by Rick Burnes and Brownie Swartwood; and Toby Hynes's newly finished #192. Terrible as they were, the losses could have been worse. Ten Wianno Seniors in the care of Karl Anderson in Harwich were spared, as were others stored in sheds and barns around the Cape.

To those who had long been involved with the fleet and who cared about its spirit and history, the losses were stunning. "If you own a Wianno Senior, it's not just *your* boat," said Ralph Lincoln, who had known the boats seemingly all his life, "they are very

*Originally purchased by Tim Fulham's father but later sold, #142 Cheerful is once again in the family. Here Tim sails in West Bay with daughter Elizabeth.*

Senior, however, was spared. *Victura*, which had for years been displayed seasonally at the JFK Library, was in a different shed. "That was just a matter of luck," Malcolm Crosby remembered. "When I brought it back from Boston for the winter, I put it where there was space."

Don Law's impeccably maintained #125 was gone and so was Brad and Jeff Tracy's #171, among those last wooden Seniors built in 1976. Richard "Dick" Taylor's bright red *Owl*, #164, was destroyed. Taylor had bought his boat not for racing but for cruising, and he'd had *Owl* outfitted with Pullman-style pull-down berths, a propane stove, and a basic lighting system. Between 1985 and 2003, Taylor had cruised his Senior to Maine and Nova Scotia, covering some 13,000 miles in the process. The Edmonds family's #136, winner of three Scudder Cups, was destroyed and so was #143, initially purchased by Francis Lloyd and successfully raced by his sons Frank, Boardy, and Malcolm, but now owned by Tim Fulham. Three fiberglass Seniors burned: the Johnsons' #178, Nantucket-moored but in storage in Osterville; #185,

*Photographer Norman Fortier caught #143 Pertelote on a hazy summer day in 1976, fresh from her Scudder Cup victory the previous season. Boardy, Frank, and Malcolm Lloyd all took turns at the helm, and Pertelote won two more Scudder Cups.*

important to all of us." Lincoln's experiences commenced pre-World War II in Bass River when he was just five years old and, seventy years later, he could still rattle off the names of the many Seniors he had crewed on, including *Dimbula, Patricia, Pinafore, Valkyrie, Winita, Surprise,* and those he and his family had owned: *Sally Ann, Saltworks,* and *Odin.*

George Edmonds tried to quantify what the fire had taken. He calculated that the lost Seniors had won twenty-seven Scudder Cups, eighteen H. Manley Crosby Memorial Trophies, fourteen Ross W. Richards Memorial Trophies, and seventeen Long Distance Races. The Edmondses and John Fallon may have been the first to immediately order a new Wianno Senior, but eventually, two-thirds of those whose boats were destroyed, followed suit. All those boats were fiberglass — all but two. Of those two, only one was a total rebuild.

"I was on my way to Boston in my car when John Fallon called to tell me about the fire," Tim Fulham remembered. "It was about seven in the morning."

Like many in the fleet, Tim Fulham had grown up in a water-oriented family. His father John "Jack" Fulham had been born in Winthrop in 1918 and would later enter the family's commercial fishing business in Boston. In Winthrop, Jack introduced the Star Class at the Cottage Park Yacht Club, and after World War II he began racing at the Eastern Yacht Club in Marblehead. There, he met his wife Margery. "He thought a good way to meet her was to buy her father's boat, which she was selling," Tim remembered.

In 1965 Jack and Margery Fulham began spending summers in Hyannis Port. "It was natural for my folks to choose Hyannis Port," Tim Fulham recalled. "We kids could walk everywhere we needed to go. The water was warm. There was a good one-design fleet in the Wianno Senior and a learn-to-sail program at the Hyannis Port Yacht Club. What's more, it was a small community where we couldn't get into too much trouble!"

While Tim began learning to sail at age eight under the firm hand of John Linehan, his parents chartered a Wianno Senior through the Crosby Yacht Building & Storage Co. Chartering of boats was not unusual in the fleet and was handled both formally and informally. In this case, a formal agreement was drawn up by Wilton "Bill" Crosby, Jr., for the charter of Lawrence "Renny" Damon's #113 *West Wind* to John Fulham. The cost was $800.

"Mr. Fulham advises me," Crosby wrote Damon, "he has arranged for a mooring in Hyannis Port and would like us to deliver her over on June 28, [1965]. I trust before this date you will have someone bring the sails up to us so they may be placed aboard prior to the charter." Thus began the Fulhams' experience with the Wianno Senior. "I sincerely hope you and your family will derive much fun and satisfaction," Damon wrote Fulham, "and hopefully keep up the good racing record *West Wind* has enjoyed."

The Fulhams chartered #113 again in 1966, but in 1968 Jack Fulham bought a new Senior of his own and #142 *Cheerful* entered the HPYC fleet. Three years later, however, weary of commuting from his Wellesley home to the Cape, Jack Fulham made the

*Here is #157* Chanzia *in the summer of 2003. From the stern forward are skipper Lloyd "Mac" McManus, Scott McManus, Joe O'Neal, and Dan Vullemier.* Chanzia *placed tenth of twenty-three boats in the 2003 Scudder Cup series, just behind Brad Tracy's #171* Lady Luck *and just ahead of* Tim Fulham in #143 Pertelote. *All three boats were lost in the Crosby boatyard fire that December.*

same mistake several other Wianno Senior owners had committed. He sold #142 without consulting his wife. Margery Fulham was anything but cheerful when she heard the news. Out at the Bass River Yacht Club, however, the new owner Bobby Churchill was delighted. He renamed the Fulhams' boat *Eight Ball* and kept her for some seventeen years before selling to Karl Anderson.

"Well," said Tim, "what happened was she made him build #165." Thus did a new *Cheerful* emerge in 1975, but this time the boat was listed in the class handbook under Margery Fulham's name. As for Tim,

his career took him away from the class for a period of time, but he returned to the fleet in 1990. In 1993, Tim Fulham bought #143 *Pertelote*. She was a proven boat. Boardy, Francis (Frank), and Malcolm Lloyd took turns at the tiller of #143 and won the Scudder Cup in 1975, 1982, and 1983.

As soon as he heard the news from John Fallon about the devastating fire at Crosby's, Fulham knew *Pertelote* was gone, and his immediate thought was to do whatever he could to support the class. "That night, my wife Lise and I were talking about the situation," Fulham remembered. "Just as we were going to bed, she came up with the idea to call Karl Anderson, and see if he'd sell my parents' old boat."

By the time of the devastating fire in Osterville, Wianno Senior #142 was thirty-five years old. After years of hard racing by Anderson and his partners — and despite having a refastened bottom and many new frames — the boat was a candidate for a total rebuild. Fulham could have opted to buy a new fiberglass boat. Instead he committed to the more costly project of restoring a classic plank-on-frame Wianno Senior as created by Manley Crosby. "The yard," remembered Fulham, "wanted it to be perfect."

Off came the deck and out came the centerboard trunk whose removal during a rebuild is really the only way to ensure a watertight boat. "Oggie suggested we really didn't want any sistered frames," said Fulham, "as they'd add unnecessary weight." One by one, #142 was reframed from the inside out, each frame removed and replaced by a new one made of laminated mahogany that would restore the strength of the boat.

"The boat has twenty-six frames per side," Tim Fulham noted. "The aft frames were fine, so they wound up needing to only put in sixteen or seventeen." Most of the yacht's mahogany planks could be saved, but a new deck structure, deck, and cabin were built. The boat was pretty much complete by late summer of 2004, and as *Pertelote*'s rig had not been destroyed in the fire, it was used when #142 was launched for the 2005 season. On the varnished transom, the yacht's name was applied in gold leaf. It was the same name Jack and Margery Fulham had given the boat thirty-seven years earlier — *Cheerful*.

OVER THE NEXT FEW YEARS, fifteen new fiberglass Seniors entered the fleet. Arrangements had been made with Shaw Yacht to provide the hull and deck units at a competitive price for finishing at Crosby Yacht. A Wianno Senior sailor who finished his own boat from a bare hull was William "Bill" Lawrence. Together with his wife Ellie, Lawrence had been nursing along #135 for years while competing in races and actively collecting all manner of memorabilia, historical materials, and maintaining the class database. Like so many in the fleet, Bill and Ellie were brought together by the Wianno Senior, though in an unusual manner. "Our families knew each other for generations," Lawrence said, "but the two of us never made a connection until Ellie took my place on the

*Wianno Senior #196* Aegir *was finished from a bare hull/deck by her owner Bill Lawrence. Here, at Edgartown in 2006, Bill is at the helm with Colin Silverio to his right and Rick O'Leary in the yellow vest. Ellie Lawrence is visible to leeward.*

crew one day. We always say that we met on the day I wasn't there."

An engineer and handy with boats, Lawrence had worked with Bernie Shaw on some of the issues involved in restarting production using the refurbished molds in 2001. "Bernie," Lawrence said, "kept after me, asking, 'When am I going to build a boat for you?' We eventually agreed on a price I could afford, which included me finishing the boat and transferring all of the parts possible from #135." In the fall of 2003, not long before the fire, #196 was delivered to the Lawrences' yard in South Yarmouth. A tarp was rigged between trees, permitting Lawrence to work on rainy days. The project took ten weeks.

So, one by one, the lost Wianno Seniors were replaced and, while some may have lamented the reality that *Cheerful* was the only completely renovated wooden boat, all were thankful that the fleet was fortunate to have so many sailors who could regroup and support such a resurgence. What's more, the retooled fiberglass boat eventually attracted attention

*The trio behind Wianno Senior Italia: Seen here at the Portofino boat show are Federico Nardi, Yula Sambuy, and her husband Mauro Piani.*

from a surprising place far from Osterville in Porto Santo Stefano, Italy, about two hours north of Rome on the western coast of Tuscany.

"We first saw the wooden Wianno Senior around 1999 or 2000 at the Cantiere Navale dell' Argentario," said Yula Sambuy.

One never could tell what unusual boats might await discovery at this storied boatyard in a medieval fortress town with its colorful old buildings. Dell' Argentario was renowned for its impeccable restoration of classic wooden yachts. The boat that Yula and her husband Mauro Piani — an *America*'s Cup-level sailor — saw that day was #108, built in 1947 and in need of a full restoration. That is exactly what the yard's technical coordinator Federico Nardi planned to do. In fact, #108 was just a beginning. Nardi had also acquired Peter O'Keeffe's #127 *Rapparee*.

Yula, Mauro, and Federico were all fascinated by the Wianno Senior and as the restorations of the first two wooden boats were completed, they began discussing the feasibility of building fiberglass Wianno Seniors. "In Italy," said Yula, "a centerboard boat is useful for mooring in shallow parts of harbors. Also, the size of the boat makes it easy to trailer and park at home."

After a preliminary meeting in Boston with George Edmonds in 2007, Yula and Mauro returned in April 2008 and signed an agreement with the Wianno Senior Class Association, giving them the right to acquire molds and build fiberglass Wianno Seniors. "We put all the tooling in a container and bought two more wooden boats on the Cape, #41 *Halcyon* and #77 *Tail Wind II*, and took it all back home," Yula recalled. Wianno Senior Italia was now in business. "Our idea was to create a movement," Yula said. They began displaying the boat at shows stressing the connection of the Wianno Senior to President Kennedy, an important marketing strategy. "The Boat of the President" was the headline of one magazine article.

The Italian-built Seniors differ in some ways from their American counterparts. Halyards go through the cabin rather than over the cabintop, and a replica bronze Merriman winch and wood-shell blocks are used, all made at the yard. The hardware gives the boat an immediate traditional appearance, a certain "old world" look when viewed in the boat's native surroundings. "Because you can't sail into harbor according to law," said Yula, "the boat is fitted with a one-cylinder 7-horsepower Nanni diesel and a folding propeller. We were granted exceptions by the class for the routing of the rigging and the engine."

"As for sailing performance," Mauro noted, "they would be the equal of the American-built boat. I didn't win the *America*'s Cup, but maybe sometime I can win the Scudder Cup!"

IN THE END, when enough time had passed after the great fire, when the new boats were racing, people could look back and reflect on the terrible destruction caused and its aftermath. When they did, and with the perspective offered by all that happened in the years that followed that night in December 2003, most saw the event in a new way. "Well," said Ralph Lincoln, "that fire probably saved the fleet."

*Old and new in the Mediterranean Sea. To port is #41 Halcyon (1918), most beautifully restored, and #216 (2010), among the fiberglass Wianno Seniors built in Italy.*

*Wianno Senior Italia received an exemption from the class permitting the routing of lines through the cabin.*

173

CHAPTER FOURTEEN

# All in the Family

## *"For me, it's all about family. Not just our family but all the others in the class."*

— *Holly Edmonds*

*"That was a crazy day that lots of people remember well," said Holly Edmonds of the Edgartown Regatta in 1996. By the end of the Scudder Cup Series, Holly and crew placed second in* Cirrus *behind Oggie Pesek in* Cochenoe *and ahead of third-place Ian McNiece in* Eight Ball. *(l–r): Holly Edmonds, Alden Edmonds, Joe Lotuff, Natalie Edmonds.*

Although it was expected that new rules governing sails would narrow the competitive gap within the Scudder Cup fleet, topmost tier boats continued to dominate. Yet this did little to squelch enthusiasm for racing. "Each little section of the fleet has battles within it," said Kevin Cain. "That's what keeps you coming back. Sometimes, too, you have a really good race. That also keeps you going. There is also the chance of serendipity thanks to the places we sail with their currents and shallows. It's a bit like an ocean race in the sense that you might just get lucky."

175

But for Don Law and the fleet's other top-ranked skippers, luck seemed a peripheral concern. Thinking back to the time he began crewing aboard *Cochenoe* in the early '80s, Oggie Pesek said, "Don seemed able to win at will which, considering the competition, was stunning." After winning his fifth Scudder Cup in 1994, Law decided the time had come to give his talented crew its own opportunities. "Don," said Kevin Cain, "is an extremely generous and appreciative person. After he had won the Scudder Cup a number of times with Sara, Oggie, and me as crew, he wanted to reward our commitment with the opportunity to

drive the boat with *him* as crew. Only Oggie was able to replicate the success of winning the Scudder Cup as a helmsman, but both Sara and I managed top three finishes." In 1991, Cain won the H. Manley Crosby Memorial Trophy (and the Bass River Yacht Club Regatta) and in 1994, Law's wife, Sara Molyneaux, relieved from her accustomed foredeck duties, won the Manley as well. By now, it seemed like it was just a matter of time before a "girl" — what the *Barnstable Patriot* had referred to in 1914 as a "young lady of Wianno" — would win the Scudder Cup.

Down through all the decades of racing, the young ladies had been competitive. From the prewar skipper era when Anne Halliday, Carolyn Crossett, Jean Hinkle, Dot Winship, and Mary Parlett were racing, to the postwar years of Connie Tracy, Lee Williams, Jean O'Toole, and others, there was nothing unusual about women competing at a high level. "Going back to the late '50s where my experience starts," remembered the BRYC's Jimmy Bartlett, "there were always women skippers in the fleet. Barbara Barrett from Stonehorse skippered *High Barbaree* and has her name on the Bass River Scudder Cup event as skipper."

What's more, the Wianno Senior women did more than skipper. "There have always been women among the crews, support boats, and shore parties," Bartlett pointed out. "The latter two categories never get enough credit for helping manage the races, shuttle people back and forth, and putting on the lunches after races, which gives our fleet a chance to unite. Ellie Lawrence from Bass River is a great example of a former Race Committee chairman without whom

*Launched in 1976 and owned since 1995 by Maxwell Kennedy, #173* Ptarmigan *was the last wooden Senior to be built. Here, #173 competes at the 2011 Scudder Cup event hosted by the Hyannis Port Yacht Club. Starting forward: Max Kennedy, Jr., Ted Kennedy, Jr., Sarah Kennedy (daughter of Christopher Kennedy, one of Robert and Ethel's sons), and Kiley Kennedy, Ted's daughter.*

we probably wouldn't have raced in recent years. And the late Muriel Townsend, Race Committee secretary at the BRYC, was a gem. She spent a good portion of her weekends for twenty-five years in a leaky wooden boat without adequate toilet facilities bouncing up and down at anchor at the start/finish line."

Sara Molyneaux's winning of the H. Manley Crosby Memorial Trophy in 1994 followed that of twenty-four-year-old Holly Edmonds in *Cirrus* — with crew Joe Lotuff, Natalie Edmonds, and Rick Burnes, Jr's. daughter, Sara — in 1993 and suggested to many that it was just a matter of time before a young lady

of Wianno won the Scudder Cup itself. "I know I was very proud to be second, but that was because I was young, rather than because I was female," Holly remembered of the 1993 season. "There had been lots of great women sailors in the fleet."

Joe Lotuff, who ran the foredeck on *Cirrus* during the 1993 Scudder Cup, remembers that year's campaign for what might have been. Lotuff, whose recall of placings in every race he's sailed is seemingly total, noted that *Cirrus* had taken a fifth and a first at Edgartown, and a second and first at Wianno. Sandwiched between those regattas, however, was

Hyannis Port. There, *Cirrus* placed tenth on the first day but didn't finish the next day's race. "We broke a backstay shackle at the mast," he said, "but we still came second in the Scudder Cup despite sailing one less race!"

Holly Edmonds had grown up in the seemingly perfect environment for a would-be sailboat racer. The daughter of class stalwarts George and Sally Edmonds, Holly and her sister Natalie and brothers Alden and Penn had, like many in the fleet, begun learning the Wianno Senior as children.

"Both my parents taught my sister and me about sailing the same way they did our brothers," Holly said. "Alden and I crewed for our parents, and I took sailing classes at the WYC where Oggie Pesek was one of my instructors. My parents were tenacious. In 1984 my mother became the first woman commodore of the WYC, and having her as a role model made it seem normal for me to expect to be successful in the boat."

By the late '80s George Edmonds and his wife Sally were ready to scale back their racing aboard their wonderful *Cirrus* and were generous — as Senior parents always have been — in letting their kids use the boat. In 1991, Alden Edmonds won the Scudder Cup in the boat. In 1996, three years after winning the Manley, it seemed to Holly that the stars were aligning nicely for her to finally win the Scudder Cup, too. Not only did she have experience on her side, but she had superstition as well. A couple years earlier she had approached her friend Kevin Cain and asked him a simple question regarding her one-time sailing instructor.

"Holly approached me at a party," Cain remembered, "and asked me how she could get Oggie Pesek to ask her on a date. I told her Oggie was too shy and might never ask but if she asked *him*, he'd accept and things would go fine after that."

By 1996 Oggie and Holly were engaged, the latest in the long line of couples — a line that included Holly's parents — to meet and marry thanks to their involvement with the Wianno Senior. In a class that had long cherished the old myth about Manley Crosby's bet, another developed in later years that had to do with people who became engaged. "There was," said Holly, "a legend that when you got engaged, you would win the Scudder Cup. We had seen that work for John Fallon in 1991, and I could see it coming true again. I said to myself: 'It's gonna work. It's happening.'"

In fact, the magic did seem to be happening. By the time the 1996 Scudder Cup series entered its last event, Holly was on the cusp of winning. All she needed to do was finish in the top ten. "Well," Oggie recalled, "I won that race and Holly came in eleventh or twelfth. The rest, as they say, is history. One of the engaged people won, but the legend never said *which* one it would be."

With competition among the top-level Wianno Senior sailors as intense as any in the one-design world, Holly came back for more. As always, the fleet's leading skippers were *really* good sailors. John Fallon was always a threat. Peter O'Keeffe, with his years of experience and steady crew, was, too. So was Burt McManus. Holly's brother Alden remained in top form, and Karl Anderson's boat preparation and

"BECAUSE IT'S A HEAVY BOAT and has a gaff rig," Karl Anderson said, "racing a Wianno Senior is almost a different sport than other one-design classes. You need to put in the time to learn the feel of the boat in order to sail it well." Anderson's partners aboard #188 *Pieces of 8* — the boat that replaced #142 *Eight Ball* — learned fast. After crewing aboard #188 during the Scudder Cup win in 2003, Todd Kittredge skippered the boat to Scudder Cup wins in 2004 and 2006. Later, when two SHYC sailors — John and Heather Gregg — joined Anderson, they learned fast, too.

"Lew Gunn was a family friend," said Heather Gregg, who grew up in Harwich Port and became an All-American at Tufts and then an Olympic-class sailor — among her other sailing achievements — "and he was always saying that he really wanted me to sail the Wianno. And he just kept at it. After awhile, I'd say, 'Oh, there he goes again.'"

But when her brother John became partners with Karl Anderson in *Eight Ball*, it was natural for Heather to finally fulfill Gunn's wish. His intuition about her success was quickly verified. As her brother's job kept him from being a regular aboard the boat, Heather soon was at the helm and discovered that Anderson's comment about a learning curve was accurate. "There's an art to driving it — it drives more like a keel boat — and to figuring it out," she said. "One of the things I've found is that the gaff rig is kind of addictive. But the rig was less an issue for me than understanding how to get the boat moving and keep it moving by not pinching and by anticipating puffs."

Whatever the challenge presented by the boat, Gregg's experience and success in other classes

*In her father's footsteps—Clare O'Keeffe tends the foredeck on #177 Rapparee. "From 1964 to 2010, I would have been up there handling the spinnaker," said Tim O'Keeffe, "but when my brother Pete went on injured reserve in 2011, I took over the helm and recruited Clare for the foredeck. It was a different but proud experience watching her fill my old shoes."*

tactical skills represented a challenge to everyone in the fleet. In 1997, Holly finished ninth; in 1998, fourth: in 1999, eleventh. The quest went on until 2005. That year, Holly Edmonds became the first woman skipper to win the Scudder Cup. She took first in two events to ultimately edge out Jeffrey Tracy and Todd Kittredge. The win was achieved in the new family boat, the fiberglass #200 *Aurora*. "I was sentimental about the wooden boat we'd lost in the fire," Holly said. "But then, I wasn't paying the maintenance bills."

## Portrait of the Fleet
## 2005 Scudder Cup Results

| Rank | Sail # | Yacht Name | Helmsman | Points | Affiliation |
|---|---|---|---|---|---|
| 1 | 200 | *Aurora* | Holly Edmonds | 513 | WYC |
| 2 | 195 | *Dauntless* | Jeff Tracy | 501 | HYC |
| 3 | 188 | *Pieces of 8* | Todd Kittredge | 592 | HYC |
| 4 | 150 | *Yankee Dime* | Joe Lotuff | 492 | WYC |
| 5 | 142 | *Cheerful* | Lloyd B. McManus, Jr. | 486 | WYC |
| 6 | 199 | *Heritage* | John T. Fallon | 476 | WYC |
| 7 | 177 | *Rapparee* | Peter L. O'Keeffe | 470 | HPYC |
| 8 | 202 | *Eowyn* | George F. Largay | 468 | WYC |
| 9 | 197 | *Cochenoe* | Donald F. Law | 457 | WYC |
| 10 | 182 | *Lindy* | David McDonough | 451 | WYC |
| 11 | 196 | *Aegir* | William G. Lawrence | 418 | BRYC |
| 12 | 174 | *Sea Lyon* | Charles M. Lyons | 411 | HPYC |
| 13 | 184 | *Lente Festina* | G. Kent Pluckett | 407 | WYC |
| 14 | 190 | *Golden Summer* | Pat Lentell | 406 | WYC |
| 15 | 191 | *Novanglus* | Chris Wolfington | 405 | HPYC |
| 16 | 187 | *Quartermain II* | Jack Campo | 399 | HPYC |
| 17 | 180 | *Touch o'Gray* | Lewis J. H. Gunn | 394 | SHYC |
| 18 | 203 | *Dingle* | Andy Schneider | 387 | WYC |
| 19 | 175 | *Lucinda* | Chip Niehoff | 370 | HPYC |
| 20 | 201 | *Shadowfax* | Toby S. Hynes | 356 | WYC |
| 21 | 149 | *Akela* | Carter S. Bacon III | 350 | HPYC |
| 22 | 193 | *Ghost* | Dave Trimble | 341 | WYC |

including the J/24 and International One Design served her well. Double-handing with Anderson to compete at Edgartown in 2010, the two had *Pieces of 8* planing "just for the heck of it." In her first Scudder Cup Series that year, Gregg won the Edgartown Regatta, the Bass River Challenge Cup, and the H. Manley Crosby Memorial Trophy. It was a remarkable first season, but what impressed Heather Gregg most was what she learned about the class at post-race get-togethers.

"People would tell me this was their thirty-fifth Scudder Cup and I would say, 'Well, that's just not possible.' Of all the classes I sail in, I can't think of one with that sort of longevity and passion. I was also impressed that people were very warm, open, and inviting to me, given I was a total newcomer and they'd sailed the boat forever. There's a friendliness and a welcoming that not all classes have. Other classes would die to have what the Wianno Seniors have."

During her second campaign for the Scudder

*Recalling this breezy summer day on the Maine coast in the summer of 2005, Robin Lincoln said: "Dean Young and I sailed down to WoodenBoat from the Benjamin River to check out the boats as they were leaving from the race the previous day. Then we just sailed around the islands. It was fun." Built in 1933, #25* Saltworks *is still going strong.*

Cup in 2011, Heather Gregg became the second woman to win the Wianno Senior Class's ultimate prize.

MIDNIGHT ON MONDAY, September 20, 1982, found a Wianno Senior underway alone in the dark Atlantic between Bass River and Highland Light. In light wind, the boat was making 2.5 knots on a compass heading of 350 degrees. *Saltworks* was headed Down East. "Sighted whales," read the log entry of 1015 that morning. That night, the boat encountered pouring rain and increasing wind that drove her along at 6 knots. Midnight on Tuesday came with 15–20 knots, 45-degree temperatures, and the need to "pump the boat every hour or so." The crew headed into Cape Porpoise Harbor and took a 24-hour rest.

"I knew Seniors from having sailed them in fair weather and foul," said Jim Light, who was skippering *Saltworks* together with a small, cheerful woman named Chris Johnson. "We had sandwiches and stuff you could eat with one hand, water, and a case of beer. The head was a bucket. The head is always a bucket on a Wianno Senior."

On their fifth day out of Bass River, at 2120 on September 23, Light and Johnson hove-to in a thunderstorm by backing the jib and luffing the main. A few hours later, they were making 6–7 knots in a 15–20 southwesterly breeze and they passed due north of Monhegan. "We are both freezing cold," read the log. When the wind increased to 20–25, they dropped the main into the lazyjacks to reduce strain on the boat and slow the leaking. They saw the aurora borealis. At 1449 on Friday, September 24, the voyage ended when *Saltworks* moored at the dock of boatbuilder Joel White in Center Harbor.

*Saltworks*'s journey — navigation was by chart, watch, chip log, and compass — was more than a cruise or a yacht delivery. It was another chapter in the long and often circuitous story of keeping a Wianno Senior in the family. Eighteen years earlier, the boat — built in 1933 — had been purchased by Ralph Lincoln, whose experience with Wianno Seniors at Bass River extended to pre-World War II days. When Chris Johnson bought the boat, she found it too big for her to handle. That's when Ralph's cousin Robert bought the boat from Chris for his daughter, Brooklin, Maine, sailmaker Robin Lincoln.

Robin now became *Saltworks*'s caretaker. Rot found in the base of the mast was repaired, and the boat has been maintained and upgraded as necessary. "It doesn't owe me anything," said Robin. "My idea of heaven is to spend a night by myself at an island, to take four-to-five-hour day sails, and sometimes do the Eggemoggin Reach Regatta."

As the Wianno Senior Class approached its one-hundredth anniversary, Robin Lincoln was but one of several young ladies of Wianno who didn't live in Osterville or even on Cape Cod. Another off-Cape Senior, and among the few to receive a complete restoration, found a home in the old fishing port of Gloucester. It is owned by Steve Lindo, a onetime racer of vintage hydroplanes who, when he moved his law practice from New York to Rockport, Massachusetts, decided he would finally learn to be a sailor.

"I had worked with Chris Mattoon at Berkshire Wooden Boat on a couple of projects," said Lindo, "and learned he had a number of Wianno Seniors awaiting restoration including #60. I was taken with its seaworthiness and that you could single-hand it, and my brother, a life long sailor, gave me a lot of encouragement."

Wianno Senior #60 was eighty-four years old in 2008 when Chris Mattoon and the staff at Berkshire Wooden Boat began a rebuild that was completed in 2010. Considering the original boat's construction methods and the limited availability of timber that had been routinely used by the Crosbys, such a project is not for the faint-hearted.

"Given the size, weight, and the expense of the white oak materials," said boatbuilder Mattoon, "the specialized tools required for materials of this size, and the complexity of the keel/horn timber/centerboard trunk assembly, it is little wonder that successful restoration of a Wianno Senior is a challenge."

But Stephen Lindo has had no regrets. "It's been about the best thing I've done since leaving New York," Lindo said of his boat named *Twila*. "I've learned so much about seamanship, made wonderful new friendships, and had some amazing sails."

As the Class approached its one hundredth anniversary, *Twila* was one of several Wianno Seniors fortunate enough to have found a dedicated owner with the will, skills, and resources to undertake an ambitious restoration. During the period 1990–92, Thomas Morse extensively rebuilt #114 in his Wrentham barn. That project was followed by Morse's restoration of the storied #73, so successful

*Here is #60* Twila *after her restoration at Berkshire Wooden Boat. Owner Steve Lindo sails the boat out of Gloucester, Massachusetts.*

*Nantucket woodworker and Wentworth Institute graduate Chris Vallett spent two years' worth of nights and weekends to complete a meticulous restoration of #146* Defiance *(1969) in his specially prepared shop that allowed the boat to be lowered beneath floor level to more comfortably access the topsides.*

*Seen here at Edgartown in 2009 is #200* Aurora, *the boat that replaced the Edmonds family's #136* Cirrus. *At the tiller is Holly Edmonds. Tony Will is trimming the mainsheet. Matt Cannistraro is to leeward in "the pit," and Natalie Edmonds is in her familiar work space on the foredeck.* Aurora *won the Scudder Cup in 2005.*

in the hands of Ben Baxter and the Moores. In the summer of 2012, Nantucket-based woodworker Chris Vallett completed the meticulous restoration of #146 in his specially designed shop.

ALWAYS IN THE CLASS, there has been family. There has been immediate family and the extended family that embraces all those who sail aboard a Wianno Senior. "Five generations of in-breeding!" quipped Jimmy Bartlett. "There are some sailing today whose great-grandparents had a connection to the boat. And people in the fleet married, divorced, and moved on. It's a fleet full of five generations of grudges, most of which we can't even remember why they started but we still can't forget — at least not when we're out racing."

Seventy-three years after Robert Stewart Kilborne, Jr., won the WYC championship in 1922, his daughter Belle and her husband Richard Taylor presented a new silver model of a Wianno Senior to be mounted atop the Scudder Trophy. The original version had, oddly, been marconi-rigged, more of a generic sailboat than a Wianno Senior. The new one, however, was a nice replica of Kilborne's #43 and was engraved with the sail number and the yacht's distinctive name, *Unquomonk*. Now, a boat instantly recognizable as a Wianno Senior sailed atop the class's most coveted trophy, and the memory of Belle's father was enshrined.

The social orb that has the boat at its center has, from the earliest days of the fleet, brought people together to become friends, business partners, or spouses and, in the case of Joe Lotuff, all three. "My

*The Tracy family is but one example of multi-generational Wianno Senior sailors. Standing in front of #195 are three Tracy generations, photographed in the winter of 2012. (l–r) Christian Tracy is the son of Brad and the grandson of Jay and Connie. Jeffrey Tracy is Jay and Connie Tracy's son. Jay H. Tracy and Connie Moore Tracy come next. On Connie's right is her son Brad with his kids Leah and Matthew. Not in the picture is Connie's Scudder Cup–winning brother Stan Moore.*

summer job was working at the WYC," said Lotuff, "and one day when I was sixteen, Sally Edmonds plucked me off the dock to crew. She knew me anyhow because we were neighbors."

Joe now began learning the ins and outs aboard #136 *Cirrus*, one of the fleet's top boats skippered by one of the fleet's greatest gentlemen. A rocket scientist with Draper Labs in Cambridge, George Edmonds often commuted in a little seaplane he owned — first a Marchetti Riviera and later a yellow STOL Twin Bee — usually taxiing through the Seapuit River to take off from Cotuit Bay. He approached sailboat racing in a predictably methodical, calm, and intelligent manner. Little or nothing upset his composure, although eventually Joe, who was responsible for the foredeck, did so. "I heard George swear for what might be the first and only time in his life," Joe remembered, "when I hoisted the spinnaker without attaching the halyard to the sail. I scampered up that mast to get it."

It was a great Wianno Senior education for a teenager and continued as the Edmonds parents phased out and Holly — who was on the women's varsity sailing team at Harvard — began skippering. "We were great upwind," remembered Lotuff. "We taped our backstays so they wouldn't flap. We'd go fast enough that Karl Anderson would watch."

When Holly began sailing with her husband, Joe Lotuff took his knowledge of the foredeck to #145 *Yankee Dime,* owned by B. Francis "Frank" Saul III. Lotuff now began to apply and further develop what he'd learned with the Edmonds family, focusing on how to adjust the centerboard in varying conditions, on mast rake, sail trim, and crew weight, "the hundred little things involved in setting up a boat and sailing it that all add up in the end."

As things developed, Lotuff was doing more than joining a new Wianno Senior crew. He met and married Frank Saul's sister, Tia, in 1997. "There was a condition attached," Lotuff said. "And the condition was no more sailing with 'competitors.'" "Competitors" now included #136, but to remind him of all the good times, the Edmondses — Lotuff also became business partners with Alden Edmonds — presented him with a beautiful half model of *Cirrus.*

Now, another in the long line of rivalries in the Wianno Senior fleet commenced. *Yankee Dime* was a formidable boat. "We rotated at the helm," said Gordon Burnes, who had learned to sail as a six-year-old in a refurbished Optimist pram. After crewing for his parents aboard their #148, Burnes became a three-time All-American at Harvard and joined #145 when he was thirty-four in 1999. "Frank, Alden, and

*Steep seas at the mark:*
Yankee Dime II *is crewed by (l–r) Frank Saul, Ben Sullivan, Kevin Cain, and Joe Lotuff. In 2007,* Yankee Dime II *became the last wooden Senior to win the Scudder Cup. Kevin Cain recalled that "we sailed upwind with a car battery powering two pumps, which ran the entire race. The boom was so bendy that the cabin hatch had to be pushed forward to allow the boom to be trimmed lower than the cabin top when fully sheeted in. The open hatch also allowed for a fairly steady flow of water to the pumps! Still, that was a fast boat."*

I took turns but Joe Lotuff always handled the fore-deck," he said. In 2002 *Yankee Dime* won the Scudder Cup, and the competition continued.

"We were tied with Holly in '05 going into the last Scudder Cup race," Lotuff recalled of that year's series final weekend at Wianno. *Yankee Dime* finished that race sixteenth while *Aurora* came ninth, sealing Holly's win. "Well," Lotuff remarked, noting what every sailboat racer quickly learns, "it can all turn on such a little bit, a little something that makes all the difference in the end."

After Frank Saul lost #145 in the Crosby boat-yard fire, he replaced it with #150, which he named *Yankee Dime II.* The thirty-three-year-old boat gave him and his crew all they could handle in terms of competing at a high level. "It was an out-of-whack boat," Lotuff remembered. "It had been stored sitting on its keel rather than properly blocked up, and it leaked so much it took four pumps to keep it afloat." Although Lotuff and Saul didn't undertake the complete rebuild that Tim Fulham had with #142, they significantly upgraded #150 for the 2005 season at

Ned Crosby's yard. Whatever *Yankee Dime II*'s remaining issues, the boat was sailed to Scudder Cup victory in 2007. "You don't need a fancy boat to win," Lotuff said. "You need great sailors. As of 2013, there are at least ten boats that could win the Scudder Cup."

Even after the adoption of the one-sail rule, the challenge to keeping the boat a one-design continued, and regulations were updated in an ongoing fashion. Windows were made permissible for both main and jib. The relocation of the mainsheet block to the end of the boom was okayed as was the installation of sister frames on wooden yachts. Although the tooling for the fiberglass yacht ensured hulls and decks would be identical, there remained the chance for variables in assembly. In addition to Crosby Yacht, both Shaw Yacht and the West Barnstable yard of E. M. "Ned" Crosby — grandson of Chester Crosby and great-grandson of Joseph who had briefly accompanied Manley to Brooklyn in 1895 — became authorized finishers.

By 2012, potential variables identified by the class involved such details as centerboard slot width, location of the centerboard pin, ballast keel alignment, the gap between the rudder and the hull, and forestay length. The importance of keeping these factors consistent was, if anything, underscored in early 2013 with the retirement from boatbuilding of Bernie Shaw and the need to find a new builder to construct the fiberglass components. Oversight of technical matters relating to important yacht dimensions is the responsibility of the class Subcommittee on Rules and Measurements currently guided by boat designer John C. Kiley III.

The importance of such a committee had been recognized years earlier. At a class meeting held on December 17, 2003, just one week after the Crosby boatyard fire, Brad Tracy expressed concern regarding his new boat, then under construction. He "was concerned that certain aspects of his new boat's rigging and equipment plan could conflict [with] the one-design rules that may evolve over the winter. He expressed his strong view that a meeting of the Subcommittee on Rules & Measurements be held as soon as possible…the Class Committee unanimously agreed…." Nine years later, the mandate for the Measurements Committee remained: Be attentive to all matters that might dilute the one-design nature of the class as it entered upon the start of its second century.

IN 2012, AFTER HAVING been lost for ninety-seven years, the Commodore's Trophy — introduced at the WYC by William B. H. Dowse in 1915 and won by James Gaff Hinkle when he was seventeen years old — was placed back in competition. The trophy had been discovered in the attic of the late Townsend

*The Peseks' #220* Scout *was the newest boat in the fleet in 2012. Here Oggie crews for daughter Sophie at the Wianno Yacht Club's Scudder Cup event.*

*Here is #220 awaiting completion at the shop of E. M. Crosby during the summer of 2011.*

Hornor and, seven years after his death in 2005, it was presented to the club by its then-owner, yachtsman Bill Koch. A longtime resident of Osterville and a former Wianno Senior owner, Koch was the 1992 winner of the *America's Cup* in *America3*. In turning Dowse's splendid old trophy back to the WYC, Koch's only stipulation was that it be supported by a new race series.

The new WYC Commodore's Trophy series was established with the goal of giving younger sailors experience of sailing a boat significantly larger and more demanding than the Optimist Prams and 420 dinghies prevalent in youth sailing programs. "The Senior fleet," said Oggie Pesek, "is missing sailors in their twenties and thirties. Many of the teens active in WYC programs are children of current Wianno Senior sailors, and we want to introduce them to the Senior fleet, hoping that the experience will 'take' and they will stay local as they grow out of Junior sailing."

As currently administered, the series has a minimum of three races and a maximum of ten. Skippers and crew must be under thirty years of age, although the majority are currently teenagers no older than eighteen. The role of an experienced adult aboard the boats was still being refined as this book went to press, but the goal is to do nothing more than provide verbal direction if needed and offer encouragement. In the summer of 2012, seven boats — #142, #197, #199, #200, #212, #214, and #220 — competed and it was common for the third generation of a Wianno Senior family to be aboard. "It was all kids, and they looked like drowned rats with big smiles," Pesek said of the 2012 event.

*Here is Joe Lotuff's #214* Smoke, *winner of the 2012 Scudder Cup, in action. From aft: Richard Feeny, Ben Sullivan, Brent Jansen, Joe Lotuff.*

AS THE WIANNO SENIOR Class entered 2014, the boat had been sailing safely through the waters of Nantucket Sound and the Atlantic Coast — and through the ever-uncharted waters of time — for a century. In the decades since the inception of the class, America experienced two world wars, the assassination of a president who grew up in the fleet, space flight, Vietnam, September 11th and the wars that followed, profound societal evolution, and technological change unprecedented in its pace and scope. The Cape Cod of the first Wianno Senior sailors — a dreamtime of sun-splashed summers, horse-drawn buggies, steam trains, and wooden boats with cotton sails — lived only in history. Yet, the Wianno Senior of 2014 would be instantly recognizable to Manley Crosby and the Osterville pioneers who had started the whole wonderful game, having no idea it would continue for so

*Number 210* Roscommon *was sailed to a satisfying fifth in the 2012 Max Crosby Regatta and finished thirteenth in that year's Scudder Cup series. "Everyone has been willing to take time and share their expertise to help novice sailors," said David Kelly, the boat's owner, seen here in the light-colored hat. "No wonder the fleet is so strong after 100 years!" David is flanked by his sons Robert Kelly and David Kelly, Jr., at the tiller. To leeward is trimmer Colin Sullivan.*

long. Yes, the fine, wood-shelled blocks might be gone; the rigging would look colorful yet generally familiar; the sails would feel oddly slippery; there would be, for the most part, an absence of mahogany planks and caulked seams. But the boat is still the boat. There are still the same familiar curves and shapes, the same coamings, the familiar bronze hardware. Of course, there remain the varnished wooden spars of a gaff rig, a rig that has always fostered seamanship while, in this case, also inciting intensely competitive tuning. The new boat, like Manley Crosby's original boat, remains a thing of beauty.

But most of all, what the past generations of Wianno Seniors would have remarked upon was the tradition begun in 1914 that continued for one hundred years. "Mr. Hinkle was a wonderful old man," remembered Pam Fallon Jagla of James Gaff Hinkle. "He was a really quiet skipper. He was out there to have fun, so it wasn't like the pressure pot of sailing with Dad. And there was one thing Mr. Hinkle made sure to have aboard his boat — kids."

*Scudder Cup race, July 2011: Chasing the fleet in light air, skipper Brad Tracy and crew guide #195 Dauntless downwind. Brad's brother Jeff is holding down the boom while Burt McManus keeps an eye on spinnaker trim. On the mainsheet is Charlie Downey, a longtime competitor in the class who sailed with Brad's grandfather Stan Moore to a number of Scudder Cup victories.*

*The Burnes family's #207 Madeline has just placed fifth at Wianno's 2009 Scudder Cup race. Sarah Burnes (left) and her brother Gordon (standing) grew up racing aboard the family's wooden Wianno Senior. Sarah's daughter Lily and Gordon's sons Henry (sitting on the cabin) and Eli handled the jib.*

*Action aboard #149 Ripple at the 2012 Wianno Yacht Club Scudder Cup event.*

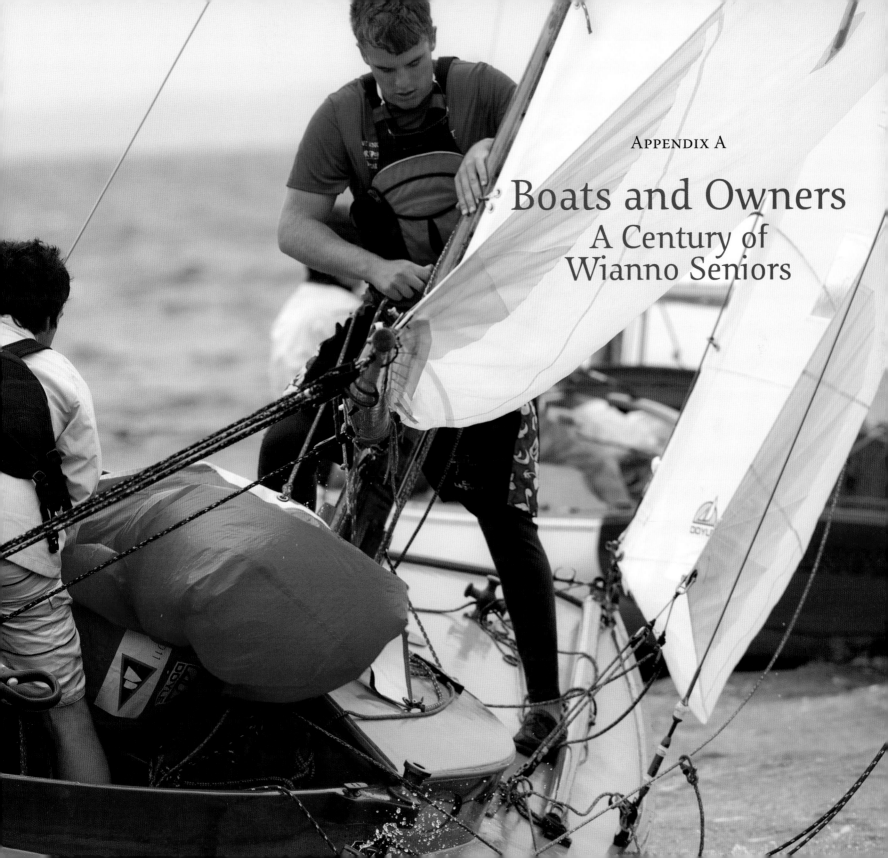

Boats and Owners
A Century of
Wianno Seniors

The following list traces the ownership of each Wianno Senior from 1914 to the present. The goal: to gather in one place information that will enlighten current and past owners about each boat's history and provide a basis for ongoing research into specific yachts and their owners. This list should be viewed as an historically oriented document rather than an effort to replace the fleet rosters long familiar to Wianno Senior owners.

## Remarks on Boat Numbering

Any list of Wianno Seniors raises the thorny question of boat numbering. This is a longstanding issue that dates back to the earliest days of the class. The problem began with the assigning of the first boats' sail numbers and was complicated by efforts starting in 1935 to sequentially number the entire fleet as it then existed. That said, all surviving prewar documents of the Wianno Yacht Club reveal that boats were always identified by sail number and owner's first initial and last name. There is nothing to suggest that those who founded the class cared about the specific order in which a boat was built or having them numbered sequentially. In fact, the boats were constructed simultaneously and there is nothing to indicate that the question ever arose.

The method by which sail numbers were first allotted or chosen is unknown. Perhaps the best that can be said is that the initial run of boats in 1914 — usually said to total fourteen — had sail numbers that, with two exceptions, were 14 or below. These numbers *could* have been drawn by lot by owners, *could* have

been selected by owners, or the owners *could* have simply accepted the sail bags put aboard their boats by the builder. Subsequently, sail numbers followed a generally chronological pattern but there were exceptions and sail numbers were sometimes skipped, leaving what became perplexing gaps. What's more, some boats changed sail numbers and while these renumberings doubtless had meaning to the owners, they further complicated efforts to understand and rationalize the matter.

At least two of the 1914 boats had sail numbers that bore no relation to chronology, and no boat ever carried #1. What Class Chairman James Gaff Hinkle would eventually (and confusingly) refer to as "boat #1 later #37," originally owned by Commodore Dowse, carried sail #23 throughout Dowse's entire period of ownership. Hinkle's own boat, #11, started life as #19. Why was Dowse's boat #23? Was #23, in fact, the first Wianno Senior to be completed? Was #19 a favorite of the Hinkle family? We simply don't know. Neither can one hazard a guess as to how the subsequent sail numbers for these boats were selected. The number 37 was chosen by the person who purchased Dowse's boat. The number 11 was chosen by the Hinkles. These particular renumberings occurred in the immediate post–World War I period that saw several other boats change their sail numbers as well.

In 1935, the Crosby Yacht Building and Storage Company compiled a list of the existing "Wianno One-Design Yachts." For reasons now unknown, this list attempted to create a sequential number system that began with #1 and ended with #103 (the most recently launched boat) irrespective, in a number of cases, of the sail number or numbers boats had used. Study of this single-page document reveals that, even by 1935, twenty-one years after the first boats were built, mystery had attached itself to boat numbering.

One result of the list's approach was that some boats appeared more than once. There is a #1 and a #37, although both #1 and #37 (and #23) were the same boat. While #11 is correctly identified on this 1935 list, its original number #19 is listed as "unknown." In fact, #11 and #19 were sail numbers used on the same boat. This approach resulted in there being more boat numbers than boats. (It also conflicted with the boat numbers that appeared in WYC documents.) In later years, compilers of the class roster might amplify "unknown" with the additional term "never built" or "not built, sail # used by...". Such comments beg questions, and inevitably confusion still attaches itself to these boats or "non-boats."

In 1962, commencing with #123, Crosby began stamping a hull number on each boat's builder's plate. But the method for determining the starting point is unknown. "It was," said Ted Crosby in a July 2010 interview, "decided 'upstairs' by Brad and Bill Jr."

It seems plausible, however, to believe that #123 was a number that closely aligned with the boat's sequential number dating all the way back to the 1935 Crosby list. (Numbers some owners have found stamped into the butt of masts—or written there in Magic Marker that usually later washed off—reflected a boat's sail number or hull number once those entered use. These numbers were intended to aid the yard men in matching a given rig to a given hull. They were an improvement over hang-tags that were sometimes lost.)

In 1972, the boat's hull number was included in its serial number as required by new Coast Guard regulations. In 1984, Rule 7 for the Scudder Cup stated: "A yacht competing in the Scudder Cup Races shall have as its sail number the hull number assigned such yacht by its builder, provided, however, that the foregoing restriction shall not apply to sail numbers in regular use prior to the 1987 season." Two exceptions to this rule were made, and they are noted in the list.

The list presented here differs from fleet rosters in that arbitrary "hull numbers" have been eliminated. This breaks with the sequential numbering process created in 1935 by Crosby, not the class itself. Boats built prior to 1962 are presented only with the sail numbers by which they were known to their owners. That is how they appeared in WYC documents. No effort has been made to stray from the historical record. If a sail number was changed, that change is reflected in the boat's entry. If a newly built boat had a sail number that didn't follow the immediately preceding boat, that is the sail number used. Beginning in 1962, both hull and sail numbers are included. All references made on fleet rosters to "unknown" or to numbers assigned to boats "not built" have been eliminated.

## The List Format

The list has six columns as follows:

| 1. Hull # | 2. Sail #(s) | 3. Year Built | 4. Name/Owner/Club or Place | 5. Ownership Period | 6. Remarks |
| --- | --- | --- | --- | --- | --- |

While the headings are self-explanatory, the following remarks may assist the reader:

**Hull Numbers:** Hull numbers do not appear until 1962 when they became official.

**Sail Numbers:** In cases when a sail number was changed, the change appears together with the date and, as appropriate, the owner responsible. If the number was later changed back to the original, that change is also reflected.

**Club or Place:** When an owner is not affiliated with a yacht club, his/her city/town of residence is used.

**Ownership Period:** The word "present" means a time frame of July 2013, when this book went to press.

**Remarks:** For space reasons, it was not practical to consistently include remarks about each boat. The included remarks are brief and subjective. They are intended to clarify specific points or explain the rare speculation about ownership. Remarks are occasionally used to explain a boat's name, note boat condition or modifications, or to include something that might assist in future research about owners.

**Abbreviations:**
The following abbreviations are used:

**c** for circa

**cb** for centerboard

**fg** for fiberglass

**BRYC** for Bass River Yacht Club

**CYC** for Canandaigua Yacht Club

**EYC** for Edgartown Yacht Club

**HYC** for Hyannis Yacht Club

**HPYC** for Hyannis Port Yacht Club

**LBYC** for Lewis Bay Yacht Club (These boats raced at the HPYC.)

**SHYC** for Stone Horse Yacht Club

**WHYC** for Woods Hole Yacht Club

**WYC** for Wianno Yacht Club

*Originally owned by Joe Hinkle, #183 was the first Hinkle family* Fantasy *built of fiberglass. Today, the boat is owned by Lee Hope. (l–r) Ery Largay, Drew Buttner, Tim Wadlow, Karen Fallon.*

## A Note on Sources

No single collection of documents existed upon which to base this list. Instead, a wide variety of sources has been drawn upon. The most important sources were WYC pre-World War II race results and rosters. Newspaper race reports of the period were also valuable. So were class association handbooks, taking into account that, for various reasons, these were not always updated in a timely manner. In addition, interviews were conducted with dozens of past owners who strove to recall, as best they could, dates and names associated with the purchase and sale of their Wianno Senior. Whenever possible, recollections have been checked against reliable, recorded dates.

## Summary

This list is presented as an historical record of the Wianno Senior fleet rather than one intended as a tool for administration of the fleet. The list does not impose a sequential numbering system but uses only the sail numbers known to the yachts' owners as revealed in class documents and other sources. Hull numbers are used beginning in 1962 when they were first officially assigned to new boats. The list is as comprehensive as possible given the information available, but it remains a document to which additional information can be added. Additional information about specific boats should be shared with the class.

| Hull # | Sail #(s) | Year Built | Name/Owner/Club or Place | Dates Owned | Remarks |
|---|---|---|---|---|---|
| | #23 | 1914 | *Dione*/William B. H. Dowse/WYC | 1914–c. 1922 | |
| | #37 | | *Fiddler*/Mary Parlett/WYC | 1922–1941 | |
| | | | *Fiddler*/William R. Scott/Unknown | 1946–1953 | |
| | | | *Peg II*/E. W. Hitchcock/Cotuit, MA | as of 1954 | Arnholt Sea Mite engine installed. |
| | | | *Peg II*/Dr. Joseph J. Angleno/Squantum, MA | as of 1970 | |
| | | | *Sirocco*/Dr. Thomas J. Anglem/Salem, MA | as of 1976 | Whereabouts unknown. |
| | #2 | 1914 | *Wendy*/Henry Brown Day/WYC | 1914–1939 | Frank A. Day, brother, also raced. |
| | | | *Wendy*/Alexander T. Brown/HPYC | as of 1941 | |
| | | | *Jessica*/Orin Tovrov/Chatham, MA | as of 1948 | |
| | | | *Barracuda*/Robert H. Ainsworth/Springfield, MA | Unknown | |
| | | | *Barracuda*/John Bassett/South Burlington, VT | as of 1970 | |
| | | | *The Aging Queen*/Robert M. Naylor/N. Pomfret, VT | 1975 | |
| | | | *Confederacy*/Pat Carney, Don Ivey, Bill Kissam/Westport, NY | 1975 | |
| | | | *Coleen*/Henry Kurtenbach/Eliot, ME | 1987–1999 | Broken up at Eliot, ME. Keel and rig said to remain. |
| | #3 | 1914 | *No. 3*/Norman Dubois/WYC | 1914–c. 1915 | No extant info for Dubois. No boat record from 1915 to 1921. |
| | | | *Alouette*/Franklin Irving Sears/BRYC, WYC | c. 1916–1928 | Raced at WYC from 1922–1926. No name associated with boat from '22–'24. *Qui Vive* in '25. |
| | | | Unknown/Harold Cross/Fitchburg, MA | 1929–1934 | Kept at Edgartown. |
| | | | *Telemark*/Crosby Yacht/Osterville, MA | 1935–1936 | |
| | | | *Telemark*/Forrest T. Ellis/WYC | 1937–1941 | Renamed *Surge* as of '41. |
| | | | *Surge*/Franklin Irving Sears/BRYC | as of 1944 | Sears appears to have kept boat at Wianno until 1944 when moved to Bass River. Lost in 1944 hurricane. |
| | #4 | 1914 | *A.P.H.*/William P. Halliday/WYC | 1914–1927 | A.P.H. for Anne Pillow Halliday. |
| | | | *A.P.H.*/F. H. Wesson/WYC | 1928–1929 | |

| Hull # | Sail #(s) | Year Built | Name/Owner/Club or Place | Dates Owned | Remarks |
|--------|-----------|------------|--------------------------|-------------|---------|
| | | | *Vic*/Unknown/WYC | 1930 | |
| | | | *Scud*/Stuart F. Scudder/WYC | 1935 | |
| | | | *Scud*/Richard Humphreys/WYC | 1936–1941 | D. M. Humphreys as of 1941. |
| | | | *Sabrina*/E. K. Graves/Huntington, NY | 1947–c. 1953 | |
| | | | *Scud*/D. M. Humphreys/HPYC | 1954–1956 | Presumed boat left Cape by 1960. |
| | | | *Scud*/R. Hartjen/Rochester, NY | as of 1970 | |
| | | | *Sabrina*/Dr. Edward M. McDonald/Whitney Point, NY | c. 1976–1979 | Lost, Whitney Point, 1979. |
| | #5 | 1914 | *Commy*/Frank and Abby S. Hagerman/WYC | 1914–1935 | Bought for Abby upon her graduation from Vassar in 1914. Campaigned by Jack Tiernan in 1921 season. |
| | | | *Commy*/A. S. Hagerman and Morrison Shafroth/WYC | 1936–1968 | Shafroth was Abby Hagerman's married name. |
| | | | *Cinque*/K. E. DeLong/HPYC | 1969–1970 | |
| | | | Unknown/Unknown/Woods Hole, MA | as of 1975 | |
| | | | *Salvage*/Phillip Westra/WHYC | c. 1976–1978 | Cb removed. Used for sailing to the Vineyard and Elizabeth Islands. |
| | | | *Cinque*/Leonard Westra/Harpswell, ME | 1978–1993 | Broken up at Harpswell, ME, following some 15 years ashore after several planned restorations failed to occur. Phillip and Leonard Westra are brothers. |
| | #6 | 1914 | *Snookums*/Andrew Adie/WYC | 1914–1921 | |
| | | | *Snookums*/P. Brown/WYC | 1922–c. 1929 | |
| | | | *Snookums*/Henry Ullman/WHYC | 1930 | |
| | | | *Snookums*/Walter O. Luscombe/WHYC | 1931–1934 | May have carried #34 for a period at WHYC. |
| | | | *Bellina*/Walter O. Luscombe/WHYC | 1935–unknown | |
| | | | *JaJac*/Unknown/Unknown | Unknown | |
| | | | *Roberly*/H. G.Blake, Jr./HYC | 1947–c. 1954 | |
| | | | *Roberly*/Unknown/Old Lyme, CT | Unknown–1966 | |
| | | | *Shambles*/James Hayes and Peter Cannistraro/Scituate, MA | c. 1966–1977 | |

| Hull # | Sail #(s) | Year Built | Name/Owner/Club or Place | Dates Owned | Remarks |
|---|---|---|---|---|---|
| | | | *Shambles*/Unknown/Unknown | 1977–1983 | Owner a Coast Guardsman. Believed never launched. Missing since 1983. |
| | #7 | 1914 | *Bobwhite*/Franklin Robinson/WYC | 1914–1915 | |
| | | | *Patsy*/Jack Tiernan/WYC | 1915–1929 | Campaigned by W. S. Day of WYC in 1919 and 1920 as #29 *Gannett*. |
| | #29 | | *Patsy*/Morris Ernst/Nantucket, MA | c. 1930–1937 | |
| | | | *Valkyrie*/Carl Barus/BRYC | 1938–1952 | |
| | | | *Valkyrie*/Robert W. Small/BRYC | 1953–1959 | |
| | #7 | | *Valkyrie*/Arthur W. Frostholm/BRYC | 1959–1961 | Purchased in Oct. Assumed original sail number. |
| | | | *Valkyrie*/James and Meg Ryan/Jamaica Plain, MA | 1961–1962 | Moored at Quincy. |
| | | | *Valkyrie*/Doug Higham/WYC | 1962–1964 | |
| | | | *Valkyrie*/Giles Wanamaker/Orleans, MA | 1965–1966 | |
| | | | *Tirza*/Richard "Deke" Ulian/WYC | 1967–2005 | Tirzah: Hebrew for "She is my delight." (It was also the name of boatbuilder Horace Manley Crosby's grandmother.) Dropping of the "h" is more modern spelling. |
| | | | *Tirza*/Museum of Yachting/Newport, RI | 2005–2013 | |
| | | | *Tirza*/Mark Sutherland/S. Yarmouth, MA | 2013–present | |
| | #8 | 1914 | *Snark*/J. P. Burton/WYC. | c. 1915–1921 | Speculative that boat not sold until 1915 or later to Burton who appears as owner in 1921. Photo in *The Rudder* for April 1915 but no name on transom. |
| | | | *Snark*/Ed Sheet/WYC | 1922–1925 | |
| | | | *Sea Dog*/John W. and De Witt Hornor/WYC | 1926–1937 | |
| | | | *Sea Dog*/William A. Hickey/HYC | 1936–1940 | |
| | | | *Jarec*/Robert Harris/WYC | 1941–1946 | Name from first initials of Harris siblings. |
| | | | *Sea Dog*/Heywood Fox/WYC | 1947–1960 | |
| | | | *Sea Dog*/Drake/WYC | 1961–c. 1965 | |
| | | | *Sea Dog*/Herbert Towle/Cohasset, MA | 1966–1970 | |
| | | | *Sea Dog*/William Spence/HPYC | 1970–1973 | Broken up at Hyannis Port, MA. |

| Hull # | Sail #(s) | Year Built | Name/Owner/Club or Place | Dates Owned | Remarks |
|---|---|---|---|---|---|
| #9 | 1914 | | *Harriet C.*/Joel S. Coffin/WYC | 1914–1918 | Presumed original owner. Coffin of New York, NY. |
| | | | *Harriet C.*/George Sicard/WYC | 1919–1920 | |
| | | | *Suno*/George Sicard/WYC | 1921–1923 | |
| | | | *Marie*/Dr. A.C. Wilson/WYC | 1924–1933 | |
| | | | *Marie*/R. D. Forgan, Jr./HPYC | 1934 | |
| | | | *Marie*/Dr. John Northrop/WYC | c. 1935–1938 | Damaged in 1938 hurricane. Further information unknown. |
| | | | *Mooncusser*/J. Whittaker/SHYC | 1947–1948 | Further information unknown. |
| | | | *Marie*/Wilton Crosby/Osterville, MA | as of 1953 | |
| | | | Unknown/Unknown/Unknown | Unknown | Wrecked at Hyannis Port, 1954 |
| #10 | 1914 | | *Scarab*/Tony Redfield/WYC | Unknown | Speculative. |
| | | | *Scarab*/Wilton Crosby/WYC | as of 1917 | |
| | | | *Qui Vive*/Franklin A. Park/WHYC | 1931–1936 | |
| | | | *Qui Vive*/David Barber/WYC | 1941 | |
| | | | *Mae Jay*/Unknown/BRYC | Unknown | |
| | | | *Heritage*/Unknown/Unknown | Unknown | |
| | | | *Sea Wings*/Charles "Chuck" Rowley/SHYC | as of 1947 | |
| | | | *Scrimshaw*/Hans Kahn/Kew Gardens, New York | 1970–1975 | |
| | | | *Shangri-La*/Dr. Lawrence Lubotta/Babylon, NY | 1976 | |
| | | | *Shangri-La*/Philip Strong/NYC | Unknown–2007 | |
| | | | *Shangri-La*/M. Christopher Mattoon/Dalton, MA | 2007–2011 | |
| | | | *Sea Wings*/M. Christopher Mattoon and Ed Stockman/Dalton, MA | 2012–present | |
| | #19 | 1914 | *Fantasy*/James Gaff Hinkle/WYC | 1914–1918 | |
| | #11 | | *Fantasy*/James Gaff Hinkle/WYC | 1918–1965 | Year of # change speculative. |
| | | | *Fantasy*/Mystic Seaport Museum | 1965–present | |
| | #12 | 1914 | Unknown/Unknown/Unknown | 1914–1926 | |
| | | | Unknown/B. W. Godsoe/WYC | 1927–1929 | Godsoe of Boston |

| Hull # | Sail #(s) | Year Built | Name/Owner/Club or Place | Dates Owned | Remarks |
|---|---|---|---|---|---|
| | | | *Whistle Wing*/Halfan Lee/WYC | 1929–1931 | |
| | | | *Whistle Wing*/Henry M. Kidder, Jr./WHYC | 1932–c. 1945 | |
| | | | *Pegasus*/Gardner Jackson/WYC | 1947–1948 | |
| | | | *Pegasus*/Walter Winship and family/WYC | c. 1949–1961 | |
| | | | *Pegasus*/Hevzio/Unknown | 1962–c. 1970 | |
| | | | *Pegasus*/David Kilroy/Newport, RI | Unknown | |
| | | | *Pegasus*/John F. Mazza/Newport, RI | as of 1976 | Rebuilt and returned to a previous owner. Missing since 1977. Possibly converted to a motor launch before falling into disrepair. Rig used in a home-built boat by Bob Wilkins of Bass River. |
| | #13 | 1914 | *Maxixe*/G. H. Fiske/WYC | 1914–1916 | Name could have derived from Maxixe candy consisting of chocolate-covered cherries. |
| | #25 | | *Maxixe*/G. H. Fiske/WYC | 1917–1919 | A painting by Cape Cod artist Charles Drew Cahoon (1861–1951) shows the boat with sail #25. See also #25 *Jolly Roger*. |
| | #13 | | *Maxixe*/G. H. Fiske/WYC | 1920–1925 | |
| | | | *Cockachoice*/N. Foster/WYC | 1926–1928 | Ownership/location after Foster unknown until postwar. See #13 of 1929. |
| | | | *Maxixe*/G. P. Wright and Betty Connors/SHYC | as of 1947 | Sailed by H.P. Gidney of HPYC in 1947 Edgartown Regatta, dnf. |
| | | | *Maxixe*/G. P. and W. H. Wright/Menauhant, MA | 1948–unknown | |
| | | | *Maxixe*/Eldon Workman/Scituate, MA | 1966–1968 | Workman of Norwell. |
| | | | *Bolero II*/George Curley/Scituate, MA | 1969–1971 | |
| | | | *Bolero II*/Gardiner Miner/Norwell, MA | 1971 | Broken up at Norwell, 1971. |
| | #20 | 1914 | *Ethyl*/Percy Melville/WYC | 1914–1918 | Melville appears in 1916 season as #20. |
| | #14 | | *Ethyl*/Robert M. Roloson/HPYC | 1919–1930 | Appears in race 1928–1931 results as #14. Robert was stepfather of Richard Burnes. |
| | | | *Ethyl*/Richard M. "Bunny" Burnes/WYC | 1931–c. 1952 | *Ethyl* was essentially a Roloson/Roloson, Jr. and Burnes family boat. Further dates unknown. |

| Hull # | Sail #(s) | Year Built | Name/Owner/Club or Place | Dates Owned | Remarks |
|---|---|---|---|---|---|
| | | | *Ethyl*/Paine/E. Greenwich, RI | 1970–1975 | |
| | | | *Foxy II*/Oscar G. Smits/Warwick, RI | 1975–1987 | Missing since 1987. |
| | #15 | 1915 | *Viking*/Horace S. Sears/WYC | 1915–1921 | Sears lived in Weston, died 1923. He may, or may not, have been the original owner. |
| | | | *Viking*/Harry L. and C. W. Bailey/WYC | 1927–1956 | H. L. was on 1928 regatta committee. |
| | | | *Syren*/Robert F. Hayden, Jr./Cotuit, MA | c. 1957–1968 | Boat ashore for unknown period before purchased by Hayden, Sr. |
| | | | *Viking*/Unknown/Mashpee, MA | Unknown | Believed never launched because of poor condition. |
| | | | *Rosemary*/Daniel R. Walus/Falmouth, MA | 1976 –1988 | |
| | | | *Rosemary*/Richard L. Colburn/Unknown | 1989–1995 | Missing since 1995. |
| | #16 | 1915 | *Mistral*/Gardner/WYC | As of 1917 | Built with mahogany planking and coamings. |
| | | | *Mistral*/Frederick.A. Day/WYC | 1920–1927 | |
| | | | *Mistral*/H. Gardiner Bridge/WYC | 1928–c. 1947 | |
| | | | *Mistral*/John Reed/Avon, MA | Unknown–1961 | Satuit Boat Club |
| | | | *Mistral*/David Hall and Ed Craig/Scituate, MA | 1961–1975 | Satuit Boat Club |
| | | | *Mistral*/Robert Vogel, Patricia Gilligan/Scituate, MA | 1976–1980 | Satuit Boat Club |
| | | | *Mistral*/Peter Gow/Belmont, MA | 1980–1989 | |
| | | | *Mistral*/Joanne "Joni" Bergen/Mattapoisett, MA | 1989–present | |
| | #17 | 1915 | *Ruth*/Thomas F. Baxter/WYC | 1915–1923 | H. H. Langenberg used the boat in 1921 and Chapin in 1923. |
| | | | *Mabel*/D. Stimpson/WYC | c. 1924–1929 | |
| | | | *Ruth*/Donald Ross/Easton, MD | c. 1930–c. 1941 | |
| | | | *Whisper*/Peter Murr/Osterville, MA | Unknown–1957 | Abandoned at Osterville, MA. |
| | #21 | 1916 | *Gull*/Channing McGregory Wells/WYC | 1916–1918 | No known relation between Channing Wells and W. F. and J. E. Wells who entered two races in July 1916, sailing *Peggy*. |
| | #28 | | *Gull*/Channing McGregory Wells/WYC | 1919–1929 | |
| | | | *Gull*/Greg and Betty Wells/WYC | 1930–1934 | |
| | | | *Gull*/C. M. Wells, Jr./WYC | 1935–1938 | |

| Hull # | Sail #(s) | Year Built | Name/Owner/Club or Place | Dates Owned | Remarks |
|--------|-----------|------------|--------------------------|-------------|---------|
| | | | *Gull*/George A. Parsons/WYC | 1939–c.1946 | |
| | | | *Gull*/Archibald Clark/SHYC | 1947–1951 | |
| | | | *Sea Star*/Carter B. Helton/HPYC | 1952–1955 | |
| | | | *Sea Star*/Charles Francis Loutrel/HPYC | c. 1956 | |
| | | | *Sea Star*/R. Woodward/Mystic, CT | c. 1972 | |
| | | | Unknown/Timothy Bailey/Chatham, MA | 1980 | |
| | | | *Persephone*/Christopher Page/HPYC | 1973–1978 | |
| | | | *Persephone*/Unknown/Unknown | 1979–1982 | |
| | | | *Persephone*/David Bourque/HPYC | 1983–1990 | |
| | | | No name/Jay Christopher/Forestdale, MA | 1991–1994 | Broken up at Forestdale, MA. |
| | #22 | 1916 | *Tomboy*/Edward C. Crossett/WYC | 1916–1935 | |
| | | | *Tomboy*/James Robertson MacColl III/WYC | 1936–1939 | Jack Kennedy crewed on the boat. Not listed in 1940 roster. |
| | | | *Barnacle Belle*/William M. Shedden/WYC | 1941–1946 | |
| | | | *Tomboy*/R. Smith/Cotuit, MA | 1947–1948 | Further dates unknown. |
| | | | *Tomboy*/Manter Hall School/Wianno, MA | 1954–1961 | |
| | | | *Tomboy*/Robert O'Rourke/HPYC | as of 1966–1969 | |
| | | | *Defiance*/Raymond O. Kittila/Lewis Bay, MA | 1970–c. 1975 | |
| | | | *Ambition*/Douglas Cameron/BRYC | as of 1976 | |
| | | | No name/William P. Boland, Jr. family/W. Yarmouth, MA | 1988–1994 | Broken up at Yarmouth, MA. |
| | #24 | 1916 | *Which*/Arthur H. Gilbert/WYC | 1916–1921 | First reference is a race in August 1917. |
| | | | *Mary L*/J. F. Syme/WYC | 1921–1931 | |
| | | | *Dimbula*/Theo. Frothingham/BRYC | 1933–1938 | *Dimbula* was name of the vessel in Rudyard Kipling's impressive story "The Ship that Found Herself" published in 1898. |
| | | | *Dimbula*/Earle Fox/BRYC | 1939–c. 1946 | Last reference to #24 was 1940. |
| | #27 | | *Rhapsody*/Lebaron Church/SHYC | 1947–1956 | |
| | | | *Dauntless*/Dr. Rodger Currie/HPYC | 1961 | |

| Hull # | Sail #(s) | Year Built | Name/Owner/Club or Place | Dates Owned | Remarks |
|---|---|---|---|---|---|
| | #109 | | *Watch Out*/Eddie Gallagher/HPYC | 1962–1965 | Sold fall '64–winter '65. Raced w/#109 sails provided by owner of #109. |
| | #27 | | *Watch Out*/Michael A. Trotto/Hyannis, MA | 1966–1990 | |
| | | | *Watch Out*/Christopher R. Scott/Unknown | 1990–1991 | Broken up at Hyannis, MA |
| | #26 | 1917 | *Whisper*/George T. Cobb/BRYC | 1917–unknown | |
| | | | *Whisper*/O. Lawton/WYC | as of 1928 | |
| | | | *Whisper*/Mrs. B. F. Sturtevant/Branford, CT | 1935–1948 | |
| | | | *Whisper*/Peter Stanford/CT | 1947–1970 | Cabin modified for cruising. |
| | | | *Whisper*/Stuart Craig/W. Haven, CT | 1970–1975 | |
| | | | *Whisper*/Christopher Duhaime/Guilford, CT | 1975–1982 | Cb removed. |
| | | | *Whisper*/Peter and Norman Stanford, Taylor Montgomery/CT | 1982–2010 | |
| | | | *Whisper*/M. Christopher Mattoon/Dalton, MA | 2010–present | |
| | #30 | 1917 | Unknown/Unknown/Unknown | Unknown | Owner may have been George T. Cobb if he didn't own #26. |
| | | | Unknown/Joseph King/Chicago, IL | as of 1935 | |
| | | | *Fancy Free*/Bruce Loucks and Richard Freund/Traverse City, MI | 1976–1989 | |
| | | | *Fancy Free*/Elaine Brigman/Traverse City, MI | 1990 | Sold after brief ownership. |
| | | | *Fancy Free*/Norman Dill/Traverse City, MI | 1990–1994 | Sold c. 1994 to two partners with plans to rebuild. Whereabouts/status unknown. |
| | #31 | 1917 | *Iky*/Irving K. Taylor/BRYC | 1917–unknown | |
| | | | *Spindrift*/Smith O. Dexter/Westport. CT | 1935–1939 | No relation to #61 *Spindrift*. |
| | | | *Riptide*/Dorothy "Dot" Winship/HPYC | 1939–1948 | |
| | | | *Riptide*/Ralph H. Lincoln/Manchester YC | Unknown–1957 | Cb removed. Bill Crosby note of Nov. 1975: "Sold—last seen at Crocker's Yard—Manchester, MA—Poor condition." |
| | #33 | 1917 | *Water Nymph*/Dr. Fritz Talbot/WYC | 1917–1932 | |
| | | | *Water Nymph*/Herbert D. Merrick/HPYC | 1933–1935 | Further dates unknown. |
| | | | *Pinafore*/Spencer Gordon/BRYC | 1947–1948 | |
| | | | *Allegro III*/Seymour/BRYC | Unknown | |

| Hull # | Sail #(s) | Year Built | Name/Owner/Club or Place | Dates Owned | Remarks |
|---|---|---|---|---|---|
| | | | *Limpopo*/John P. Ianiello/Mystic, CT | c. 1970–1979 | |
| | | | *Limpopo*/Ned Reynolds/Newport, RI | as of 1980 | |
| | | | *Limpopo*/Keith McManus/Newport, RI | as of 1988 | Further dates unknown. |
| | #35 | 1917 | *Sylmar*/George C. Graves/WYC | 1917–1925 | |
| | | | *Sylmar*/H. H. Langenberg/WYC | 1926 | |
| | | | *Lindy*/H. H. Langenberg/WYC | 1927–1934 | Charles Lindbergh, "Lucky Lindy," flew the Atlantic in 1927. |
| | | | *Jane*/John A. Holmes/HPYC | 1934–1935 | |
| | | | *Jane*/Harold W. Dodds/Waquoit, MA | 1935–1955 | President of Princeton University. |
| | | | *Jane*/Dana G. Munro/Waquoit, MA | c. 1970–c. 1987 | Munro and Dodds were close friends and shared boat — using it for daysailing — before Munro assumed responsibility. Boat needed extensive work and was sold through Edwards Boat Yard in E. Falmouth. Further information unknown. |
| | #36 | 1917 | Unknown/Unknown/Unknown | 1917–1918 | |
| | | | *Mimi*/W. R. "Pop" Sinclair/WYC and HPYC | 1919–1932 | Named after Sinclair's wife Emily, known as "Mimi." Campaigned with skipper Fred Scudder. |
| | | | *Mimi*/B. Ellis and R. D. Forgan/HPYC | 1933–1934 | |
| | | | *Mimi*/William R. Sinclair/HPYC | 1935–1956 | |
| | | | *Mimi*/Louis and Dody Loutrel/HPYC | 1956–1996 | Fiberglassed by Mattapoisett boatbuilder Allan Vaitses in the early '80s. |
| | | | *Mimi*/Mass. Maritime Academy | 1997–2006 | |
| | | | *Mimi*/Peter Taylor/Cotuit, MA | 2006–2009 | |
| | | | *Mimi*/Todd Palavanchi/Plymouth, MA | 2009–present | Rebuilt at Berkshire Wooden Boat. |
| | #41 | 1918 | *Buella*/Rene E. Paine/WYC | 1918–1923 | Named for Mrs. Paine. |
| | | | *Halcyon*/James R. and Norman A. MacColl/WYC | 1928–1934 | |
| | | | *Halcyon*/J. J. Daly/WYC | 1935–1941 | Lewis Bay YC as of '39. |
| | | | *Halcyon*/Cort Mather/Falmouth, MA | Unknown | Mather from Brockton. |

| Hull # | Sail #(s) | Year Built | Name/Owner/Club or Place | Dates Owned | Remarks |
|--------|-----------|------------|--------------------------|-------------|---------|
| | | | *Halcyon*/Cameron and Ann Baird/Scituate, MA | 1964–1970 | When purchased, boat was water-filled in a marsh. Some restoration including fg decks. |
| | | | *Halcyon*/Unknown/Unknown | Unknown | Further information unknown |
| | | | *Halcyon*/Saul Crasny/Megansett Yacht Club | 1975–1988 | Cb removed and boat partly renovated by cold-molding cedar over existing hull. |
| | | | *Halcyon*/M. Charles Capra/W. Wareham, MA | 1988–2008 | |
| | | | *Halcyon*/Wianno Senior Italia/Grosseto, Italy | 2008–present | Restored. |
| | #40 | 1920 | *Vashti*/William A. Thibodeau/WYC | 1920–1921 | "Vashti" is Persian for beauty or goodness. |
| | | | *Vashti*/B. V. White/WYC | 1922–1927 | |
| | | | *Vashti*/B. O. Gerrish/WYC | 1928 | Gerrish of Charlestown, MA. |
| | | | *Vashti*/Malcolm Chace and A. B. Chace III/WYC | 1929–1932 | Chace of Providence, RI. |
| | | | *Vashti*/William R. Kales/SHYC | 1933–1956 | |
| | | | *Vashti*/Watson Small/SHYC | 1956–1964 | |
| | | | *Vashti*/Steve Smalley/SHYC | 1964–1966 | |
| | | | *Vashti*/Kelley/SHYC | 1967 | 1967–1970 |
| | | | *Vashti*/Daniel J. Kelleher/HPYC | 1970–1976 | |
| | | | *Vashti*/Ken Lincoln/E. Dennis, MA | 1976–1992 | Broken up at S. Dennis, MA. |
| | #42 | 1920 | *A.R.E.M.*/Mitchell/WYC | 1921–1924 | |
| | | | *Arem*/George Field/WYC | 1925–1929 | Raced at WYC until moving to Falmouth. Field of Buffalo, NY. |
| | | | Unknown/J. L. Richards/W. Falmouth, MA | 1929 | Further dates unknown. Richards of Boston. |
| | | | *Golden Eagle*/Doug Higham/Osterville, MA | 1958–1961 | Rebuilt by Higham at Crosby's with raised flush deck, higher cabin, inboard. |
| | | | *Golden Eagle*/John Hastings/BRYC | 1961–1972 | Doghouse added. |
| | | | *Golden Eagle*/Allan Jones/Osterville, MA | 1972–1975 | |
| | | | *Golden Eagle*/Jack Smith/Osterville, MA | 1975–1978 | |
| | | | *Golden Eagle*/Mrs. Dorothy R. Smith/Osterville, MA | 1978–1995 | Given to Dorothy's brother Brian and left at Norton shipyard. Believe broken up in late '90s but date/circumstances unknown. |

| Hull # | Sail #(s) | Year Built | Name/Owner/Club or Place | Dates Owned | Remarks |
|---|---|---|---|---|---|
| #43 | 1921 | *Unquomonk*/R. Stewart Kilborne, Jr./WYC | 1919–c. 1927 | Year of sale unknown. |
| | | | *Pequod*/Louis Loutrel/WYC | 1932–1939 | |
| | | | *Pequod*/Walker F. Frederick/SHYC | 1936–1941 | |
| | | | *Pequod*/Walker/Buzzards Bay, MA | as of 1948 | Further dates unknown. |
| | | | *Rikajo*/George Spalt/BRYC | 1954–1956 | Further dates unknown. |
| | | | *Wanderer II*/George Haskins/HYC | as of 1970 | |
| | | | *Wanderer*/Robert E. J. West/Bass River, MA | 1974 | |
| | | | *Wanderer II*/Theodore M. Boorum/E. Orleans, MA | 1976–1988 | Broken up at Wellfleet, MA. |
| #44 | 1921 | *Allegro*/N. Talbot/WYC | 1921–1929 | |
| | | | *Allegro*/J. Gates Williams/WYC | 1930–1939 | Raced at HPYC in 1933 by Allan Gardner. |
| | | | *Spindrift*/Rowland/Mattapoisett, MA | 1940–1945 | |
| | | | *Surprise*/Dr. Benjamin Aldrich/BRYC | 1946–c. 1948 | Date of sale unknown. |
| | | | *Ruthie*/J. R. Ruggles/HPYC | 1954–1956 | Further dates unknown. |
| | | | Unknown/Bob St. Jaques/Unknown | 1960s | |
| | | | *Namet*/Joe Baptiste/S. Dartmouth, MA | 1970 | Name composed of Baptiste's daughters' and wife's initials. Daysailing and overnights to Cuttyhunk. |
| | | | *White Pearl*/William P. Senna/New Bedford, MA | as of 1976–1984 | Cb removed. Lost at Assonett, MA. |
| #45 | 1921 | *Phalarope*/C. A. Hardy/WYC | 1921–1928 | |
| | | | *Phalarope*/Phillip and Dorothy Goodell and family/WYC | 1929–1944 | |
| | | | *Phalarope*/Rick Keeler/Edgartown, MA | 1944–1946 | Keeler given boat to repair after '44 hurricane. |
| | | | *Argo*/Dr. S. Dana Weeder/HPYC | 1947–1956 | *See* also #121. |
| | | | *Evelina*/Gordon/HPYC | 1961–1970 | Centerboard removed. |
| | | | *Evelina*/Richard Haskins/HPYC | as of 1975 | |
| | | | *Evelina*/Penn Colbert/E. Orleans, MA | 1976–1978 | Broken up at Orleans, MA. |
| #46 | 1921 | Unknown/Unknown/Unknown | | No pre-war ownership history. |
| | | | *Blue Boy III*/F. Gardner Schirmer/HPYC | 1947–1955 | |

| Hull # | Sail #(s) | Year Built | Name/Owner/Club or Place | Dates Owned | Remarks |
|--------|-----------|------------|--------------------------|-------------|---------|
| | | | *Freelance*/Frank. M. Babbitt, Jr./Westport, MA | Unknown | Further information unknown. |
| | | | *Freelance*/Maxwell F. Turner/Westport, MA | Unknown | Further information unknown. |
| | | | *Kari*/Robert Metcalf/S. Dartmouth, MA | as of 1970 | Further information unknown. |
| | | | *Kari*/Jeffrey T. Fanning/Scituate, MA | as of 1977 | Broken up at Warehouse Point, CT. |
| #47 | | 1923 | No name/Benjamin H. Hallowell/WYC | 1923 | Son of James Mott Hallowell (see #67). |
| | | | *Dorothy II*/Benjamin H. Hallowell/WYC | 1924 | |
| | | | *Janabe*/Benjamin H. Hallowell/WYC | 1925–1935 | |
| | | | Unknown/L. Smith/Wollaston, MA | c. 1936–1948 | Further dates unknown. |
| | | | *Janabe*/Lewis Goddard/Wollaston, MA | as of 1970–1975 | |
| | | | *Ozly*/Erik Will/Sodus Point, NY | 1976–1988 | No cb. |
| | | | *Ozly*/David Young/Newark, NY | 1989–present | |
| #48 | | 1923 | No name/K.L. Green/WYC | 1923–1929 | A few races in '23 and '24 only. |
| | | | *Gogetta*/A. E. Van Bibber/WYC | 1930–1931 | |
| | | | *Gogetta*/Sidney and Mary Kirkman/WYC | 1932–1941 | |
| | | | *Rainbow's End*/Dr. Pickford/Chesapeake Bay | 1948 | |
| | | | *Bessie II*/Kenneth M. McIlvin/SHYC | 1961–1962 | |
| | | | *Bessie II*/Bruce Hammatt/Pleasant Bay | 1963 | |
| | | | *Pyxis*/G. Hammatt/Chatham, MA | as of 1970 | |
| | | | *Pyxis*/R. Hammatt, Sr./Orleans, MA | as of 1976–1978 | |
| | | | *Pyxis*/Glenn Plimpton/E. Orleans, MA | 1979–present | |
| #49 | | 1922 | *Peggy M.*/Morse/WYC | 1922–1924 | |
| | | | *Peggy M.*/Frederick G. Crane/WYC | 1925–1926 | |
| | | | *Thekla*/Frederick G. Crane/WYC | 1927–1937 | Renamed for Crane's wife. Pronounced "Tekla." No record for 1938–1946. |
| | | | *Bettahad*/Ross Richards/HPYC | 1946–1949 | Further dates unknown. |
| | | | *Bettahad*/Joseph Theriault/Cousins Island, ME | as of 1970 | Broken up at Cousins Island, ME. |
| #50 | | 1923 | *Felyrial*/Alexis du Pont/WYC | 1923–1953 | Name composed of the du Pont children's initials: Fe: Felix, ly: Lydia, ri: Richard, al: Alice. Bahamas by 1947. |

| Hull # | Sail #(s) | Year Built | Name/Owner/Club or Place | Dates Owned | Remarks |
|---|---|---|---|---|---|
| | | | *Good News*/Tuttle/Nassau | 1954–1966 | Rebuilt by Brown's Boat Basin, Nassau, 1960. Wrecked off New Providence. |
| | #51 | 1923 | *King Tut*/W. P. Thayer/WYC | 1923–1929 | |
| | | | *King Tut*/J. Mettler, Jr./WYC | 1930–1931 | |
| | | | *King Tut*/Lawrason Riggs, Jr./WHYC | 1932–1948 | Further dates unknown. |
| | | | *Golden Fleece*/John Flanagan/Harwich, MA | as of 1970 | |
| | | | *Lynne*/Fred Mulligan/Westport, CT | as of 1975 | |
| | | | *Simba*/Eric Neuman/Stony Creek, CT | as of 1976 | |
| | | | *Corsair*/Henry A. Young, Jr./Lake Minnetonka, MN | 1982–1990 | Restored. |
| | | | *Hilda*/Victor M. Tyler II/Chatham, MA | 1991–present | |
| | #52 | 1924 | *Green Dragon*/W. Y. Humphreys/WYC | 1924–c. 1931 | Presumed to be original name. |
| | | | *Green Dragon*/Eric P. Swenson/WYC | 1932–1949 | |
| | | | *Green Dragon*/H. and J. Moye/Unknown | 1946 | |
| | | | *Green Dragon*/B. and S. Graf/SHYC | 1947–c. 1953 | |
| | | | *Green Dragon*/Warren Wilhelm/Winthrop, MA | as of 1970 | |
| | | | *Aquarius*/Irving Gurwitz/Winthrop, MA | 1976–1983 | Rebuilt. Missing since '83. |
| | #53 | 1924 | *Altair*/George C. Hitchcock/WYC | 1924–1937 | Did not race. |
| | | | *Altair*/Gilbert P. Wright/WYC | 1938–c. 1940 | |
| | | | *Altair*/Mrs. F. L. Barton/WYC | 1941 | |
| | | | *Akela*/Donald Sutphin/Hyannis Port, MA | c. 1942–1954 | Wrecked in Hurricane Carol. |
| | #54 | 1924 | *Dovekie*/Charles N. and George Loveland/ W. Falmouth, MA | 1924–1937 | |
| | | | *Winita*/Robert E. Chapman/BRYC | 1938–1940 | Chapman raced during '38 but '40 was last date of ownership record. |
| | | | *Chaperon IV*/John C. Wells, Jr./SHYC | 1954–1956 | Further dates unknown. |
| | | | *Ro-Jan*/Dan Jackson/SHYC | c. 1961–c. 1974 | Fiberglassed. |
| | | | *Masada*/Richard Barton/SHYC | 1975 | Broken up at Harwich Port, MA. |
| | #55 | 1924 | *Dolphin*/Frederic M. Schaefer (Sr.)/WYC | 1924–1938 | |
| | | | *Saidee*/Wilbur C. Cook/WYC | 1938–c. 1945 | |

| Hull # | Sail #(s) | Year Built | Name/Owner/Club or Place | Dates Owned | Remarks |
|---|---|---|---|---|---|
| | | | *Maxixe II*/P. Letchford/WYC | 1946–1948 | |
| | | | *Gail*/Arthur Kettle/SHYC | 1954–1956 | |
| | | | *Gail*/George Spalt/SHYC | 1957–1960 | |
| | | | *Sea Witch*/Allan Ruggles/SHYC | 1961 | |
| | | | *Naughty Miss*/James Bartlett/BRYC | 1962–1973 | |
| | | | *Naughty Miss*/Eugene Prolux/BRYC | 1974 | |
| | | | *Naughty Miss*/Unknown/WHYC | c. 1975 | |
| | | | *Dolphin*/Maine Maritime Museum/Bath, ME | as of 1989–1994 | |
| | | | *Dolphin*/Stephen R. Kent/Boothbay Harbor, ME | 1994–present | |
| #56 | | 1924 | *Suno II*/George M. Sicard/WYC | 1924–1940 | Re-rigged marconi in 1927. Further dates unknown. |
| | | | *Ebb*/George Rockwood/SHYC | 1947–1964 | |
| | | | *Ebb*/George Spalt/SHYC | 1964–1973 | |
| | | | *Ebb*/Robert and Diane Meyer/Pocasset, MA | 1977–1982 | |
| | | | Unknown/Unknown/Unknown | 1982–1989 | |
| | | | *Ebb*/Daniel James II/HYC | 1989–present | |
| #57 | | 1924 | *Second Fiddler*/F. Edna Parlett/WYC | 1924–1941 | |
| | | | *Second Fiddler*/William Scott Sneath/SHYC | 1947–1956 | |
| | | | *Naiad*/Unknown/Unknown | | |
| | | | *Second Fiddler*/Walter Clark/Mattapoisett, MA | 1970–1974 | |
| | | | *Polly Ann*/Charles A. Maxfield/Mattapoisett, MA | 1975–1998 | Yawl rig. Engine installed. Raised cabin. |
| | | | *Polly Ann*/Carl Hoines/Fairhaven, MA | 1998–1999 | |
| | | | *Polly Ann*/Frank Webb/Mattapoisett, MA | 2000–2001 | |
| | | | *Polly Ann*/John Piernont/Unknown | 2001 | |
| | | | *Polly Ann*/John J. Gallagher/Scituate, MA | 2002–present | Poor condition. Ashore for many years. |
| #60 | | 1924 | *Malolo*/Harry F. Stimpson/WYC | 1924–1936 | |
| | | | *Suitzme*/H. H. Bernard/WYC | 1937–1939 | |
| | | | *Allecto*/Frederick E. Platt/WYC | 1940–1948 | |

| Hull # | Sail #(s) | Year Built | Name/Owner/Club or Place | Dates Owned | Remarks |
|--------|-----------|------------|--------------------------|-------------|---------|
| | | | *Allecto*/Mariana Lowell Barzun and Francis C. Lowell/WYC | 1949–1962 | |
| | | | *Allecto*/Robert Charles Butman/Nantucket, MA | 1962–1972 | |
| | | | *Challenge*/Roger Barzun/Concord, MA | 1972–1988 | |
| | | | *Resurrection*/Jeremy Robbins and Steven Brown/Osterville, MA | 1989–2000 | |
| | | | *Resurrection*/Thomas Griffin/Newport, RI | 2000–2004 | |
| | | | *Resurrection*/M. Christopher Mattoon/Dalton, MA | 2004–2008 | |
| | | | *Twila*/Stephen Lindo/Eastern Point YC. | 2008–present | Restored. |
| | #61 | 1926 | *Is Zat So*/Michael Lester Madden/WYC | 1926–1929 | Initially raced with no name on transom. *Is Zat So* was adopted by 1930. Father of John, Robert, James, William, and Grace Madden, Michael often went by the name "L." Boat raced by "L's" kids. Marconi in 1927. |
| | | | *Is Zat So*/John and Robert Madden/WYC | 1930–1934 | Practical joker John entered the boat as *Is Satan* in race on Sept. 3, 1930, finishing 20th of 24. |
| | | | *Spindrift*/John Madden/WYC | 1935–1954 | Michael Lester Madden also raced boat on occasion. Wrecked in Hurricane Carol. |
| | | | *Spindrift*/Boden/WYC | 1961–1965 | Rebuilt after storm damage. |
| | | | *Spindrift*/John Stewart/Scituate, MA | 1966–1969 | |
| | | | *Spindrift*/Francis X. Walsh, Jr./LBYC | 1970–1974 | Wrecked at Pt. Gannon, MA. |
| | #62 | 1926 | *El Cid*/John Lester Madden/WYC | 1926–1928 | El Cid was an 11th-century Spanish military hero and champion. Marconi rig in 1927. |
| | | | *El Cid*/Jean Kiley/WYC | 1929–1933 | |
| | | | *El Cid*/Jean and John "Jock" Kiley/WYC | 1934–1945 | John (b. 1917) and Jean were brother and sister. |
| | | | *Rondot*/Roland Derosier/WYC | 1946–1960 | |
| | | | *Rondot*/Dauphinee/HPYC | 1961–1965 | |
| | | | *Sea Bird*/George W. Beale/Osterville, MA | 1966–1972 | |
| | | | *Sea Bird*/Thomas Duncan/Osterville, MA | 1973–1974 | |
| | | | *Tir Na Nog*/Thomas Duncan/Osterville, MA | 1975–1984 | Broken up at Osterville, MA. |

| Hull # | Sail #(s) | Year Built | Name/Owner/Club or Place | Dates Owned | Remarks |
|--------|-----------|------------|--------------------------|-------------|---------|
| #63 | | 1926 | *Mimi II*/R. F. Richards/HPYC | 1926–1939 | |
| | | | *Mimi II*/John Eyre/HPYC | 1940–1941 | |
| | | | *Aeolus*/F. W. Packard/HPYC | c. 1954–1961 | |
| | | | *Yellow Bird*/Richard La Morte/HPYC | 1968–1975 | |
| | | | *Spring Bok*/William H. Wiseman/Chatham, MA | 1976–1983 | |
| | | | *Crow*/William Harney/Bass River, MA | 1983–1988 | Rebuilt keel, removed cb. |
| | | | *Crow*/Daniel Rowntree/Hyannis Port, MA | 1988–1992 | |
| | | | *Crow*/Steven N. Smith/Eastham, MA | 1992–2005 | Broken up at Eastham, MA. |
| #64 | | 1926 | *Natanis*/Kent and F. W. Matteson/WYC | 1926–1930 | Marconi-rigged for part of the 1927 season. |
| | | | *Natanis*/F.J.W. Diller/Huntington, NY | 1931–1948 | Further dates unknown. |
| | | | *Natanis*/James P. Jensen/Osterville, MA | c. 1960–1980 | |
| | | | *Anjou Away*/Jonathan Jensen/Mill Reef, Antigua | 1980–present | Son of James P. Jensen. |
| #65 | | 1927 | *Nonie*/S. B. Sutphin/WYC | 1927–1935 | Marconi. |
| | | | *Nonchy*/Dan Pettingill/SHYC | c. 1936–1948 | *Nonchy* for "nonchalance." |
| | | | *Nonchy*/J. W. Scarbrough, Jr./SHYC | c. 1954–1964 | |
| | | | *Nonchy*/T. M. Borum/Antrim, NH | c. 1965–1967 | Broken up at Antrim, NH. |
| #66 | | 1927 | *Peajay*/Owen D. Young/Riverside, CT | 1935–1940 | Further dates unknown. |
| | | | *Missy*/Martin Hird/Brooklyn, NY | 1970–1976 | Missing since '76. |
| #67 | | 1928 | *Wild Goose*/James Mott Hallowell, Jr./WYC | 1928 | |
| | | | *Wild Goose*/W. J. K. Vanston/Peconic Bay, NY | 1929–1940 | |
| | | | *Wild Goose*/Harold Lundin/New Suffolk, NY | 1970 | |
| | | | *Wild Duck*/James Bitses/Southold, NY | 1976–1992 | Broken up at Southold, NY, after tree fell on the boat during the "No Name" storm. |
| #68 | | 1928 | *Eleanor*/Dr. R. H. Wilds/WYC | 1928–1933 | |
| | | | *Eleanor*/H. V. Morris/WYC | 1934 | |
| | | | *Xara III*/J. Y. Means/WHYC | 1935–c.1946 | |
| | | | *Margo*/Robert Nordblom/SHYC | 1947–1954 | |
| | | | *Margo*/Robert C. Linnel/SHYC | 1954–1956 | Further dates unknown. |

| Hull # | Sail #(s) | Year Built | Name/Owner/Club or Place | Dates Owned | Remarks |
|---|---|---|---|---|---|
| | | | *Margo*/Raymond B. Carey, Jr./Rumson, NJ | 1957–unknown | |
| | | | *Margo*/Atlantic Highlands Sea Scouts | Unknown–1970 | |
| | | | *Salty Dog*/Keith Alfier/Sea Bright, NJ | c. 1971–1975 | |
| | | | *Bete Noir*/Frederick W. Gander, Jr./Scituate, MA | 1975–1980 | Sailed from NJ to MA. Uncovered at time of '78 blizzard, damaged by ice. |
| | | | *Bete Noir*/Robert F. Erickson/Scituate, MA | 1989–1996 | Broken up at Scituate, MA. Cypress planks in good shape but frames broken or rotted as were horn timber, deadwood, etc. |
| | #69 | 1928 | *Sunny*/W. C. Rich/WYC | 1928–1930 | |
| | | | *Sunny*/Henry S. Stone/WYC | 1931–1955 | E. C. Stone also raced. |
| | | | *Sunny*/John W. White/WYC | 1956–c. 1960 | |
| | | | *Sandpiper*/John Stathos/NYC | 1961 | |
| | | | *Sandpiper*/Bryce Kirk/City Island, NY | 1975–1988 | |
| | | | *Sandpiper*/Geoffrey C. Rodstrom/City Island, NY | 1989–1992 | |
| | | | *Sandpiper*/Edward C. Fullerton/Media, PA | 1993–2004 | Berthed at Rock Hall, and St. Michaels, MD. |
| | | | *Sandpiper*/Brian M. Connelly/Lewis Bay, MA | 2004–2006 | Sistering of frames and rewiring at Karl's Boat Shop. |
| | | | *Sandpiper*/Peter Fraser/Hingham, MA | 2006–present | |
| | #70 | 1928 | *Shuttle*/Clare H. Draper/WYC | 1928–1936 | |
| | | | *Shuttle*/Richard O'Leary/HYC | 1937–1938 | |
| | | | *Shuttle*/A. T. Simonds/WYC | 1939–1940 | |
| | | | *Sari*/Rudolph Homan and family/SHYC | 1941–1947 | |
| | | | *Sari*/Paul Brown/SHYC | 1947–1955 | |
| | | | *Sari*/Nicols/WYC | 1956–1960 | |
| | | | *Sky Sweeper*/Bob Lenk/WYC | 1961–1971 | |
| | | | *Hannah Screechum*/David A. Lewis/Osterville, MA | c. 1972–1975 | Converted to a launch. |
| | | | *Phoenix*/Frederick J. Ellis/WYC | 1976–1978 | |
| | | | *Phoenix*/Ken Shaughnessy/Bass River, MA | 1978–1987 | |
| | | | *Phoenix*/Ken Lincoln/S. Dennis, MA | 1987–1992 | Broken up at S. Dennis, MA. |

| Hull # | Sail #(s) | Year Built | Name/Owner/Club or Place | Dates Owned | Remarks |
|--------|-----------|------------|--------------------------|-------------|---------|
| #71 | | 1928 | Unknown/H. E. Griswold/WYC | 1928–c. 1931 | Cypress-planked. |
| | | | *Whisper III*/Mrs. Edward Roth, Jr./Vineyard Haven, MA | c 1932–1940 | |
| | | | *Whereaway*/Dr. E. P. Brown/Wianno, MA | 1956 | |
| | | | *Happy Thought*/Dr. C. Wesley Watson/Osterville, MA | 1970–1973 | |
| | | | *Happy Thought*/Ged Delaney/WHYC | 1973–1975 | |
| | | | *Swab*/Gary LeDuc/S. Dartmouth, MA | 1976–1980 | New laminated deckbeams at mast, refastened garboards, repair of rust-damaged deadwood. Sail cut w/o roach to balance boat. |
| | | | Unknown/Unknown/Woods Hole, MA | 1981–1982 | Missing since 1982. |
| #72 | | 1928 | *Alva II*/Harold and B. Blossom/WYC | 1929–1934 | No boat name for #72 appeared on roster until 1934. |
| | | | *A and P*/F. A. Waterhouse/Cotuit, MA | 1935–1939 | |
| | | | *Plover*/A .H. Castonguay/HYC | 1940 | |
| | | | *Mischief*/Joe Horne and Joe Horne, Jr./HPYC | 1947–1975 | Finished bright. |
| | | | *Mischief*/Richard Brand and Gordon Kraft/HPYC | 1976–1988 | |
| | | | *Mischief*/Andrew Mele/Kingston, NY | 1989–1993 | |
| | | | *Mischief*/Yourji Donskoj/Rondot, NY | 1993–2010 | |
| | | | *Bonnieux*/Rob and Anne Ames/Hyannis, MA | 2010–2012 | |
| | | | *Bonnieux*/M. Christopher Mattoon/Dalton, MA | 2012–2013 | Broken up April, at Dalton, MA. |
| #73 | | 1928 | No name/A. C. Brown/WYC | 1928–1930 | Owner also appeared as "Broome" on roster. |
| | | | *Skokie*/E. R. Johnston/WYC | 1931–1934 | |
| | | | *Vitamin D*/Herbert C. Morris/WYC | 1935–1941 | |
| | | | *Rosalie II*/Roswell Bassett/HYC | 1941–1942 | Boat rebuilt. Named for Ros and his wife Alie. |
| | | | No name/Ben Baxter/HYC | 1942–1955 | Ben had crewed for Ros Bassett. |
| | | | *Uncle Benny*/Connie Moore/HYC | 1956–1960 | Named in honor of Ben Baxter. |
| | | | *Uncle Benny*/Stan Moore/HYC | 1961–1973 | |

| Hull # | Sail #(s) | Year Built | Name/Owner/Club or Place | Dates Owned | Remarks |
|--------|-----------|-----------|--------------------------|-------------|---------|
| | | | *Uncle Benny*/Tabor Academy | 1973–c. 1979 | New maststep installed at Tabor by Eric Bacon, then a junior, in 1976. Wrecked at Cleveland Ledge. Litigation followed. |
| | | | Unknown/Unknown/Woods Hole, MA | As of 1980 | Owner was a carpenter. |
| | | | *Uncle Benny*/Karen Uhlaender/W. Yarmouth, MA | c. 1981–1991 | Green hull with white-painted coamings. Sailed for a few seasons and then stored in back yard. |
| | | | *Uncle Benny*/Thomas H. Morse, Jr./Wrentham, MA | 1992–present | Purchased for parts but fully restored 1994–1997 and hull painted the original red. |
| | #13 | 1929 | *Rajaam*/R. A. Amerman, Jr./WYC | 1929–1931 | While this hull would nominally have been a number in the 70s, it appears the owner adopted sail #13, an opportunity available because the original #13 was no longer racing and may have left Cape. Details unknown. In rosters, #13A has been applied both to this 1929 boat and the 1914 boat that originally carried sail #13. |
| | | | *Prodigal Pig*/Norman H. Batchelder and N. H. Batchelder Jr./WYC | 1932–1965 | |
| | | | *Live Yankee*/Howard E. North/Scituate, MA | 1975–1988 | Further dates unknown. |
| | | | *Live Yankee*/Paul Twohig/Scituate, MA | 1989–1996 | Missing since 1996. |
| | #74 | 1929 | *Firefly*/Henry A. Gardner, Jr./HPYC | 1929–c. 1960 | Presumed original owner. In 1939 only, Gardner listed as WYC, not HPYC. He may, or may not, have owned the boat for period 1941–1945. Raced by James Huidekoper on Aug. 31, 1935. Charles Shephard of HPYC placed 9th of 14 in the 1946 Edgartown Regatta. |
| | | | Unknown/Unknown/Milford, CT | unknown–1966 | |
| | | | *Firefly*/Robert Baldwin/Bristol, RI | 1967–1970 | |
| | | | *Firefly*/Robert W. McGuire, Jr./BRYC | c. 1971–1980 | |
| | | | *Ukelele Lady*/Jack Glynn/Lewis Bay, MA | 1980–1999 | Heavily damaged in 1991's Hurricane Bob. |
| | | | *Ukelele Lady*/Karl Anderson/HYC | 2000–2004 | Broken up at Harwich, MA. |
| | #75 | 1929 | *Senorita*/John H. Nichols/W. Falmouth, MA | 1929–1945 | |
| | | | *Tudie*/William Kimball/SHYC | 1946–1953 | |

| Hull # | Sail #(s) | Year Built | Name/Owner/Club or Place | Dates Owned | Remarks |
|--------|-----------|------------|--------------------------|-------------|---------|
| | | | *Kim*/R. M. Kimball/SHYC | 1954–c. 1969 | |
| | | | *Kim*/Eugene Thompson/Sandwich, MA | 1970–1974 | |
| | | | *Mint*/Harry Schaller/Hyannis, MA | 1975–1991 | Schaller is Thompson's nephew. |
| | | | *Mint*/Richard Sheehy/Osterville, MA | 1991–2003 | |
| | | | *Mint*/Richard Egan/Crosby Yacht/Osterville, MA | 2004–2005 | |
| | | | *Mint*/Stephen Bussiere/Bath, NC | 2005–2006 | |
| | | | *Mint*/Crosby Yacht/Osterville, MA | 2006–2007 | |
| | | | *Mint*/IYRS/Newport, RI | 2007–2013 | Broken up (April) at Newport, RI. |
| | #76 | 1929 | *Curlew*/Kenneth D. Steere/WYC and SHYC | 1929–1939 | Raced in '38 and '39 by Robert G. Guest, Jr of WYC and HPYC. |
| | | | *Hermanos*/Allan and Stan Priddy/BRYC | 1940–1975 | Name is Spanish for "brothers." |
| | | | *Hermanos*/David and Gregory Rehe/BRYC | 1976–c. 1988 | |
| | | | *Curlew*/Dr. William H. Langfield, Jr./Somerset, MA | 1988–1991 | |
| | | | *Curlew*/Robert McCauley/Bristol, RI | 1992–1995 | |
| | | | *Curlew*/Jeffery P. Cronin/Charlton, MA | 1996–present | |
| | #77 | 1929 | *Rita*/R. A. Stephenson/WYC | 1929–1939 | |
| | | | *Seagie*/Jerome Powell/LBYC | 1940 | |
| | | | *Dimbula III*/Ted Frothingham/BRYC | 1947–1949 | |
| | | | *Tail Wind II*/Frederick D. and Tom King/BRYC | 1950–2008 | Glassed c. 1975. |
| | | | *Tail Wind II*/Wianno Senior Italia | 2008–present | |
| | #78 | 1929 | *Seeadler*/Stanley R. Morton/WYC | 1929–1937 | |
| | | | *Seeadler*/William M. Taussig/WYC | 1938 | |
| | | | *Lancer*/William M. Taussig and William M. Taussig, Jr./WYC | 1939–c. 1953 | Sailed by John Bentinck-Smith for some races in 1940. |
| | | | *Lancer*/Charles G. Carter/WYC | 1954–c. 1960 | |
| | | | *Lancer*/Jeffrey Foster/WYC | 1961–c. 1969 | |
| | | | *Nancy*/Wayne Bellinger/Cotuit, MA | 1970–1976 | |

| Hull # | Sail #(s) | Year Built | Name/Owner/Club or Place | Dates Owned | Remarks |
|--------|-----------|------------|--------------------------|-------------|---------|
| | | | *Lancer*/David S. Isenberg/Woods Hole, MA | 1976–1978 | Keel area between cb and maststep reinforced with steel rod, fg, and epoxy. New hatch and gooseneck. |
| | | | *Manu La*/Dr. Robert G. Miller/Botsford, CT | 1978–2007 | |
| | | | *Manu La*/Shannon Collins/Cotuit, MA | 2008–2011 | Purchased sight unseen to restore. Boat was too far gone. Broken up at Cotuit, MA. |
| | #79 | 1929 | *Southlook*/W. Crane and W. M. Crane, Jr./WYC | 1929–1941 | |
| | | | *Southlook*/W. H. Snow/Unknown | 1945–1947 | |
| | | | *Snowbird*/K. Payne Martin/BRYC | 1948 | |
| | | | *Snow Bird*/John Young/BRYC | 1949–1969 | |
| | | | *Snow Bird*/Bruce Heick/BRYC | 1970–1975 | Fiberglassed. No cb. |
| | | | *Snow Bird*/Jim Goldsmith/BRYC | 1976–1987 | |
| | | | *Snow Bird*/Carlo M. DiPersio/Cotuit, MA | 1988 | |
| | | | *Snow Bird*/Michael A. Gallo/Chatham, MA | 1989 | |
| | | | *Snow Bird*/Karen Uhlaender/W. Yarmouth, MA | 1989–1992 | Purchased in June to use rig on #73. |
| | #43 | | *Southlook*/Daniel R. Adams/BRYC | 1992–1999 | |
| | #79 | | *Southlook*/Jon E. Knudson/Cotuit, MA | 2000–2011 | Broken up at Cotuit, MA. |
| | #80 | 1930 | *Neonym*/Whitney Wright/HPYC | 1930–c. 1960 | |
| | | | *Anniversary*/Hartwell/HPYC | 1961–c. 1969 | |
| | | | *Anniversary*/Ken North/Scituate, MA | 1969–1974 | |
| | | | *Sunshine*/Richard "Dick" Farrell/Scituate, MA | 1975–1976 | |
| | | | *Stephanie*/Francis E. Callahan/Dorchester, MA | 1976 | |
| | | | *Elizabeth*/Unknown/Pembroke, MA | Unknown–Oct. '86 | Owner had been a merchant mariner. |
| | | | *Ardent*/Philip J. Holbrook/HYC | 1986–present | Restored by owner from 1986 to 1989, cold-molded cedar over the refastened, faired hull. New mahogany keel. |
| | #81 | 1930 | *Ariel*/William T. Brown/EYC | 1930–1935 | |
| | | | *Jivaro*/Paul and Doris Bander/WYC | 1936–1938 | |
| | | | *Jivaro*/Richard Russell/WYC | c. 1939–1988 | |

| Hull # | Sail #(s) | Year Built | Name/Owner/Club or Place | Dates Owned | Remarks |
|--------|-----------|------------|--------------------------|-------------|---------|
| | | | *Jivaro*/Billy Sullivan, Jr./Cotuit, MA | 1990–1991 | Sullivan was son of New England Patriots owner. Boat needed repairs. Not launched. |
| | | | *Jivaro*/Dr. Michael R. Coppe/Cotuit, MA | 1992–2007 | Never launched. Broken up at Cotuit, MA. Remains buried in the back yard. |
| | #82 | 1930 | *Cave Canum*/J. P. Carney and family/WYC | 1930–c. 1953 | *Cave Canum*: Latin for "Beware of the Dog." |
| | | | *Gosling IV*/G. Cronin/WYC | c. 1954–1959 | |
| | | | *Lello Baby III*/Koch/HPYC | 1960–c. 1969 | |
| | | | *La Belle Esprit*/G. Everett Howes/SHYC | 1970–1979 | Broken up at W. Yarmouth, MA. |
| | #83 | 1930 | *Ippy*/Benjamin A. Rowland/WYC | 1930–1936 | Benjamin was older brother of George Rowland, husband of Carolyn Crossett Rowland. |
| | | | *Nandabid*/David Homan/SHYC | 1937–1940 | |
| | | | *Sovereign IV*/H. D. Meincke, Jr./SHYC | c. 1954–1960 | |
| | | | *Sovereign IV*/Harrison P. Bridge, Jr./WYC | c. 1960–1977 | Missing since 1977. |
| | #84 | 1930 | *Kypris*/W. E. A. Bulkeley/WYC | 1930–1934 | |
| | | | *Kypris*/A. and C. MacLeod, Jr./WYC | 1935 | |
| | | | *Kypris*/Joseph Mattison, Jr./WYC | 1936–c. 1950 | |
| | | | *Carol*/J. E. McKelvey, Jr./HPYC | 1954–1960 | |
| | | | *Carol*/William Gulliver/HPYC | 1961–1974 | |
| | | | *Summa*/Chris Blauvelt/WYC | 1974–1983 | |
| | | | *Summa*/Walter Schmid/Cotuit, MA | 1983–1985 | |
| | | | *Summa*/Unknown/Dennis, MA | 1985–1988 | Broken up at E. Dennis, MA. |
| | #85 | 1930 | *Venture*/David D. Steere/SHYC | 1930–1986 | |
| | | | *Venture*/John Kiley III/WYC | 1988–1998 | |
| | | | *Venture*/Osterville Historical Soc. | 1998–present | |
| | #86 | 1930 | *Fifty Fifty*/John R. Vanderbogart/WYC | 1930–1935 | Record unclear post-1932. |
| | | | *Omar*/W. G. Tyler/Baltimore, MD | c. 1947 | Further dates unknown. |
| | | | *Ulua*/Gerald F. Ursitti/Annapolis, MD | c. 1970–1996 | Broken up at Annapolis, MD. Rig and hardware remain. |

| Hull # | Sail #(s) | Year Built | Name/Owner/Club or Place | Dates Owned | Remarks |
|--------|-----------|-----------|--------------------------|-------------|---------|
| #87 | | 1930 | *Eroica*/Francis J. Danforth/Edgartown YC | 1930–1941 | Extended cabin and cypress planking. |
| | | | *Alert*/Edward "Eddie" F. O'Leary/SHYC | 1941–1953 | Used for a honeymoon cruise to Nantucket. First winner of BRYC Challenge Cup in 1956. |
| | | | *Alert*/Richard "Dick" P. O'Leary/BRYC | as of 1954–1956 | Brother of Eddie. Joined SHYC by 1956. Hull color changed from white to black because of bleeding iron fasteners. |
| | | | *Alert*/John and Anthony Correa/BRYC | 1957–1978 | Boat purchased by Edgardo A. Correa for his sons John and Anthony who raced and cruised. They refastened boat and replaced the keelbolts. Sailed to Westport Island, Maine, by 1971 and then to Bar Harbor. |
| | | | *Alert*/Nathaniel Bray/Brooklin, ME | 1978–2004 | |
| | | | *Alert*/Richard P. O'Leary, Jr./Dalton, MA | 2009–present | Boat spent over 30 years ashore awaiting restoration by different caretakers including Atlantic Challenge and IYRS (2004–2009) before being acquired by owner. |
| #88 | | 1930 | *Haze*/Henry K. McVickar/EYC | 1930–1942 | Extended cabin. Further dates unknown. |
| | | | Unknown/Unknown/Unknown | 1943–1945 | |
| | | | *Mitsipupu*/Richard Southgate/HPYC | 1946–1948 | |
| | | | Unknown/Hewing/Unknown | 1948–1956 | |
| | | | *Ocean*/James Melcher, Jr./Chatham, MA | 1956–1971 | Rebuilt 1961–62 with keel and raised deck. |
| | | | *Ocean*/Philip L. Azoy/HPYC | 1971–1988 | |
| | | | *Ocean*/Crosby Yacht/Osterville, MA | 1989–1993 | |
| | | | *Ocean*/Par-Tee Freeze Ice Cream/Hyannis, MA | 1993–present | Donated by Crosby Yacht to become a prop at miniature golf course. |
| #89 | | 1930 | *Adios*/Gerald Chittenden/EYC | 1930–1938 | Extended cabin. |
| | | | *Stymie II*/James Churchill/BRYC | 1938–1945 | |
| | | | *Blue Boy II*/F. Gardner Schirmer/HPYC | 1946–1947 | Believed that Schirmer chartered from Churchill. |
| | | | *Stymie II*/James Churchill/SHYC | 1948–1953 | |
| | | | *Lady B.*/J. P. Heinemann/Lyme, CT | 1953–1963 | |

| Hull # | Sail #(s) | Year Built | Name/Owner/Club or Place | Dates Owned | Remarks |
|--------|-----------|------------|--------------------------|-------------|---------|
| | | | *Spinster*/Thomas Marston/Essex, CT | 1964–1968 | Boatbuilder Marston wooded and caulked hull, added a foredeck hatch and used boat for cruising. Lost in boatyard fire at Essex, CT, Jan. 20, 1968. |
| | #90 | 1930 | *Hobgoblin*/Alex O. Vietor/EYC | 1930–1935 | Extended cabin. |
| | | | *Topaz*/J. Connant/N. Falmouth, MA | c. 1936–1940 | |
| | | | *Gemini*/Henry Hope/Chatham, MA | 1970–1989 | |
| | | | *Gemini*/Sarah-Anne Hope-Davis/Chatham, MA | 1989–1993 | Boat rebuilt. |
| | | | *Gemini*/Edson Eldridge/Chatham, MA | 1994 | |
| | | | *Gemini*/Charles L. Harrington/E. Dennis, MA | 1995–present | Derelict discovered by Sam Lawrence on 8/31/2013 |
| | #91 | 1931 | *Moby Dick*/William R. Scott/WYC | 1931–1941 | |
| | | | *Moby Dick*/H. J. Clapp/SHYC | 1947–c. 1953 | |
| | | | *Robwind*/Rodger P. Nordblom/SHYC | 1954–1974 | Given to Tabor Academy. |
| | | | *Robwind*/Tabor Academy/Marion, MA | 1974–1976 | |
| | | | *Due East*/Kenneth E. Hudson/HYC | 1976–1980 | |
| | | | *T.H.E. Guands*/Richard Guandalini/Lewis Bay, MA | 1980–1988 | Lost on mooring in 1988 storm when keelbolts failed. |
| | #92 | 1931 | *Francis*/Mrs. T. Thornhill Broome/WYC | 1931–1935 | |
| | | | *Varuna*/J. Stanley Churchill/BRYC | c. 1936–1946 | Varuna: a Vedic god of sky, water, and ocean. Stanley was grandfather of Robert Churchill. |
| | | | *Varuna*/Barbara Herrick/SHYC | 1947–c. 1953 | |
| | | | *Varuna*/H. D. Meincke/SHYC | 1954–1956 | |
| | | | *Varuna*/Earl C. "Chan" Hughes, Jr./SHYC | 1957–c. 1969 | |
| | | | *Varuna*/Donald Wright/Osterville, MA | 1970–1973 | |
| | | | *River Rat*/Charles "Chas" Orr/Centerville, MA | 1974–1975 | |
| | | | *Varuna*/Arnold B. Chace, Jr./W. Yarmouth, MA | 1976–1979 | |
| | | | No name/Douglas Pinney/Nantucket, MA | 1980–present | Fully restored by owner. |
| | #93 | 1931 | *Wiki Wiki*/F. Gardner Schirmer/HPYC | 1931–1938 | |
| | | | *Wiki Wiki*/Dr. Paul Henson/HYC | 1939–1948 | |

| Hull # | Sail #(s) | Year Built | Name/Owner/Club or Place | Dates Owned | Remarks |
|---|---|---|---|---|---|
| | | | *Wiki Wiki*/unknown | 1949–1954 | |
| | | | *Shangri-La*/Dr. Herbert M. Blanchard/Scituate, MA | 1954–1985 | Bought through Crosby's. |
| | | | *Shangri-La*/Christopher Scott/Scituate, MA | 1985–1991 | Broken up at Scituate, MA. |
| | #94 | 1932 | *Victura*/John F. Kennedy, Joseph P. Kennedy, Jr., Edward M. Kennedy/HPYC | 1932–1975 | |
| | | | *Victura*/John F. Kennedy Library/Boston, MA | 1976–present | Displayed seasonally at the JFK Presidential Library and Museum. |
| | #95 | 1931 | *Beacon*/Ann and Francis W. Bird/WYC | 1931–1941 | |
| | | | *Beacon*/Albert Rockwood/WYC | Unknown–1946 | |
| | | | *Sea Beast II*/Joel B. Davis/WYC | c. 1947–c. 1953 | *Sea Beast I* had been a Star boat struck and sunk by lightning. |
| | | | *Roweida VII*/S. A. Beggs/WYC | 1954–1955 | |
| | | | *Roweida VII*/William Danforth/WYC | 1956–c. 1963 | Renamed *Fleetwind*. |
| | | | *Fleetwind*/Manter Hall School/Cambridge, MA | 1964–1988 | |
| | | | *Fleetwind*/Osterville Historical Museum | 1989–1998 | Broken up at Osterville, MA. |
| | #96 | 1932 | *Patricia*/F. J. Hartwick/Oak Bluffs, MA | 1932–1942 | |
| | | | *Patricia*/Franklin Irving Sears/BRYC | 1947–1952 | |
| | | | *Patricia*/George E. Robertson/BRYC | 1953–c. 1972. | |
| | | | *Annabel Lee*/Anthony Olivieri/BRYC | c. 1973–1980 | |
| | | | *Del Viento*/Doug Nemeth/Phippsburg, ME | 1980–2004 | Broken up at Phippsburg, ME. |
| | #97 | 1932 | *Taravao*/Frank S. Bissell/WYC | 1932–1940 | Cypress planked. Originally built with 5 winches. |
| | | | *Sally Ann*/Richard E. Lincoln/BRYC | 1941–1988 | Sailed by Richard's son Ralph in later years. Named for Ralph's sister. |
| | | | *Barbara Ann*/Robert Haas/Yarmouth, ME | 1989–2004 | Broken up at Yarmouth, ME. |
| | #98 | 1932 | No name/E. F. Creekmore/W. Falmouth, MA | 1932–1936 | First Senior to be bronze-fastened and mahogany planked. |
| | | | *Gammoner*/Ward Detweiler/WYC | 1937–c. 1956 | George and Peter Detweiler also associated with boat. |
| | | | *Barca-de-Oro*/Unknown/Unknown | c.1957–c. 1965 | |

| Hull # | Sail #(s) | Year Built | Name/Owner/Club or Place | Dates Owned | Remarks |
|---|---|---|---|---|---|
| | | | *Barca-de-Oro*/William Southworth and Robert Cleary/Scituate, MA | 1966 | |
| | | | *Easterling*/William Southworth and Robert Cleary/Scituate, MA | 1967–c.1973 | Dewy Mark associated with boat as of 1969. |
| | | | *Hoot Mon II*/William R. Reeve/Quincy, MA | 1973–1981 | Lost at Wollaston, MA. |
| | #99 | 1931 | *Wiggle*/Harry and Gordon Wheeler/HPYC | 1931–1939 | Galvanized fastenings. Reaching the Wheelers' mooring required navigating a twisting channel, hence the name. |
| | | | *Wiggle*/H. Gates Lloyd,/WYC | 1940–1986 | |
| | | | *Wiggle*/Crosby Yacht/Osterville, MA | 1986–1993 | Abandoned due to cost to rebuild. Used as prop at miniature golf course. |
| | | | *Wiggle*/Par-Tee Freeze Ice Cream/Hyannis, MA | 1993–present | |
| | #100 | 1931 | *Hajo*/C. F. and W. A. Coffin/WYC | 1931–c. 1950 | Believed last boat to use galvanized fastenings after a remaining package was found at Crosby's and used for #100 and #99. |
| | | | *Hajo*/Floyd Coffin/Osterville, MA | 1950–1955 | |
| | | | Unknown/Unknown/Unknown | 1955–1970 | |
| | | | *Allambi*/Dr. Leighton Johnson/New York, NY | 1970–1974 | Marconi rig. |
| | | | *Allambi*/Mark Gere/Long Beach, NY | 1974–1975 | |
| | | | *Shadow*/Raymond Mitchell/Island Park, NY | 1975–1995 | Rebuilt winter of '75–'76. Painted black. |
| | | | *Shadow*/Charkowski/Island Park, NY | 1995–2000 | |
| | | | Unknown/Unknown/Mystic, CT | 2000–2005 | Missing since 2005. |
| | #101 | 1931 | *Quip*/Kenneth Boyd and family/WYC | 1931–1948 | |
| | | | *Quip*/R. R. Hallowell II/BRYC | c. 1949–1957 | |
| | | | *Scotch and Sofa*/Unknown/Unknown | Unknown | Further information unknown. |
| | | | *Le-Ri*/John L. Rugo/BRYC | by 1962–1966 | |
| | | | *Thunderbird*/C. and Esther Edwards/HPYC | 1967–1975 | |
| | | | *Thunderbird*/Earle Blinn/HYC | as of 1976 | Cb removed. Missing since 1977. |

| Hull # | Sail #(s) | Year Built | Name/Owner/Club or Place | Dates Owned | Remarks |
|--------|-----------|------------|--------------------------|-------------|---------|
| #25 | | 1933 | *Jolly Roger*/James R. and James A. Waller/WYC | 1933–1956 | Number 25 had been used on #13 for period 1919–1921 and then dropped. This #25 has been referred to on rosters as #101a, the number it has been more generally associated with. Sails exist with #101 and #25. |
| | | | *Estelle*/Evan Whalley/BRYC | c. 1957–1963 | |
| | | | *Saltworks*/Ralph M. and Robert B. Lincoln/BRYC | 1964–c. 1975 | |
| | | | *Maine Stay*/Theodore Weigand/BRYC | 1976–1980 | |
| | | | *Saltworks*/Chris Johnson/W. Dennis, MA | 1981–1982 | |
| | | | *Saltworks*/Robin Lincoln/Brooklin, ME | 1982–present | |
| #102 | | 1933 | *Letty B.*/J. L. Ladd/Pocasset, MA | 1933–1938 | |
| | | | *Winkle*/Dr. John Northrop/WYC | 1939–1948 | |
| | | | *Alito*/E. N. Oakes/Wianno, MA | 1954–1955 | |
| | | | *Eight Ball*/Robert R. Churchill/BRYC | c. 1959–1969 | |
| | | | *Black Slip*/Robert F. Hayden, Jr./Cotuit, MA | 1970–1985 | Name later changed back to *Eight Ball*. Broken up 1986. Fittings used on #181. |
| #103 | | 1935 | No name/John L. Handy/Barnstable, MA | 1935 | |
| | | | *Zephyrine*/Mr. and Mrs. Homer P. Clark/WYC | 1938–1985 | |
| | | | *Zephyrine*/Tom Hammatt/Orleans, MA | 1986–1989 | |
| | | | *Zephryine*/Robert T. Booth/W. Warwick, RI | c. 1989–1994 | |
| | | | *Zephyrine*/Kevin Curry and Bill Crane/Middletown, RI | 1994–2004 | Restoration partnership failed and boat destroyed. Rig donated to IYRS. |
| #104 | | 1936 | *Sea Hawk*/Montgomery/Black Pt., CT | 1936–c. 1942 | Further information unknown. |
| | | | *Sea Hawk*/George Lee Ulrick/Madison, CT | c. 1942–c. 1946 | |
| | | | *Sea Hawk*/Dr. H. B. Bradburn/Branford, CT | c. 1946–c. 1948 | |
| | | | *Hawk*/Stephen Tafeen/Norfolk, VA | c. 1948–1970 | |
| | | | *Hawk*/Lee's Yacht Harbor/Portsmouth, VA | 1970–1974 | |
| | | | *Hawk*/Douglas M. Armstrong/Virginia Beach, VA | 1974–1978 | Restoration hopes. Broken up at Virginia Beach. |
| #105 | | 1936 | *Fire Chief*/Raymond W. Lapham/WYC | 1936–1946 | |
| | | | *Fire Chief*/Joseph J. Bodell and J. Bodell, Jr./WYC | 1946–1955 | |

| Hull # | Sail #(s) | Year Built | Name/Owner/Club or Place | Dates Owned | Remarks |
|---|---|---|---|---|---|
| | | | *Fire Chief*/Joseph Bodell, Jr. and Vincent Bailey/ WYC | 1956–1966 | |
| | | | *Williwaw*/Steve Lawson/HPYC | 1966–1970 | Owner removed rig when he bought #152. Jeff Lawson (WYC) associated with boat in 1967. |
| | | | *Absinthe*/Randy Peffer/Chatham, MA | c. 1971–1975 | Rig replaced with that of #13 when it was broken up in 1971. |
| | | | *Williwaw*/Graham H. Ero/Stony Creek, CT | 1976–1988 | |
| | | | *Williwaw*/Paul D. Smith/Plymouth, MA | 1989 | |
| | | | *Williwaw*/John and Sean Kelley/Barnstable, MA | 1990–1992 | |
| | | | *Williwaw*/Mass. Maritime Academy | 1992 | |
| | | | *Williwaw*/Paul J. Rhude/Barnstable, MA | 1992–1995 | Broken up at Barnstable. Rig used on #152. |
| | #106 | 1939 | *El Cid*/John C. Kiley, Jr./WYC | 1939–1954 | The second *El Cid*. |
| | | | *Grand Rouge*/John Madden/WYC | 1954–1975 | |
| | | | *Blue*/Eliza Moore/WYC | 1975–1988 | |
| | | | *Blue*/Paul E. Stewart/Cotuit, MA | 1989–1995 | Restoration begun but halted. Broken up in 1996. Hardware, spars, and sails remain. |
| | #107 | 1941 | *Cherrissimee*/J. Pitcairn/Oyster Harbors | 1941–c. 1949 | |
| | | | *Whistler*/Dr. Nathan Talbot/WYC | c. 1950–1960 | |
| | | | *Whistler*/Dr. L. M. and Ellen Phillips/BRYC | as of 1961 | |
| | | | *Judge's Girl*/George S. Thenault/SHYC | as of 1984 | |
| | | | *Judge's Girl*/Russell W. Small/SHYC | 1984–1987 | |
| | | | *Judge's Girl*/David Agnew/Chatham, MA | 1988–1999 | Boat didn't sail. Worked on at Pease's Boat Yard in Chatham. |
| | | | *Namaste*/David Sclarow/SHYC | 1999–2002 | |
| | | | *Namaste*/James Jensen/Manchester, NH | 2002–present | |
| | #108 | 1947 | *Rijoro*/Arthur H. Tichnor/SHYC | 1947–1973 | |
| | | | *Alice*/William "Woody" J. Underwood, Jr./ Westport, MA | 1973–1995 | Sistered half the frames, fg deck, cb removed. |
| | | | *Alice*/Carol Long/Westport Pt., MA | 1995–1996 | Did not commission the boat. |
| | | | *Alice*/Devin Corey/Newport, RI | 1996–1997 | |

| Hull # | Sail #(s) | Year Built | Name/Owner/Club or Place | Dates Owned | Remarks |
|--------|-----------|------------|--------------------------|-------------|---------|
| | | | *Rijoro*/Federico Nardi/Wianno Senior Italia | 1997–2006 | Restored at Cantiere Navale dell'Argentario. |
| | | | *Rijoro*/Arturo Ferruzzi/Ravenna, Italy | 2007–present | |
| | #109 | 1947 | *Dungolphin*/Durban McGraw/HPYC | 1947–1976 | |
| | | | *Shenanigans*/Richard Egan/Crosby Yacht | 1977–1992 | |
| | | | *Shenanigans*/Dave Trimble III/WYC | 1992–2003 | Lost in Crosby boatyard fire. |
| | #110 | 1947 | *Mahaja*/Jack Moye/HPYC | 1947–c. 1953 | |
| | | | *Mahaja*/Carter Helton/HPYC | 1956 | |
| | | | *Carmike*/Carter Helton/HPYC | 1957–1960 | |
| | | | *Barry G.*/George Spalt/SHYC | c. 1961–1965 | |
| | | | *Barry G.*/John Moye/HPYC | 1966 | |
| | | | *Lollypop*/William Smith/SHYC | 1967–1974 | |
| | | | *Madrigal*/Howard C. Cahoon/Chatham, MA | 1975–1988 | Boat given to Howard by William Smith after the marriage of Howard to Smith's daughter Joanna. |
| | | | *Madrigal*/George W. Douglass/Chatham, MA | 1989–c. 2006 | Sold to unknown buyer. Missing since 2006. |
| | #111 | 1947 | *Sagittarius*/George Pease/Akron, OH | 1947–1948 | |
| | | | *Sagittarius*/Andrew Edmonds, Jr./WYC | 1949–1962 | |
| | | | *Sagittarius*/John R. Taylor/HPYC | 1970–c. 1981 | |
| | | | *Sagittarius*/Chester Hartshorn/Portsmouth, RI | 1981–1987 | |
| | | | *Sagittarius*/Christopher R. Scott/Portsmouth, RI | 1987–1992 | |
| | | | No name/Walter J. Kilguss/N. Kingston, RI | 1993–1999 | Later of Wickford, RI. |
| | | | *Josephine*/George Whitehead/Lewis Bay, MA | 2000–2004 | |
| | | | *Tribute*/Will and Martha Tracey/BRYC | 2005–present | When acquired, boat had been upgraded with many sistered frames, garboard and centerboard trunk work, new keelbolts, and the canvas deck replaced by Dynel. |
| | #112 | 1947 | *Spook*/Betsy Keating/HPYC | 1947–1953 | |
| | | | *L'Avenir*/John Nichols/SHYC | 1954–1955 | |
| | | | *L'Avenir*/W. C. Cook/HPYC | 1956–1957 | |
| | | | *Curlew*/W. C. Cook/HPYC | 1958–1965 | |

| Hull # | Sail #(s) | Year Built | Name/Owner/Club or Place | Dates Owned | Remarks |
|---|---|---|---|---|---|
| | | | *Glimpse II*/John Bentley/WYC | 1966–.c 1970 | |
| | | | *Me-Je*/Dr. Vincent A. Schaefer/BRYC | c. 1970–1975 | |
| | | | *Escapade*/Barry Plunkett/HPYC | 1976–present | Derelict. |
| | #113 | 1947 | *West Wind*/W. W. Sinclair/HPYC | 1947–1955 | |
| | | | *West Wind*/Lawrence "Renny" Damon/SHYC | 1956–1974 | |
| | | | *West Wind*/Tabor Academy | 1974–1975 | |
| | | | *Westwind*/H. Clifford Lundblad/Marion, MA | 1975–1989 | |
| | #75 | | *Westwind*/Paul S. Warden/Shelburne, VT | 1989–1993 | |
| | #113 | | *Westwind*/Edson B. Hackett/St. Albans Bay, VT | 1994–2005 | |
| | | | *Westwind*/Seth Meyer/Marion, MA | 2006–2010 | |
| | | | *Westwind*/Matthew R. Meyer/Marion, MA | 2010–present | |
| | #114 | 1948 | *Marlin*/W. R. Reynolds/WYC | 1948–c. 1953 | |
| | | | *Marlin*/Byron Ramsing/WYC | 1954–c. 1960 | |
| | | | *Marlin*/Alice Horn/WYC | 1961–1963 | Fred Scudder's daughter, Maureen Scudder McNulty, sailed with Alice. |
| | | | *El Cid II*/John Kiley III/WYC | 1964–1973 | Richard "Rick" Burnes, Jr. campaigned boat circa 1971–1972. |
| | | | No name/Charles P. "Brownie" Swartwood/WYC | 1974 | Cb case lowered to reduce leaking. |
| | | | *Eurydice*/Kip Gould/WYC | 1974–1986 | Cb removed. |
| | | | *Indigo*/Matt Borden/Ipswich, MA | 1986–1990 | Cruised to Friendship, ME, in 1986. |
| | | | *Indigo*/Thomas H. Morse, Jr./Wrentham, MA | 1990–present | Restored by Morse. Wintered at Sarasota, FL, in 1993. Spent several summers at the Museum of Yachting. |
| | #115 | 1948 | *Morning Star*/J. Lloyd Hawkridge/Unknown | 1948–unknown | |
| | | | *Morning Star*/Richard Bukay/Dedham, MA | as of 1954 | |
| | | | *Morning Star*/John L. Casey, Jr./WYC | 1961–1970 | |
| | | | *Blithe Spirit*/Dr. Warren Nickerson/Cotuit, MA | c.1971–1976 | |
| | | | *Blithe Spirit*/Lynn Bouck/Menemsha, MA | 1977–1978 | |
| | | | *Hazel Coe*/Katherine Kittredge/Menemsha, MA | 1979–present | Used for daysailing, local cruising, and as a liveaboard. Currently in storage. |

| Hull # | Sail #(s) | Year Built | Name/Owner/Club or Place | Dates Owned | Remarks |
|---|---|---|---|---|---|
| #116 | | 1948 | *Turmoil*/Charles "Chuck" B. Rowley, Jr./SHYC | 1949–1970 | Purchased for Chuck by his mother, Elizabeth H. Rowley. Name chosen to reflect the typical goings-on aboard during races. Boat was raced by George Rockwood of SHYC in 1969. |
| | | | *Turmoil*/Williams College/Williamstown, MA | 1970–unknown | Given to Williams by alum Charles Rowley. |
| | | | *Yonder*/Veronica Worthington/BRYC | 1976–1988 | |
| | | | *Yonder*/Alan C. Battit/East Hampton, CT | 1989–1994 | Woodworker Battit had reunited the boat with its keel and was restoring it at the time of his death. Boat deteriorated until broken up in 2002 by those who purchased the Battit home with boat still on the property. |
| #117 | | 1948 | Unknown/Ralph C. McLeod/Waquoit, MA | Unknown | |
| | | | *Bettayet*/Ross W. Richards/HPYC | 1954–c. 1960 | |
| | | | *Phebe*/Robert Gill/WYC | 1961–1972 | |
| | | | *Nemo*/Richard S. Cohen/Harvey Cedars, NJ | 1973–1982 | |
| | | | *Nemo*/Scott Freidgenevitch/Cheney, PA | 1983–2005 | |
| | | | *Justin B*/Howard A. Bauer/Palm Beach Gardens, FL | 2006–present | Restored. |
| #118 | | 1948 | No name/Crosby Yacht/Osterville, MA | 1948 | |
| | | | *Melody*/Hugo G. Huettig, Jr./SHYC | 1949–1964 | Bought for Huettig children Hugo "Kitt" and Deedee who raced. |
| | | | *Kim II*/William Kimball/SHYC | 1965–1975 | |
| | | | *Sea Lyon*/Thomas J. Lyons, Jr./BRYC | 1976–1988 | |
| | | | *Sea Lyon*/Charles M. Lyons/BRYC | 1989–2003 | Lost in Crosby boatyard fire. |
| #119 | | 1948 | No name/Crosby Yacht/Osterville, MA | 1948 | |
| | | | *High Barbaree*/E. T. "Ted" Barrett/SHYC | 1949–1969 | |
| | | | *High Barbaree*/Arthur and Jane Coté/SHYC | 1970–1988 | |
| | | | *Gretchen*/Edwin H. Yeo III/Harwich Port, MA | 1988–2002 | |
| | | | *Gretchen*/James Everson/Unknown | 2003–2005 | |
| | | | *Gretchen*/Karl Anderson/HYC | 2006–present | Derelict. Rig sold for use in #206 and hardware sold to Wianno Senior Italia. |

| Hull # | Sail #(s) | Year Built | Name/Owner/Club or Place | Dates Owned | Remarks |
|--------|-----------|------------|--------------------------|-------------|---------|
| | #120 | 1950 | *Marna*/Marjorie and Nate Hunt/HPYC | 1950–1955 | |
| | | | *Marna*/John T. "Jack" Fallon/WYC | 1956–2003 | Lost in Crosby boatyard fire. |
| | #128 | 1951 | *Gull II*/Archibald E. Clarke/SHYC | 1951–1956 | Although nominally #121, the boat's sail carried #128 in deference to Clarke's previous boat, #28. |
| | #45 | | *Argo II*/Dr. S. Dana Weeder/HPYC | 1957–1959 | Weeder used his old boat's (*Argo*) sail # for racing during this period without conflict with #45's then owner. |
| | #121 | | *Argo II*/Dr. S. Dana Weeder, Jr./HPYC | 1960–c. 1965 | |
| | | | *Argo II*/Dr. S. Dana Weeder descendants/HPYC | 1966–2006 | |
| | | | *Argo II*/Caroline Weeder Bickel/HPYC | 2007–present | Keel area fiberglassed by Dana Nixon Weeder. Some new frames circa 1992. Daysailing. |
| | #122 | 1952 | *Ko-We-Ze*/Safetee Glass Co./HPYC | 1952–1962 | |
| | | | *Ko-We-Ze*/Ralph Gibbs/HPYC | 1963–1965 | |
| | | | *Ko-We-Ze*/Larry Singmaster/HPYC | 1966–1969 | Appeared on 1967 EYC race results as "Go-E-Z." |
| | | | *Ko-We-Ze*/Mass. Maritime Academy/Buzzards Bay, MA | 1970–1971 | |
| | | | *Therapy*/Joe Grazulis/Scituate, MA | 1972–1974 | |
| | | | *Sundance*/Christopher V. Davis/Round Pond, ME | 1974–present | |
| #123 | #123 | 1962 | *Kialoa*/Mattison family/WYC | 1962–2007 | Longtime boat of the Mattison family, #123 was also sailed by the Rowland family in the late '70s. |
| | | | No name/Gerard Fournier/Centerville, MA | c. 2007–2013 | Broken up (May) at Centerville, MA. |
| #124 | #124 | 1962 | No name/Edward R. True, Jr/WYC | 1962 | Boat sold before construction was complete. |
| | | | *The Junk*/Stephen Morris/WYC | 1962–1976 | |
| | | | *Fayerweather*/Penn Edmonds/WYC | 1976–1979 | |
| | | | *You'll See*/Edward and Brent McFarland/Centerville, MA | 1979–c. 1991 | Boat midway through rebuild when sold. |

| Hull # | Sail #(s) | Year Built | Name/Owner/Club or Place | Dates Owned | Remarks |
|---|---|---|---|---|---|
| | | | *Avalon*/Thomas Quinn/Hyannis, MA | 1991–1998 | Rebuild completed by Karl's Boat Shop, Harwich, MA. |
| | | | *Twenty Two*/Boland Family/West Yarmouth, MA | 1998–present | |
| #125 | #125 | 1962 | *Fleetwind II*/William Danforth, Jr./WYC | 1962–1976 | |
| | | | *Cochenoe*/Donald F. Law and family/WYC | 1977–2003 | Lost in Crosby boatyard fire. |
| #126 | #126 | 1962 | *Tamwock*/Alan Ruggles/SHYC | 1962–1969 | |
| | | | *Gone Broker*/Lawrence G. Singmaster/HPYC | 1970–1979 | |
| | | | *Xiphias*/George and Richard Largay/WYC | 1980–1992 | Name is Latin for swordfish. Pronounced "see–p–ahs." |
| | | | *Ceallach*/Sean P. Kelley/HYC | 1993–present | |
| #127 | #127 | 1962 | *Rapparee*/Peter and Tim O'Keeffe/HPYC | 1962–1998 | |
| | | | *Rapparee*/Wianno Senior Italia | 1999–2000 | |
| | | | *Rapparee*/Mauro Piani/Grosseto, Italy | 2000–present | Fully restored by Cantiere Cerulli, Porto S. Stefano. |
| #128 | #128 | 1963 | *Dauntless*/L. Rodger Currie/HPYC | 1963–1977 | |
| | | | *Last Chance*/S. Richard Brand and Gordon Kraft/HPYC | 1977–1993 | Brand became sole owner in 1989. |
| | | | *Last Chance*/John C. Finglas/HYC | 1994 | Changed white hull to royal blue. Rebuilt deck and sistered frames. Added fg board and rudder. |
| | | | *Mariah*/John Rice/WYC | 1995–1999 | |
| | | | *Mariah*/Steve Wholly/Salem, MA | 2001–2004 | Changed hull back to white. Daysailer. |
| | | | *Mariah*/Kingston family/HPYC | 2004–present | Refastened, new decks. |
| #129 | #129 | 1964 | *Apres Moi*/Dr. W. Lawrence Wilde/WYC | 1964–1971 | |
| | | | *We're Here*/Connie Tracy/HYC | 1972–1976 | |
| | | | No name/Mellon Family/Osterville, MA | c. 1977–1988 | |
| | | | *Tradition*/Jackson W. Robinson/Brooksville, ME | 1989–present | |
| #130 | #130 | 1964 | *Manana*/J. W. and David Scarbrough/SHYC | 1964–1984 | |
| | | | *Avocet*/Bruce Hammatt, Jr./Pleasant Bay | 1985–2002 | Refastened, new keelbolts, and sistered 24 frames. |

| Hull # | Sail #(s) | Year Built | Name/Owner/Club or Place | Dates Owned | Remarks |
|--------|-----------|------------|--------------------------|-------------|---------|
| | | | *Avocet*/Louis Foy/Osterville, MA | 2002–unknown | Foy associated with Suzanne (last name unknown). |
| | | | *Avocet*/Dave Helmer/Harwich, MA | before 2007 | |
| | | | *Sorceress*/Karen Uhlaender/W. Yarmouth, MA | 2007–present | Restored. Maiden voyage in 2011. |
| #131 | #131 | 1964 | *Zurba*/Dr. Joseph A. Valatka/Scituate, MA | 1964–c. 1975 | |
| | | | *Pioneer*/Al Whritenour/Cotuit, MA | 1975–1980 | |
| | | | *Rima*/Warren A. Locke/Milton, MA | 1980–1990 | |
| | | | *Thea*/Peter Lane/Kittery Point, ME | 1991–1999 | |
| | | | *Thea*/David Lampton/S. Bristol, ME | 2000–present | |
| #132 | #132 | 1965 | *Resolute*/Robert and Ethel Kennedy/HPYC | 1965–2003 | Lost in Crosby boatyard fire. |
| #133 | #133 | 1965 | *The Stork*/Dr. Joseph N. Russo/WYC | 1965–1989 | |
| | | | *Circe*/John J. Spillane/HYC | 1989–2003 | Lost in Crosby boatyard fire. |
| #134 | #134 | 1965 | *Invader*/Lew Gunn/SHYC | 1965–1974 | Boat was painted Gunn's signature dark blue. |
| | | | *Kim III*/William S. Kimball/SHYC | 1975–1984 | |
| | | | *Heron*/David Sundelin/Mattapoissett, MA | 1985–1987 | |
| | | | *Kim II*/George Delaney/Falmouth, MA | 1988 | |
| | | | *Heron*/Lee Taylor/Mattapoissett, MA | 1989 | |
| | | | *Heron*/Lee Taylor and Dave Thompson/Menemsha, MA | 1990–1993 | |
| | | | *Heron*/Walter S. Teller/Chilmark, MA | 1993–2005 | Attorney Teller is son of Joshua Slocum biographer Walter Magnes Teller. Boat used for daysailing. |
| | | | *Blue Sky*/Rick Trotto/HPYC | 2005–present | |
| #135 | #135 | 1965 | *Hoya*/Fred B. Williams/HPYC | 1965–1979 | |
| | | | *Hoya*/Christopher B. Morrison/WHYC | 1980–1982 | |
| | | | *Kobold*/Lawrence family/BRYC | 1982–1990 | |
| | | | *Kobold*/Bill and Ellie Lawrence/BRYC | 1990–2004 | Bill and Ellie bought out shares owned by uncle, cousin, and brother. |
| | | | *Kobold*/Independence Seaport Museum | 2004–2012 | Broken up (May) at Philadelphia, PA. |
| #136 | #136 | 1965 | *Cirrus*/George Edmonds and family/WYC | 1965–2003 | Lost in Crosby boatyard fire. |

| Hull # | Sail #(s) | Year Built | Name/Owner/Club or Place | Dates Owned | Remarks |
|--------|-----------|------------|--------------------------|-------------|---------|
| #137 | #137 | 1966 | *Fantasy II*/Joseph D. Hinkle/WYC | 1966–1989 | |
| | | | *Fantasy*/Marcus Sherman/Hyannis, MA | 1989–2004 | Restored boat for resale. |
| | | | *Mistress*/Andrew J. Naporano, Jr./Short Hills, NJ | 1994–2002 | Missing since 2002. |
| | | | *Mistress*/Mass. Maritime Academy/Buzzards Bay, MA | 2003 | |
| | | | *Mistress*/Crosby Yacht Yard/Osterville, MA | 2004 | Missing since 2004. |
| #138 | #138 | 1966 | *Forget It*/Dr. Lawrence M. McCartin/WYC | 1966–1976 | Name based on Mrs. McCartin's reaction when her husband informed her he'd just bought a Wianno Senior. |
| | | | *Unforgettable*/Michael McCartin/WYC | 1977–1991 | Michael received the boat from his father and slightly altered the name. |
| | | | *Unforgettable*/Mass. Maritime Academy | 1991–1994 | |
| | | | *Unforgettable*/Christopher Macort/Unknown | 1995–1996 | |
| | | | *Unforgettable*/Barry Clifford/Provincetown, MA | 1996–1998 | |
| | | | *Unforgettable*/Steven Smith/Eastham, MA | 1998–present | Bought without ballast keel. Derelict. |
| #139 | #139 | 1967 | *Head Start*/Mrs. R. Sargent Shriver/HPYC | 1967–2003 | Lost in Crosby boatyard fire. |
| #140 | #140 | 1968 | *Snafu II*/Alton Churbuck/WYC | 1968–1992 | |
| | | | *Snafu III*/Marcus Sherman/Hyannis, MA | 1992–2003 | Restored. |
| | | | *Spirit*/Richard Egan/WYC | 2003–present | |
| #141 | #141 | 1968 | *Bettawin*/Ross Richards/HPYC | 1968–1973 | |
| | | | *Bettawin*/Spencer Richards/HPYC | 1973–1984 | Assumed ownership after father's death and daysailed on occasion. Raced by Steve Andrews of HPYC for several years. |
| | | | *Bettawin*/Dr. Robert A. MacBeth/BRYC | 1984–1997 | |
| | | | *Bettawin*/James A. Hardman III/Pleasant Bay, MA | 1998–2012 | New drifts, keel, and garboard. For sale as of spring 2013. |
| #142 | #142 | 1968 | *Cheerful*/John Fulham/HPYC | 1968–1971 | |
| | | | *Eight Ball*/Robert R. Churchill, Jr./BRYC | 1971–1987 | Co-owned with Kenneth Shaughnessy. |
| | | | *Eight Ball*/Karl Anderson/HYC | 1988–2003 | Co-owners: Henry Dane, Chris Cooney, Ian McNiece, Rick Bishop. Rig used in #188 after hull became unseaworthy. |
| | | | *Cheerful*/Timothy Fulham/WYC | 2004–present | Restored and rig from #143 (lost in fire) installed. |

| Hull # | Sail #(s) | Year Built | Name/Owner/Club or Place | Dates Owned | Remarks |
|---|---|---|---|---|---|
| #143 | #143 | 1968 | *Pertelote*/Francis V. Lloyd, Jr./BRYC | 1968–1990 | |
| | | | *Pertelote*/Timothy Fulham/WYC | 1991–2003 | Lost in Crosby boatyard fire. |
| #144 | #144 | 1968 | *Shamrock*/Dr. Francis O'Neil and Francis O'Neil, Jr./HPYC | 1968–2010 | |
| | | | *Shamrock*/Dr. John D. Fisk/Seattle, WA | 2011–present | |
| #145 | #145 | 1969 | *Tern*/Sigourney B. Romaine/W. Falmouth, MA | 1969–1979 | |
| | | | *Sovereign V*/Harrison G. Bridge, Jr./WYC | 1980–1989 | |
| | | | *Yankee Dime*/B. Francis Saul III/WYC | 1990–2003 | Lost in Crosby boatyard fire. |
| #146 | #146 | 1969 | *Brigadoon*/George M. Shannon/HPYC | 1969–1975 | |
| | | | *Defiance*/Dr. Robert W. O'Brien/BRYC | 1976–1995 | |
| | | | *Defiance*/Christopher J. Vallett/Nantucket, MA | 1996–present | Restored. |
| #147 | #147 | 1969 | *Intuition*/Robert Glenworth, Peter Ream/HPYC | 1969–1983 | |
| | | | *Incubus*/James H. "Jim" Light/BRYC | 1983–1986 | |
| | | | *Intuition*/James H. "Jim" Light/HPYC | 1986–1992 | |
| | | | *Intuition*/Jeff Hanaway, Ted, Barry, Colin Hoffmeister/HPYC | 1993–2003 | Lost in Crosby boatyard fire. |
| #148 | #148 | 1969 | *Madeline*/Richard M. Burnes, Jr./WYC | 1969–1991 | |
| | | | *Payster*/Chip Niehoff/HPYC | 1992–1999 | |
| | | | *Payster*/Christopher Wolfington/HPYC | 2000 | |
| | | | No name/Karl Anderson/HYC | 2001–2004 | |
| | | | No name/William Regan/E. Dennis, MA | 2005–2009 | |
| | | | No name/Karl Anderson/HYC | 2010–present | Derelict. |
| #149 | #149 | 1970 | *Akela*/Karen Bacon and Carter "Bink" Bacon, Jr./HPYC | 1970–2009 | |
| | | | *Ripple*/Bradford W. Tracy/HYC | 2009–present | |
| #150 | #150 | 1970 | *Orange Aid*/Lois Birmingham/WYC | 1970–1975 | |
| | | | *Orange Aid*/Lois and Frederick Wrightson/WYC | 1976–2001 | |
| | | | *Bella*/Robert Mangiaratti/Wellfleet, MA | 2001–2003 | |
| | | | *Yankee Dime II*/B. Francis Saul III/WYC | 2003–present | |

| Hull # | Sail #(s) | Year Built | Name/Owner/Club or Place | Dates Owned | Remarks |
|--------|-----------|------------|--------------------------|-------------|---------|
| #151 | #151 | 1971 | *Evergreen II*/Morton Rechler/Kings Pt., NY | 1971–2003 | Some winters in Manalapan, FL. |
| | | | *Evergreen*/Robert Limoggio/Osterville, MA | 2003–present | Damaged in Crosby boatyard fire. May be restored. |
| #152 | #152 | 1971 | *Vantage*/Stephen B. Lawson/HPYC | 1971–1977 | |
| | | | *Mathemagic*/John J. King/SHYC | 1977–1987 | |
| | | | *Spartan*/Mike and Brad Pease/Chatham, MA | 1987–1988 | Fully restored. |
| | | | *Spartan*/Richard J. Guandalini/Lewis Bay, MA | 1988–present | Family boat, daysailer. |
| #153 | #153 | 1972 | No name/Arthur R. "Randy" Greene/SHYC | 1972–present | |
| #154 | #154 | 1972 | *Lovely Lady*/Bruce Brown/Canandaigua Lake, NY | 1972–1988 | |
| | | | *Panay*/John C. Janowicz/Cotuit, MA | 1989–2007 | |
| | | | *Willow*/Rebecca Perry/Cotuit, MA | 2007–present | Frames repaired, recanvas deck, cosmetics. |
| #155 | #155 | 1973 | *Relentless*/Jeff Hurst and family/SHYC | 1973–2003 | |
| | | | *Relentless*/Ted Titcomb/Cotuit, MA | 2004–present | |
| #156 | #156 | 1973 | *Never Miss*/James P. Bartlett/BRYC | 1973–1993 | |
| | | | *Never Miss*/James P. Shay and Shannon S. Hayden/HPYC | 1993–2003 | Lost in Crosby boatyard fire. |
| #157 | #157 | 1973 | *About Time*/Gerarda Fulham/WYC | 1973–1985 | |
| | | | *Troika*/John Conathan II, Philip Danby, Michael Deeley/WYC | 1986–1988 | |
| | | | *Chanzia*/Lloyd "Mac" McManus/WYC | 1989–2003 | Lost in Crosby boatyard fire. |
| #158 | #158 | 1973 | *Molly*/Alan T. McDonough/WYC | 1973–1998 | |
| | | | *Molly*/Thomas Kennedy/Osterville, MA | 1998–2003 | Lost in Crosby boatyard fire. |
| #159 | #159 | 1973 | *Hibou II*/Theodore Nemeth/Sag Harbor, NY | 1973–1975 | Ordered boat but did not take delivery. |
| | | | *Quest*/William T. Kilbourne and William L. Henry/S. Yarmouth, MA | 1975–1980 | |
| | | | *Quest*/William L. Henry/S. Yarmouth, MA | 1981–2003 | Lost in Crosby boatyard fire. |

| Hull # | Sail #(s) | Year Built | Name/Owner/Club or Place | Dates Owned | Remarks |
|--------|-----------|------------|--------------------------|-------------|---------|
| #160 | #160 | 1974 | *High Barbaree*/Arthur V. Coté/SHYC | 1974–2007 | #160 was originally bought by Bruce Steere at the same time Arthur Coté bought #161. As #160 was Arthur's lucky number, the two agreed to alter their purchase arrangements and swap numbers. Boat campaigned by Mark Robinson in several Scudder Cup events in the late '80s. |
| | | | *Gretchen*/Edwin H. Yeo III/Harwich Port, MA | 2007–present | Daysailing. |
| #161 | #161 | 1974 | *Snow Goose*/Bruce M. Steere/SHYC | 1974–1994 | |
| | | | *Invader*/Lewis H. Gunn and William O'Connor/SHYC | 1995–1999 | |
| | | | *Snow Goose*/William O'Connor/WYC | 2000–2010 | |
| | | | *Sea Lion*/Peter McClennen/Chatham, MA | 2010–present | |
| #162 | #168 | 1974 | *Odin*/Rodger P. Nordblom/SHYC | 1974–1987 | In deference to the ownership of #68 by Rodger's father, class permitted use of sail #168 on this hull. |
| | #162 | | *Odin*/Ralph M. Lincoln/BRYC | 1988–present | |
| #163 | #173 | 1974 | *Stanley Steamer*/Stanley Moore/HYC | 1974–1980 | Built as replacement for #73 and permitted to sail as "173" so existing sails could be used. |
| | | | *Scarlet*/Dr. William O'Toole/HYC | 1980–1985 | |
| | | | *Scarlet*/Thomas and Jeanne O'Toole/HYC | 1986–1993 | |
| | | | *Scarlet*/L. Burt and Jeanne McManus III/HYC | 1994–2010 | |
| | #163 | | *Scarlet*/O'Toole families/HYC | 2011–present | As of Sept. 2011, required by Class to race with sail # that matched hull #. Day sailing in Duxbury Bay. |
| #164 | #164 | 1974 | *Flame*/Joseph L. Gallagher/SHYC | 1975–1985 | |
| | | | *Owl*/Richard S. Taylor/WYC | 1985–2003 | Lost in Crosby boatyard fire. |
| #165 | #165 | 1975 | *Cheerful*/Margery Fulham/HPYC | 1975–1981 | |
| | | | *Winnie*/Stephen H. and Samuel C. Croll III/WYC | 1982–1988 | |
| | | | *Catalina*/Robert W. Morey, Jr./HPYC | 1989–2002 | |
| | | | *Catalina*/George J. Kimmerle/Stonington, CT | 2002–present | |

| Hull # | Sail #(s) | Year Built | Name/Owner/Club or Place | Dates Owned | Remarks |
|---|---|---|---|---|---|
| #166 | #166 | 1975 | *Frieche*/Charles P. "Brownie" Swartwood III/ WYC | 1975–1979 | |
| | | | *Cheetah*/Eric K. Bacon/HPYC | 1980–2006 | |
| | | | *Cheetah*/Dr. Victor Cillis/HPYC | 2007–present | |
| #167 | #194 | 1975 | *Victura*/Sen. Edward Kennedy/HPYC | 1975–2009 | Sail # exemption granted by class in order to carry on tradition of #94 *Victura*. |
| | | | *Victura*/Chris Kennedy/HPYC | Present | |
| #168 | #216 | 1975 | *Turmoil Too*/James F. Ruhan, William Servos/ BRYC | 1975–1988 | |
| | | | *Turmoil Too*/Thomas B. Kivney/HYC | 1988–1991 | |
| | #168 | | *Perfect Timing*/Dr. Brooke Seckel/HYC | 1992–1999 | |
| | #168 | | *Buckeye*/Dr. Brooke Seckel/HYC | 2000–present | |
| #169 | #169 | 1975 | *Invader*/Lewis J.H. Gunn/SHYC | 1975–1981 | |
| | | | *Eowyn*/George Largay/WYC | 1981–2003 | Lost in Crosby boatyard fire. |
| #170 | #170 | 1976 | *Irish Mist*/Frederick J. O'Neal, Jr./Cataumet, MA | 1976–1982 | |
| | | | *Irish Mist*/Robert D. and Frederick Q. Watt/ HPYC | 1982–1995 | |
| | | | *Irish Mist*/Thomas White/Sandwich, MA | 1995–present | Last sailed in 1995. Derelict. |
| #171 | #171 | 1976 | *Sanderling*/Col. Dana G. Mead/BRYC | 1976–1990 | |
| | | | *Sanderling*/David Bourque/HPYC | 1991–2000 | Chartered by Peter Eastman for '97 season |
| | | | *Lady Luck*/Brad and Jeff Tracy/HYC | 2001–2003 | Lost in Crosby boatyard fire. |
| #172 | #172 | 1976 | *Lucky Lady*/Jay and Connie Tracy/HYC | 1976–1999 | Tracy family boat also raced by Brad and Jeff. |
| | | | *Athena*/Joseph E. Driscoll/HPYC | 2000–2001 | |
| | | | *Dixie*/Lucy Steere/SHYC | 2002–present | |
| #173 | #173 | 1976 | *Wynsome*/Jeff Clark/Irvington, VA | 1976–1987 | |
| | | | *As Time Goes By*/Robert J. Solomon/Portsmouth, VA | 1988–1994 | |
| | | | *Ptarmigan*/Maxwell T. Kennedy and Dirk Ziff/ HPYC | 1995–present | |
| #174 | #174 | 1986 | *Invader*/Lewis J.H. Gunn/SHYC | 1985–1990 | |
| | | | *Sea Lyon*/Charles M. Lyons/HPYC | 1990–present | |

| Hull # | Sail #(s) | Year Built | Name/Owner/Club or Place | Dates Owned | Remarks |
|--------|-----------|-----------|--------------------------|-------------|---------|
| #175 | #175 | 1986 | *Kikiriki*/Robert B. Horner/Nantucket | 1986–1997 | |
| | | | *Lucinda*/Chip and Kelly Niehoff/HPYC | 1998–present | |
| #176 | #176 | 1986 | *Lovely Lady*/Bruce Brown/Canandaigua Lake, NY | | |
| | | | *Lovely Lady*/Christine Brown/CYC | 1987–present | |
| #177 | #177 | 1987 | *Resin D'Etre*/David Johnson and George S. Thenault/BRYC | 1987–1994 | |
| | | | *Rapparee*/Peter L. O'Keeffe/HPYC | 1995–2012 | |
| | | | *Rebel*/Brad Tracy/HYC | 2013–present | |
| #178 | #178 | 1988 | *Betsy Ross*/John Seward Johnson III/Nantucket, MA | 1988–2003 | Lost in Crosby boatyard fire. |
| #179 | #179 | 1989 | *Outlier*/William Koch/WYC | 1989–1993 | |
| | | | *Senior Moment*/Rodger P. Nordblom/SHYC | 1993–present | |
| #180 | #180 | 1987 | *Touch o'Gray*/Fred B. and Lee S. Williams/HPYC | 1987–1999 | |
| | | | *Touch o'Gray*/Lewis Gunn/SHYC | 2000–2007 | |
| | | | *Touch o'Gray*/Carl Gustafson/BRYC | 2008–2012 | |
| | | | *Touch o'Gray*/Kevin J. Cusack/Oak Bluffs, MA | 2012–present | |
| #181 | #181 | 1987 | *Coatuet*/Robert F. Hayden, Jr./Cotuit, MA | 1987–present | Name is Native American spelling of Cotuit. |
| #182 | #182 | 1990 | *Lindy*/Alan T. McDonough/WYC | 1990–present | |
| #183 | #183 | 1990 | *Fantasy*/Joseph D. Hinkle/WYC | 1990–2005 | |
| | | | *Fantasy*/Lee W. Hope/Cotuit | 2006–present | |
| #184 | #184 | 1990 | *Invader*/Lewis J. H. Gunn/SHYC | 1990–1994 | |
| | | | *Lente Festina*/G. Kent Plunkett/HPYC | 1995–present | |
| #185 | #185 | 1990 | *Althea*/Charles B. Swartwood III and Richard "Rick" Burnes, Jr./Cotuit, MA | 1990–2003 | Lost in Crosby boatyard fire. |
| #186 | #186 | 2001 | *Amusing*/Steven Haley/Cotuit, MA | 2001–present | |
| #187 | #187 | 2001 | *Quartermain II*/John B. Wilson/HPYC | 2001–present | |
| #188 | #188 | 2001 | *Pieces of 8*/Karl Anderson and John Gregg/HYC | 2001–present | |
| #189 | #189 | 2001 | *Odette*/R. Bruce Hammatt, Jr./Tenants Harbor, ME | 2001–present | Sailed in Pleasant Bay through 2009. |

| Hull # | Sail #(s) | Year Built | Name/Owner/Club or Place | Dates Owned | Remarks |
|--------|-----------|------------|--------------------------|-------------|---------|
| #190 | #190 | 2003 | *Golden Summer*/Patrick Lentell/Cotuit, MA | 2003–2013 | |
| | | | *Golden Summer*/Bud Carmichael/Arlington, MA | Thru June 2013 | |
| | | | *Goose*/Alexander D. Whittemore/WYC | July 2013–present | |
| #191 | #191 | 2003 | *Novanglus*/Gregory Dempsey and Christopher Wolfington/HPYC | 2003–present | |
| #192 | #192 | 2003 | *Shadowfax*/Toby Hynes/WYC | 2003 | Lost in Crosby boatyard fire. |
| #193 | #193 | 2003 | *Ghost*/David C. Trimble and David C. Trimble III/WYC | 2003–present | |
| #194 | | | | See #167 | |
| #195 | #195 | 2004 | *Dauntless*/Brad and Jeff Tracy/HYC | 2004–present | |
| #196 | #196 | 2004 | *Aegir*/Bill and Ellie Lawrence/BRYC | 2004–present | |
| #197 | #197 | 2004 | *Cochenoe*/Donald F. Law, Jr./WYC | 2004–present | |
| #198 | #198 | 2004 | *Never Miss*/Shannon S. Hayden and James P. Shay/HPYC | 2004–present | |
| #199 | #199 | 2004 | *Heritage*/Antoinette "Toni" Fallon/WYC | 2004–present | |
| #200 | #200 | 2004 | *Aurora*/George P. Edmonds/WYC | 2004–present | |
| #201 | #201 | 2004 | *Shadowfax*/Toby Hynes/WYC | 2004–present | |
| #202 | #202 | 2004 | *Eowyn*/George Largay/WYC | 2004–present | |
| #203 | #203 | 2004 | *Dingle*/Thomas Kennedy/Osterville, MA | 2004–2012 | |
| | | | *Dingle*/Mark Shriver/HPYC | 2012–present | |
| #204 | #204 | 2005 | *Santa Maria*/Mrs. Eunice Shriver/HPYC | 2004–2012 | |
| | | | *Santa Maria*/Timothy P. and Anthony K. Shriver | 2012–present | |
| #205 | #205 | 2005 | *Courant*/Scott Doyle/N. Chatham, MA | 2005–present | |
| #206 | #206 | 2005 | *Mad Jack*/Jack Hamilton/HYC | 2005–present | |
| #207 | #207 | 2006 | *Madeline*/Richard W. Burnes, Jr./WYC | 2006–present | |
| #208 | #208 | 2006 | *Rhubarb*/Robert E. Schofield, Jr./Annapolis, MD | 2006–present | |
| #209 | #209 | 2006 | No name/Crosby Yacht/Osterville, MA | 2006–present | |
| #210 | #210 | 2007 | *Roscommon*/David Kelly/WYC | 2007–present | |
| #211 | #211 | 2008 | *Cairdeas*/Joe O'Neal and Ed Cusick/HYC | 2008–present | |

| Hull # | Sail #(s) | Year Built | Name/Owner/Club or Place | Dates Owned | Remarks |
|---|---|---|---|---|---|
| #212 | #212 | 2010 | *Bellona*/William O'Connor family/WYC | 2010–2011 | |
| | | | *Three Sticks*/William O'Connor family/WYC | 2012–present | |
| #213 | #213 | 2008 | *Aria*/Terry Martorana/WYC | 2008–present | |
| #214 | #214 | 2010 | *Smoke*/Joe Lotuff/WYC | 2010–present | |
| #215 | #215 | 2010 | *Koukla*/Arthur and Maureen Demoulas/HPYC | 2010–present | |
| #216 | #216 | 2010 | No name/Wianno Senior Italia/Grosseto | 2010–present | |
| #217 | #217 | 2012 | No name/Wianno Senior Italia/Grosseto | 2012–present | |
| #218 | #218 | 2012 | No name/Wianno Senior Italia/Grosseto | 2012–present | |
| #219 | #219 | 2012 | *Gretchen3*/Edwin Yeo III/Harwich Port | 2012–present | |
| #220 | #220 | 2011 | *Scout*/Sophie Pesek/WYC | 2011–present | First Senior finished by E. M. Crosby. |
| #221 | #221 | 2013 | No name/Wianno Senior Italia/Grosseto | Present | |
| #222 | #222 | 2011 | *Beltane*/James Cunningham/BRYC | 2011–present | |
| #223 | #223 | 2013 | Wianno Senior Italia/Grosseto | Present | |
| #224 | #224 | 2013 | Wianno Senior Italia/Grosseto | Present | |

# Acknowledgments

First, I must express my gratitude to Llewellyn Howland III, who not only put the class editorial committee in contact with me but read the manuscript and graciously contributed the Foreword to this book. The Wianno Senior Class Association was well served by the small committee charged with overseeing this project. Thanks to Lee Williams, and to Bill Lawrence and his son Sam. A special appreciation is due to committee member and class chairman Timothy Fulham, whose understanding, and steady support made this book possible.

As always, libraries are indispensable to a work such as this. Special thanks to Lucy Loomis and the staff of the Sturgis Library in Barnstable. Thanks to the photo staff at the New Bedford Whaling Museum including Michael Lapides, Mark Procknik, and Melanie Correia. Thanks to the John F. Kennedy Memorial Library in Boston, to Joe Tucker at Bennington College, to the New York Yacht Club Library, and to the reference staff at the Brooklyn Public Library, the Kansas City Public Library, and the Carnegie Library of Pittsburgh. Thanks to Mary Kirkpatrick, librarian at the Massachusetts School of Law, for her prompt help with some research materials, and to Jennifer Morgan Williams of the Osterville Historical Society.

A great many people shared their memories throughout this project. Only through their patience and trust was it possible to pursue the stories that reside at the heart of this book. Several people were especially important to the project as a whole and as readers of the manuscript. They include James Hinkle, Jr., Lucy Steere, Connie Tracy, Richard Ulian, Belle Taylor, Cathryn A. Wright, and Ted and Malcolm Crosby.

Within the Wianno Senior Class, the insights of Carter "Bink" Bacon were especially helpful, and so were the perspective and administrative assistance provided by Kevin Cain. Thanks also to Bob Frazee and David Trimble, holders of Wianno Yacht Club materials. At the Edgartown Yacht Club, thanks to William J. Roman. At the Woods Hole Historical Society, thanks to archivist Susan F. Witzell.

Not everyone I spoke with appears in the narrative, yet their contributions were very important. They include Paul Brown, Nick Battit, Dave Borque, Roger Barzum, Christine Brown, Joanne Cahoon, Ed Craig, Charles Capra, Murray Crane, Samuel Croll, Ged Delaney, Dabney Draper, Peter Eastman, Betsy Glanville, Richard Guandalini, Phil Holbrook, Mary Madden, Hugh and Bob MacColl, Tom Morse, Lawrence and Peter Damon, Ellen Huettig, George Kimmerle, John Kingston, Hugh MacColl, Mary Madden, Thomas and Maureen McNulty, Chris Page, Bill O'Toole, Patty Spalt Hopple, Chip Rowley, Bill Sauerbrey, Ann Barus-Seeley, Jock Shafroth, Marcus Sherman, Lee Scarbrough, Steve Smith, Richard and Belle Taylor, Walter S. Teller, Brad Tracy, Martha Twigg, Chris Vallett, Kathy Sinclair Wood, Karen Uhlaender, Woody Underwood, Dana Richards Vaitses, Len Westra, Fred Williams, and Steve Wood. I suspect there are a few others whom I've somehow overlooked, so thanks to you as well.

# Photo Credits

# Bibliography

*Barnstable Patriot*, primarily 1913–1930.

Bass River Yacht Club (BRYC), rosters and newsletters.

*Boston Globe*, various articles, 1913–1980s.

*Brooklyn Daily Eagle*, various, 1895–1900.

*Cape Cod Life*, April/May 1987.

Crosby Yacht Building & Storage Co., 1935 roster of yachts.

Crosby, Wilton ("Bill"), notecards relating to owners, author interview.

Edgartown Yacht Club, race results 1932–1938

Frothingham, Theodore, *With a Grain of Salt*, self-published, 1972.

*Hyannis Patriot*, primarily 1913–1930.

Hyannis Port Yacht Club (HPYC), "Summary of Fleet Rosters and Race Results 1932–1941."

*Kansas City Star*, December 4, 1921.

*MotorBoating*, July 1928.

*New York Times*, various articles, 1890s–1970s.

*Pittsburgh Press*, February 21, 1965.

*A Sailor's Notebook*, Richard Ulian, Van Nostrand Reinhold & Co., New York, 1982,

Sherborn Historical Society, *Dowse Scrapbook*.

Stone Horse Yacht Club (SHYC), member interviews.

*The Register*, October 9, 1986.

*The Rudder*, April 1915, January 1917.

*The Senior*, published by Wianno Senior Class Association, Inc., 1989.

*Vineyard Gazette*, various.

Wianno Senior Class Bulletins, 1948–present.

Wianno Yacht Club and Wianno Club, archived letters, yearbooks, race records, miscellaneous notes, rosters, correspondence.

*WoodenBoat*, Nos. 91, 153, 190.

Woods Hole Historical Museum, Woods Hole Yacht Club (WHYC) booklets 1930, 1931, 1932, 1933, 1940.

*Yachting*, March 1965

# Index

# About the Author

Stan Grayson is a writer widely known for his books and articles about American yachting and small-craft history, and the American marine engine and automobile industries. After receiving a master's degree in English from Pennsylvania State University followed by Army service in Vietnam, Stan pursued a career that has included stints as a newspaper reporter, photographer, automotive industry consultant, and most of all as a writer. His work has appeared in *Automobile Quarterly*, *Nautical Quarterly*, and *WoodenBoat*, among other publications. Among his best-known works are *Cape Cod Catboats*, *Ferrari, the Man, the Machines*, *Beautiful Engines*; and the *WoodenBoat* article, "The Musketaquid Mystery: In Search of Thoreau's Boat." Stan lives in Marblehead, Massachusetts.

## About Llewellyn Howland III

A publisher, antiquarian bookseller, and yachting historian, Llewellyn Howland III is the author, most recently, of *The New Bedford Yacht Club: A History* and, with Calvin Siegal, the co-author of *On the Wind: The Marine Photographs of Norman Fortier*. He is a frequent contributor to *WoodenBoat* and is currently writing a biography of the yacht designer and aviation pioneer W. Starling Burgess.